Essentials of Supervision

Essentials of Supervision

William F. Simpson, MBA, CPCU

Patricia E. Gould, CPCU, AIM

Phillip J. Hardy, CPCU

Karen J. Lindahl, CPCU

James F. Fryer, EdD, CPCU

3rd Edition • 14th Printing

The Institutes
720 Providence Road, Suite 100
Malvern, Pennsylvania 19355-3433

3rd Edition • 14th Printing • October 2010

Library of Congress Control Number: 00-111569

ISBN 978-0-89462-149-9

Foreword

The Institutes are the trusted leader in delivering proven knowledge solutions that drive powerful business results for the risk management and property-casualty insurance industry. For more than 100 years, The Institutes have been meeting the industry's changing professional development needs with customer-driven products and services.

In conjunction with industry experts and members of the academic community, our Knowledge Resources Department develops our course and program content, including Institutes study materials. Practical and technical knowledge gained from Institutes courses enhances qualifications, improves performance, and contributes to professional growth—all of which drive results.

The Institutes' proven knowledge helps individuals and organizations achieve powerful results with a variety of flexible, customer-focused options:

Recognized Credentials—The Institutes offer an unmatched range of widely recognized and industry-respected specialty credentials. The Institutes' Chartered Property Casualty Underwriter (CPCU) professional designation is designed to provide a broad understanding of the property-casualty insurance industry. Depending on professional needs, CPCU students may select either a commercial insurance focus or a personal risk management and insurance focus and may choose from a variety of electives.

In addition, The Institutes offer certificate or designation programs in a variety of disciplines, including these:

- Claims
- Commercial underwriting
- Fidelity and surety bonding
- General insurance
- Insurance accounting and finance
- Insurance information technology
- Insurance production and agency management
- Insurance regulation and compliance

- Management
- Marine insurance
- Personal insurance
- Premium auditing
- Quality insurance services
- Reinsurance
- Risk management
- Surplus lines

Flexible Online Learning—The Institutes have an unmatched variety of technical insurance content covering topics from accounting to underwriting, which we now deliver through hundreds of online courses. These cost-effective self-study courses are a convenient way to fill gaps in technical knowledge in a matter of hours without ever leaving the office.

Continuing Education—A majority of The Institutes' courses are filed for CE credit in most states. We also deliver quality, affordable, online CE courses quickly and conveniently through our newest business unit, CEU.com. Visit www.CEU.com to learn more.

College Credits—Most Institutes courses carry college credit recommendations from the American Council on Education. A variety of courses also qualify for credits toward certain associate, bachelor's, and master's degrees at several prestigious colleges and universities. More information is available in the Student Services section of our Web site, www.TheInstitutes.org.

Custom Applications—The Institutes collaborate with corporate customers to utilize our trusted course content and flexible delivery options in developing customized solutions that help them achieve their unique organizational goals.

Insightful Analysis—Our Insurance Research Council (IRC) division conducts public policy research on important contemporary issues in property-casualty insurance and risk management. Visit www.ircweb.org to learn more or purchase its most recent studies.

The Institutes look forward to serving the risk management and property-casualty insurance industry for another 100 years. We welcome comments from our students and course leaders; your feedback helps us continue to improve the quality of our study materials.

Peter L. Miller, CPCU
President and CEO
The Institutes

Preface

Many talents combined to produce this book, as is fitting for a text on supervision. The chapters were originally written by people who tapped their own rich experiences as supervisors and trainers of supervisors. Revisions for this third edition drew from the feedback and suggestions of many students and course leaders who used the previous editions. We are very grateful that they took the time to send their comments and opinions to The Institutes.

This book assumes that you currently or will in the near future supervise employees within an insurance organization. It also presumes that you have performed technical or clerical duties in a superior manner. Whatever your situation, you share with other readers the need to add supervisory skills to the many skills you now possess.

Supervisory skills are broad ranging. The ideas you learn from this text will apply in almost any setting; they will help you in your roles as both leader and follower.

As an insurance supervisor, you can make a difference in the success of your organization and in the lives of those who work for you. Your influence on their immediate well-being and their ultimate growth is significant. We hope this book helps you to achieve organizational success and to see people flourish under your leadership.

For more information about The Institutes' programs, please call our Customer Service Department at (800) 644-2101, e-mail us at customerservice@TheInstitutes.org, or visit our Web site at www.TheInstitutes.org.

James F. Fryer, EdD, CPCU

Contents

Chapter 1

The Role of the Supervisor

Imagine yourself in the following situation. You have just been offered a promotion to your first supervisory position. Your boss tells you to consider the offer carefully overnight and to come in the next day with any questions and concerns you might have about accepting the promotion. You are thrilled with the opportunity, but even before you walk out of the office, you begin to have second and third thoughts. Will you really like supervisory work? Just what does supervisory work entail, and how does it differ from nonsupervisory work? If you do take the job, what can you do to make your transition as smooth as possible?

These concerns are held by many who contemplate making the move to a supervisory position. This chapter will discuss these concerns and other concepts related to supervision.

THE NATURE OF SUPERVISION

Supervision is defined as guiding the activities of people who perform the work. It includes planning, organizing, directing, and controlling the work and the activities of subordinates or employees—the so-called four functions of management. Supervisors are defined as members of management; therefore, they must perform these four general functions. More specifically, the supervisor does the following: interviews prospective employees; trains, evaluates the performance of, and counsels subordinates; and performs other activities that help to accomplish the general management functions. Supervision also includes the idea of unit task accomplishment; that is, the supervisor is responsible for the accomplishment of the unit's objectives through others.

Let's now look at the major parts of this definition more closely:

1. Supervision is defined as guiding the activities of people who perform the work.

   Literally hundreds of technical and clerical positions exist in the insurance industry, which are filled by people with varying skills

[handwritten margin notes:]

* Supervison is... guiding the activities of people who perform the work.

* Four-functions of management: Planning, organizing, directing and controlling

* Supervision includes unit task accomplishment

and talents. In this book, we are concerned with the broad range of supervisory settings in the insurance industry—from supervising technical jobs requiring considerable training to supervising clerical tasks that may be filled by new employees.

2. Supervision includes planning, organizing, directing, and controlling the work and activities of unit employees. Following are examples of these supervisory functions:

- Planning—setting annual objectives for your unit
- Organizing—determining whether to replace a part-time filing clerk who quits
- Directing—instructing an underwriter on how to use a personal lines rating software package on a PC
- Controlling—reviewing the claim files your unit completed for completeness and accuracy

3. Supervision also includes the concept of unit task accomplishment; i.e., the supervisor is responsible for accomplishing the unit's objectives through others.

These objectives could include increasing commission income in an agency sales unit, improving quality control in a personal lines underwriting operation, or converting some data for use on a new information technology system by an agreed target date.

Insurance supervisors often have nonsupervisory tasks mixed in with their supervisory duties. To highlight this, and to further illustrate supervisory duties, we present the following list of tasks contained in supervisors' workloads. Place a check mark in front of each task that you consider to be supervisory rather than technical or clerical.

✓ 1. Reviewing the salary records for the eight commercial underwriters who work for you

___ 2. Adjusting a particularly difficult fire claim with one of your company's insureds

✓ 3. Writing a weekly report on the activities of the six external agency sales representatives who report directly to you

___ 4. Underwriting applications for small commercial business package policies

✓ 5. Notifying one of the ten claim representatives who report to you that he or she is to be promoted to senior property claim representative

___ 6. Rating private passenger automobile policies

___ 7. Preparing renewal billings for your agency's insureds

✓ 8. Outlining an employee orientation program to a new premium auditor just hired into your unit

___ 9. Programming a computer system that will rate and issue homeowners policies

✓ 10. Preparing an annual salary budget for your public relations unit

✓ 11. Counseling one of your commercial raters who has been tardy twice in the past week

___ 12. Making a loss prevention inspection of the premises of one of your company's insureds

Six of these tasks should be categorized as supervisory. This is shown in Exhibit 1-1.

Exhibit 1-1

Supervisory Tasks

Task Number	Activity	Function
1	Reviewing salary records of underwriters	Controlling
3	Writing a weekly report	Controlling
5	Notifying a claim representative of a promotion	Organizing
8	Outlining an employee orientation program to a new premium auditor	Directing
10	Preparing an annual salary budget	Planning
11	Counseling a tardy commercial rater	Directing

In all of the preceding tasks, which are performed as part of your supervisory role, you are supervising or guiding the activities of those who performed the work—underwriters, outside sales representatives, claim representatives, premium auditors, or raters. You accomplish your general supervisory task through the supervisory management functions of planning, organizing, directing, or controlling the work activities of subordinates. As we will see later, the scope and execution of these supervisory functions will vary greatly among insurance companies, agencies, and other organizations in the insurance industry.

As for the other tasks, Task 7 requires you to perform a clerical function. Tasks 2, 4, 6, 9, and 12 require you to perform technical tasks rather than supervise the work of people who are trained in a particular area. Although these six tasks require special skills and abilities, they do not require you to function at a supervisory level—you perform the task *yourself* rather than supervise/guide those who report to you.

The dictionary defines supervision as "a critical watching (and directing) of activities or a course of action." The essence of supervision, then, involves accomplishing results through others—the people who do the actual work. We will return to this key idea in this chapter and in subsequent chapters.

Supervisory Work

What do we mean by the term "supervisor," that is, the person performing the function of supervision? A supervisor is a member of the management team who has authority over technical or clerical employees and who is accountable for the results of their performance.

Let's examine the major components of this definition in detail:

1. "... a member of the management team ..."

   The supervisor is a member of the body of managers that guides the organization on its general course. Depending on its size, an organization may have senior executives and layers of middle-level managers in addition to first-line supervisors in its management group. The supervisor is the only one who guides the people who actually do the work of the organization. Those who supervise supervisors are usually called managers.

2. "... who has authority over ..."

   Authority is the right to give directions to others—underwriters, claim representatives, loss control specialists, outside sales representatives, systems analysts, accountants, raters, general clerks, and so on.

3. "... and is accountable for the results of technical or clerical employees."

   This aspect of the definition relates to part of the definition of supervision just examined; that is, the supervisor is responsible for the accomplishment of the unit's task through the efforts of others.

Although we will analyze some of the major differences between supervisory and technical work in detail in the next chapter, let's identify several of them now. What do you think these differences are? Take a moment and list them on scratch paper.

Here are some of the differences identified by new and potential supervisors from both insurance companies and agencies and brokerage organizations. Although your words may be different from those shown, you can compare your answers with theirs.

1. The nature of the job itself changes greatly when you become a supervisor. As a supervisor, your effectiveness will be judged primarily on the results achieved by your technical or clerical staff rather than on how technically proficient you are as an individual underwriter, rater, or claim representative.

2. The skills demanded of you in a supervisory job are different. Assuming that your span of control (the number of people reporting directly to you) is large enough, you will be removed from the technical or operating work of the unit.

   For example, your prior strength may have been expertise in group health insurance claims or technical knowledge of information technology. If you are now supervising ten or so health insurance claim specialists or systems analysts, you will have to become proficient as a planner or organizer rather than a technical authority. That latter role is more likely to be assumed by one or more of your senior subordinates. You probably will not have the time to maintain your past technical expertise if you are to accomplish your supervisory work.

3. Your accountability widens considerably. In your former job, whether you were a loss prevention engineer or a billing clerk, you were generally accountable only for your own work. Even if, as a senior loss prevention engineer or as a senior clerk, you had responsibility for training new people in the unit, it was still exercised under the general direction of the supervisor.

Now the situation is different. You are actively assuming responsibility for the performance of others. For example, let's assume that you supervise eight claim representatives. On Monday morning one of them calls in sick, and another is delayed by car trouble. As a supervisor, you will have to respond effectively to this situation by using a variety of supervisory actions, probably including reassigning the work or reorganizing the priorities of the work in process. In your former technical or clerical role, you were not immediately concerned with responding appropriately to staff absenteeism or tardiness, because you were primarily accountable only for your own work.

Supervisors as Members of Management

When we defined the word "supervisor," we indicated that a supervisor is a member of the organization's management team. What does the word "management" mean? It can be defined in terms of the name of a process and as the name of a group of people. Both uses apply to your supervisory role.

As a process, management means achieving results through others. In a sense, this definition is similar to but somewhat broader than that of supervision. Recall that we defined supervision as guiding the activities of people who perform the work. Management means accomplishing work through other managers, supervisors, and staff specialists, usually not directly through the people who perform the work.

As a name for a group of people, management means all those who control or guide an organization. Supervisors are usually included by most people when they use the word management to refer to a group of people within an organization. Management can range from the thousands of senior executives, middle managers, and first-line supervisors in large insurance companies to the owner or principal of a small insurance agency who may also necessarily serve as the first-line supervisor of the entire staff. Between these two extremes are any number of management groupings and configurations in companies, agencies, and other insurance organizations.

In any case, as a first-line or front-line supervisor, you are probably going to be guided in your activities by a manager. In a large organization, this person may be accountable for guiding a number of first-line supervisors. In a small agency, the owner or manager may direct you and also engage in direct personal sales production.

In a smaller company or organization, you will frequently have more scope and responsibility in your supervisory job. This is because smaller organizations often cannot afford a highly specialized division of tasks. In addition, a smaller organization will not have specialized staff units such as personnel, education, or information technology units. In such an organization, supervisors and managers will often have to learn enough about these functions to perform them adequately, or at least to know when to consult higher managers or call in an outside specialist or consultant.

SUPERVISORY FUNCTIONS

In a previous exercise, you distinguished between supervisory and technical tasks. We then matched the supervisory tasks to the four management or supervisory functions of planning, organizing, directing, and controlling. Some of the examples were as follows:

- Planning—drawing up an annual salary budget
- Organizing—notifying a claim representative of a promotion
- Directing—outlining an employee orientation program to a new premium auditor
- Controlling—writing a weekly report

We will now examine these supervisory functions in more detail. As used here, the term "function" means the activities or operations expected of a person within his or her role. For example, you would reasonably expect an experienced commercial rater to be able to rate the appropriate coverages. Similarly, you would expect an experienced, trained supervisor to be able to perform the various supervisory functions, recognizing that the scope and extent of the functions will vary with the supervisory job. For example, in a larger organization with a high degree of division of labor and specialized staff units, the supervisor may do relatively more organizing, directing, and controlling than planning. However, in a small company or agency, planning may play a larger part in the supervisor's job than do the other functions.

Supervisory Functions Defined

Let's briefly define each supervisory function, give another example or two, and then apply this knowledge to some actual situations.

Planning

Planning is defined as determining ways to achieve organizational objectives. Some specific planning tools are setting subordinate goals, establishing budgets, setting timetables, and establishing guidelines for action.

An example of an objective is to reduce the workers compensation loss ratio by 5 percent by December 31.

An example of a budget guideline is to hold telephone and postage expenses to the same level as last year without sacrificing service to policyholders.

Organizing

Organizing, the arranging of activities to attain goals, includes two subfunctions:

1. Creating the structure of the organization
2. Arranging the use of resources to achieve objectives

Creating the structure of the organization would probably require the active involvement, or at least the compliance, of the supervisor's manager or other managers. For example, the decision to add an underwriter to the staff of a personal lines underwriting unit usually requires the supervisor to seek the approval of a manager. In many cases, the unit supervisor would develop the workload, productivity, and other data necessary to justify adding a new underwriter. The final decision to add the new employee, however, would most likely be at least a shared one.

Arranging the use of resources to achieve objectives is frequently the responsibility of the supervisor. For instance, the supervisor could decide to use clerical rather than more highly paid technical staff to locate and retrieve policyholder or customer files.

Directing

Directing is defined as achieving objectives and carrying out plans by giving instructions to subordinates. Examples of this function are as follows:

*   Holding weekly meetings of the sales staff of an agency
*   Requiring that commercial underwriters spend at least two days per month visiting key agents within their territories to improve communications, troubleshoot problems, and so on

Controlling

The fourth and final supervisory function is controlling. It consists of three steps:

1. Establishing standards of performance
2. Comparing actual results against established standards
3. Taking corrective action when needed

Let's illustrate the control function with an example that follows these steps:

1. The company or agency requires that all customer complaints be acknowledged within six hours of receipt.

2. The supervisor determines that a particular customer service representative is not meeting this standard.

3. The supervisor reviews the standard with that employee and, if necessary, warns the employee of the consequences of continuing to fail to meet the standard.

Application Exercise

In the following list of eight tasks, place a "P," an "O," a "D," or a "C" (representing *planning, organizing, directing,* or *controlling*) in front of each task. If you prefer, you may do the exercise on scratch paper. After you complete the list, we will review each of the answers.

C _O_ 1. Reviewing the weekly expense accounts submitted by the field loss prevention engineers whom you supervise

O _d_ 2. Selecting two underwriters from your unit to be trained on new ratings software

_P_ 3. Setting an objective to reduce homeowners policy processing time by half a day by December 31

d _C_ 4. Requiring that field marketing specialists submit their weekly itineraries by noon each Friday

O _d_ 5. Recommending that one of your about-to-retire telephone claim representatives be replaced by a part-time employee

P _d_ 6. Requiring that photocopying and duplicating expenses be held to no more than a 2 percent increase over last year's dollar amount without sacrificing service levels

C _O_ 7. Auditing the policy files of your unit's personal lines underwriters to determine whether underwriting requirements are being met

d _C_ 8. Requiring that your newly hired commercial property under-writers complete a particular self-study course within the first month on the job

Now, let's review the answers by presenting the preferred response and rationale for each choice.

1. You should have indicated that this is an example of the control function of supervision. More than likely, as you review the expense accounts, you apply some criteria or guidelines that the employees are expected to meet.

2. Here, the preferred answer is the organizing function because you are arranging the use of resources to achieve objectives. Likely objectives here might be to reduce the expense of underwriting or to improve the quality and speed of a response.

3. The preferred answer is planning because you are determining ways to reach organizational objectives. The statement itself is an objective.

4. The desired answer is directing because here you are carrying out plans by giving instructions to subordinates.

5. Here, you are performing the organizing function of supervision because you are arranging the use of resources to achieve objectives. A probable objective here is to reduce expense.

6. The correct answer is planning because you are determining ways to reach organizational objectives. The statement itself can be considered as an objective and as a budget guideline.

7. Here, you are performing the control function because as you audit the policy files, you are applying the relevant underwriting requirements.

8. The correct answer is directing because you are carrying out plans by giving instructions to subordinates.

Of the eight tasks analyzed, two illustrated each of the supervisory functions of planning, organizing, directing, and controlling. In all of the preceding functions, you were supervising the activities of those who performed the specific technical or clerical work-loss prevention engineers, marketing specialists, telephone claim representatives, or underwriters.

SUPERVISORY SKILLS

Communicating
Listening
Counseling
Motivating
Leading
Decision Making
and Training

Complementing or supporting the supervisory functions are certain supervisory skills that you will be expected to master in your role as a supervisor. A skill is the ability to use one's knowledge in an expert way. Skill involves *doing something,* and how well that something is done is a reflection of the skill level of the person who does it. Supervisory skills, then, are abilities to perform, in an expert way, some essential tasks or processes that support the four major supervisory functions.

Application Exercise

The supervisory skills we will analyze briefly include communicating, listening, counseling, motivating, leading, decision making, and training. To introduce them, we will ask you to complete another short quiz, either here or on scratch paper. After you complete the quiz, we will review each question and develop each point more completely.

1. In a unit, accountability for initiating job-related communication rests with the
   X Supervisor___Employee

2. Asking for feedback from the receiver of a message is a useful way to ensure effective communication.
   X Agree___Disagree

3. Supervisors and managers spend more of their day listening than they do speaking or writing.

   _X_Agree___Disagree

4. Counseling is a natural skill for most supervisors.

   _X_Agree___Disagree

5. Motivating and leading are

   ___The same process _X_Different processes

6. The job itself is usually the best place to start in developing employee motivation.

   _X_Agree___Disagree

7. Leadership is an inherited characteristic.

   _X_Agree___Disagree

8. Leadership in a unit can be both formal and informal (or unofficial).

   _X_Agree___Disagree

9. Not doing anything about a chronic absenteeism problem in a unit would itself be a form of decision.

   _X_Agree___Disagree

10. Effective training almost always improves employee job performance.

   _X_Agree _X_Disagree

Let's review your answers. We will give the preferred answers followed by some comments.

1. The supervisor should initiate such communication. You hope to develop a willingness among employees to initiate communication; your job is to know what is going on within each job. We define communication as the exchange of information and understanding between one person and another. It involves conveying meaning through words, other symbols, and body language. Defined in terms of an organization, communication follows through organization, department, and unit information flows and allows all members of the organization to be knowledgeable and to feel part of the organization.

2. Assume you are giving directions or instructions to your under-writers. One quick, useful way for you to be certain that they understand what you want is for them to repeat your instructions in their own words. Unless they can do this, you cannot be certain that you have communicated clearly.

3. Surveys and estimates show that supervisors and managers spend between one-third and one-half of their days listening to others—more time than they spend speaking or writing.

* Sups/Mangs spend ⅓ – ½ of their day listening

4. Counseling, which may be defined as advising, is not usually a natural skill for a supervisor; however, it can be systematically learned and applied. One example of counseling is helping an employee decide whether to take a particular course for career advancement.

5. You should have selected *different*. The terms have quite different meanings in the field of management. Motivating means encouraging subordinates to perform by fulfilling or appealing to their needs. Motivating includes creating a climate in which employees can motivate themselves. Leadership, on the other hand, is defined as the ability to achieve desired results and, simultaneously, win the confidence, cooperation, and loyalty of others. One example of motivating is encouraging a unit member to achieve a certain level of job performance in order to be considered for promotion. An example of leadership is convincing employees to adopt new unit service objectives in order to retain policyholders or to control expenses. In the first case, motivation, people perform or work primarily for reasons important to them, such as recognition or promotion. In the second case, leadership, employees respect the supervisor and will extend themselves when the supervisor asks them to meet demanding objectives.

6. We think that the job itself is usually the best place to start when attempting to improve employee motivation. The job is where employee needs such as achievement, responsibility, recognition, growth, and the need for interesting work will or will not be met. Factors such as generous benefit plans, attractive surroundings, and pleasant co-workers are important in the work environment, but their effect may be lost on an employee who perceives the job itself as lacking. What are some things you as a supervisor can do to ensure that employees will be motivated on the job or at least will not be greatly demotivated? First, have you communicated to employees what their jobs are in sufficient detail? Do they have position descriptions or at least some type of task list to follow? Second, do they know the performance standards that they are supposed to meet? Have you spelled out, preferably in writing, your quantity, quality, and other performance expectations for them? Third, do they know what authority they have? As a rule, the degree of authority should be spelled out when an employee is hired and then reviewed periodically.

    Certainly other factors exist for you as a supervisor to consider in motivating your employees, but those we just discussed meet our present purposes. You will learn more about motivation in Chapter 3.

7. Research shows that leadership can be exercised by any person, whether male or female, short or tall, from a humble or distinguished social or economic background, and with almost any other personal characteristics.

An important point is that the leader must want to lead or at least be comfortable in the leadership role. Some effective supervisors and managers are outgoing, while others are more reserved; some project an aura of dominance or of being "in charge," while others are relatively unobtrusive; some enjoy verbal exchange, while others are reserved in their communications. In short, there isn't any master personality profile that effective managers and supervisors automatically follow in their leadership role.

Task leader
Social leader

8. Research indicates that two types of leaders will often be in a work unit or work situation. One is the task leader; the other is the social leader.

As a supervisor, your primary responsibility is to effectively guide the group in the achievement of its tasks. Although you certainly want to practice good human relations with your employees, you do not have to be the group's social leader. The critical point is that your employees respect you enough to follow your leadership in achieving the goals of the unit.

9. Electing to do nothing is itself a decision. Sometimes a supervisor will decide to wait for a problem to become more noticeable so that employees more readily see the need for change. That approach is not likely to be wise in the instance of chronic absenteeism. Ignoring or trying to avoid confronting such a problem usually makes it worse. For example, the employees who come to work on time every day often resent the extra work burden put on them by the chronic absentee(s). As a supervisor, you are expected to deal promptly and actively with such problems.

Problem-solving and decision-making techniques will be analyzed in detail in *Supervisory Skills*, the second text in the IIA Program in Supervisory Management.

10. You should have disagreed because of the phrase *almost always*. Training is appropriate if poor performance is caused by the employee's lack of knowledge or skill. Training is not likely to solve a performance problem if the problem is rooted in employee motivation or job design. Sometimes training reveals that an employee has ample knowledge and skill and serves to direct your attention to other possible causes of poor performance. The abilities to provide and monitor training are essential supervisory skills.

Major Supervisory Skills

Although other skills can be identified, the major supervisory skills suggested by the questions in the quiz are summarized below. These are the most critical skills for most supervisory positions.

Communicating

Communication refers to the exchange of information and understanding between one person or organization and another. As with other management terms taken from everyday language, the word *communication* has many meanings. The essential idea is that communication creates an understanding on the part of two or more people or groups. Communication implies the exchange of meaning but not necessarily acceptance or agreement. Reduced to the simplest terms, if you want to be a good supervisor, you must learn to communicate well. In turn, this means consciously working on your ability to communicate by getting feedback and by trying new approaches.

Listening

Listening is such an important part of communicating that it deserves to be listed as a separate supervisory skill. You can learn specific techniques to improve your ability to draw out the thoughts and feelings that people have trouble expressing. These techniques are described in Chapter 7.

Counseling

For our purposes, counseling and advising are synonymous. They are labels for the process of helping employees to make decisions about personally important matters.

Counseling often focuses on career plans or issues. Generally, a supervisor should not advise employees on family, financial, or other personal matters; however, job and career matters are often intertwined with personal matters, and it is virtually impossible to separate them. Moreover, employees see a respected supervisor as an obvious source of help when something troubles them. As a supervisor, you should expect employees to ask your advice. In turn, this means that you should develop skills in counseling employees and know your strengths and limitations in the counseling role.

Motivating

Strictly speaking, you cannot motivate an employee. Motivation is something that must come from the employee. It can be seen as the force that produces behavior.

Behavior consists of three elements: a *need* (for example, recognition from peers), the *motivation* that drives behavior to fulfill the need, and the *goal* of the behavior (for example, earning a promotion). In this view, motivation is the link between the need (recognition) and the particular need satisfier (a promotion) being sought. To repeat: You cannot motivate employees. What you *can* do is create a climate in which employees can develop their own motivation. For instance, you can provide a variety of rewards to serve as goals. You can also work to make the job itself a source of challenge and reward. Motivation and your role in employee motivation will be discussed further in Chapter 3.

(handwritten margin notes)
* Motivation is the force that produces behavior

* Behavior consists of 3 elements: a need, the motivation, and the goal.

Leading

The words *leader* and *supervisor* are not synonymous in our everyday language. Have you ever heard someone described as a "good supervisor but a poor leader"? There is a distinction between supervising competently and supervising in a way that wins the allegiance and support of others. A good supervisor is effective at planning, organizing, directing, and controlling, and he or she may exhibit many other supervisory skills. Being a good supervisor, however, does not necessarily mean being a good leader, who would have the confidence, cooperation, and loyalty of others in addition to supervisory skills.

One question often pondered is whether leaders are born or made. In other words, is leadership inherited or can it be developed? This is a traditional discussion question in supervisory and management training programs. You might want to jot down your ideas on both sides of the question. Your "leaders are made" thoughts should outweigh your "leaders are born" arguments. Put simply, you can do much to improve your effectiveness as a leader. Chapter 4 will explore the subject of leadership.

Decision Making

The essence of decision making is choosing among alternatives. Skill in decision making involves defining problems, identifying alternatives, gathering evidence, clarifying arguments, establishing criteria, and making the choice. More broadly, decision making also involves implementing choices and taking follow-up action.

Training

As a supervisor, you can expect to be a trainer in a very direct sense. That is, you will teach others in order to make them proficient in their work or to qualify them for new tasks. You will train employees in a deliberate or formal sense. You will also train them in an informal sense; they receive training as a side effect of your interactions with them.

Large insurance organizations usually have education and training specialists to design and administer employee training programs. Neither the specialists nor the programs, however, relieve you of your supervisory responsibility for training. Your responsibility is to identify and provide the training that members of your unit need to perform their tasks properly and efficiently. The training department is a resource, but the ultimate responsibility for training your employees is yours.

Becoming Proficient as a Supervisor

What can you do to become proficient in your supervisory role? We suggest that you focus on three dimensions of supervisory effectiveness:

acquiring knowledge, developing skills, and developing sensitivity to employee attitudes and performance.

Acquiring Knowledge

Knowledge is the understanding of a subject. Following are some examples of knowledge a supervisor might be expected to have:

1. Supervisors are required to set objectives annually in key areas that support the objectives of their immediate manager.

2. Supervisors are required to report weekly or biweekly on key unit productivity indices.

3. Supervisors must be aware of states in their geographic area that have no-fault automobile insurance laws.

4. Supervisors are required to conduct an annual performance appraisal interview with each of their employees.

5. Supervisors are expected to follow a "promote from within" policy whenever possible.

6. Absent or tardy employees are required to call their supervisor within fifteen or thirty minutes of their daily starting time so that the supervisor can reorganize or reassign the work.

Developing Skills

In addition to acquiring knowledge, you must sharpen your skills if you are to succeed in the supervisory role. *Skill* is the ability to use one's knowledge in an expert way. This chapter has identified seven major supervisory skills. Furthermore, we can say that skill manifests whenever knowledge is used in an efficient way and with effective results. Skills are sharpened through practice. You can speed the development of your supervisory skills by seeking feedback from others and using it to analyze your results, both good and bad.

Developing Sensitivity to Employee Attitudes and Performance

Two other key ideas—attitude and performance—should be examined as we look at the supervisor's role. You will often hear someone say that a certain employee has a poor or negative attitude. *Attitude* is defined as a mental stance, feeling, or emotion with regard to a fact or condition. An example of a counterproductive attitude is an underwriter who occasionally displays a patronizing view of trainees he or she is assigned to train. An example of a positive attitude is a telephone claim representative who conveys a desire to be helpful to claimants.

Performance is defined as results achieved on the job. As it is usually used, the term also encompasses the manner in which the job is done. In the preceding examples, you would hope that the underwriter would not allow his or her patronizing attitude to get in the way of training new underwriters. Some trainees could be repelled by such an attitude of superiority and might not absorb the training as effectively as they otherwise would. You would also expect the telephone claim representative who communicates a helpful attitude to perform all of the other aspects of the job effectively, such as developing accurate and complete claim-file data.

As a supervisor, you should be sensitive to employees' attitudes and performance. You will have to be able to distinguish between attitudes that can hamper performance (such as being abrupt or impatient with customers) and attitudes that do not undermine performance (such as an employee who prefers to begin work early or to go to lunch late under a flexible-hours plan). As long as attitudes and preferences do not hinder the performance of the unit, you should accept them.

WHAT MANAGEMENT EXPECTS OF THE SUPERVISOR

As a supervisor, you are expected to direct your unit so that it makes the greatest possible contribution to the goals of the firm. To do this, you must have a complete and realistic picture of what higher managers expect of you.

Effective Unit Performance

We saw earlier that one of the key perceived differences between supervisory and technical work is that your effectiveness as a supervisor will be judged primarily on the results your unit achieves rather than on how technically proficient you personally are. In general, this is an accurate statement of what your immediate manager and other managers and supervisors expect of you. They expect your unit to perform effectively within the organization's general guidelines. For example, if your organization has a reputation for prompt customer service, management will expect you and your staff to respond promptly to customer needs and will judge you by your unit's performance in customer service.

We defined performance as something accomplished. At the unit level, performance could be measured by the number of claims processed in a week, the number of applications processed in a day, the number of sales made in a week, or the number of policies issued in a day. You know which measures are most important to your superiors.

Productivity

In addition to their general expectations about performance, management expects a certain level of productivity from your unit. Productivity is the ratio of production to resources used. Your manager expects the unit output—for example, invoices produced and mailed—to correspond with the number and type of employees and the equipment and supplies used.

You may find that one or more ratios or measures are used by management as yardsticks of your unit's productivity; for instance, policies

Productivity is the ratio of production to resources used.

processed per employee, endorsements processed per week, or (in an agency) commission income per employee.

The standards of unit performance will probably include statements of acceptable quality levels. These statements may be quantitative, as with error counts, or qualitative, as with customer satisfaction, and they are often historically determined. Again, as a supervisor, you must have a clear grasp of both the organization's requirements and the yardsticks used by those who judge the performance of your unit.

Contribution to Profit

In addition to unit performance, management expects you to be aware of the importance of profit to the organization. Whether you work in a large insurance company or a small agency, an adequate profit must be made if the organization is to survive and to grow. You should not think in terms of unit profitability in the strict accounting sense. You are expected, however, to understand the unit's role in contributing to profit. You should think in terms of cost/benefit comparisons—a very rough idea of profitability.

For most agencies and brokerage firms, the major source of income is commission income. The expenses of operating the agency are deducted from this to determine agency profit. Visualizing the components of profitability in such small firms is not difficult; however, profitability is a more elusive concept in property-liability insurance companies. Here, the traditional ratio used to express the profitability level is the *combined ratio*. In simple terms, the combined ratio is total losses and expenses divided by premiums. The ratio shows how well the insurance company is doing in its insurance business and does not reflect investment income. If this ratio is 100 or less, the insurer is making a profit on its insurance operation. A combined ratio of 98.5 indicates that the insurer has earned an operating profit after losses and expenses have been paid. However, a combined ratio of 104 indicates that the company's losses and expenses exceed its income by 4 percent of premiums. In many cases, this shortfall or deficit is offset by the earnings on the insurer's investment portfolio. The key point is that the combined ratio serves as the informal "batting average" measure of insurer performance.

Although other units may not be as visibly involved in selling a product or service and producing revenues as a marketing or sales department, all supervisors are to some extent accountable for the expenses generated in their unit. Often, salary expense is the most common and most important expense you are asked to control. You are often expected to support higher-level organization objectives related to revenues and costs.

To summarize, management expects you to work toward the profitability of the organization. In some instances, this means being measured by the profitability of the unit. More frequently, it means that you must make cost/benefit comparisons (even if rough) or must exhibit a continuing commitment to holding costs down.

Effective Management of People

Management expects your unit to perform effectively under your direction. In other words, it expects the unit to achieve its mission however it is defined and to measure its results. At the same time, you are expected to manage the human resources for which you are accountable.

In terms of staff relations, you may be expected to do the following:

1. Recruit and select qualified applicants for job openings that occur in the unit. A personnel department may often perform preliminary screening, while much of the final accountability for the hiring decision will rest on the supervisor.

2. Orient and train new employees to the required levels of proficiency.

3. Impart the following to employees:

    *   The job duties. These are often contained in a position description or a position guide. In some situations, particularly in a small company or agency, you will develop a position description or at least a list of the duties the employee is expected to perform.

    *   The performance standards for the job. These state the expected level of performance for the various job duties.

    *   The authority the employee has.

4. Having met the preceding responsibilities, evaluate and guide the employee's performance through such techniques as periodic performance appraisal interviews, coaching, and counseling.

In addition to having these internal expectations and requirements, you must know and comply with various external ones. These arise from laws dealing with such matters as fair employment practice, employee safety, and employee privacy. There are also external requirements of a more informal nature, such as social standards of dress and behavior, that a supervisor must follow.

Mastery of a New Language

As supervisor, you must learn a new language. To win the support of employees and the cooperation of other supervisors, you must sound like a supervisor. Your language plays a major role in the way others see you and how they will respond to your supervision.

New Terms and New Meanings

As a supervisor, your vocabulary must expand. Many everyday terms have slightly different meanings when used by managers than when used by nonmanagers. Mastering the language of management often means observing these slight nuances of differences in the meaning of familiar words. As a new supervisor, you will be hampered in building relationships with other members of management if your speech suggests that you still think as you did before you were promoted to supervisor.

Line and Staff

The terms *line* and *staff* are two of the most important and common in the management vocabulary. Unfortunately, because each has two related meanings, there is often confusion about which is intended. They warrant our attention because of this confusion and because they illustrate how familiar terms are used more specifically by supervisors and managers.

Line Tasks

The terms *line tasks* and *line jobs* denote operations that are part of the major work of an organization. In a manufacturing organization, manufacturing, distributing, and marketing are likely to be the line tasks. The vast majority of the firm's employees are likely to work in the departments that perform these tasks. These line departments are supported by smaller nonline units that perform such specialized tasks as accounting, product design, market research, and legal work. In an insurance company, underwriting, claims, and marketing are likely to be the line divisions. The information technology division may also be considered a line unit in an insurance company, in part because of its size and overall effect on the company. In an insurance agency, the sales and customer service staffs perform the line tasks.

Staff Tasks

The nonline support activities mentioned above are called staff tasks. In a manufacturing company, these tasks are accounting, product design, market research, and legal work and are essential to the overall success of the firm. They are labeled staff, however, to signify that they are more specialized tasks that require particular expertise and support rather than being the major activities of the firm. People who serve as personal assistants are also acknowledged as holding staff positions.

In an insurance company, human resources, actuarial, education, mail room, accounting, and corporate legal departments are some of the many staff units. Some of the staff units a large insurance agency may have include accounting and claims. In a small agency, managers perform the staff functions along with their other duties.

Line Authority

A direct reporting relationship is said to be one of *line authority*. A boss always has line authority over his or her subordinates. Line authority involves giving directions to subordinates, representing them to higher management, appraising their performance, and assuming responsibility for their work.

Staff Authority

The term *staff authority* is used to denote the relationship within an organization of a person or unit that performs staff tasks. In essence, staff authority means the absence of line authority. Staff people lack line authority over the people with whom they must collaborate. For example, accountants do not normally have the right to order line managers or other personnel to provide data. Instead, the accountants must request their cooperation. Because they lack line authority, staff people achieve influence over others by asking, persuading, cajoling, and sometimes by bargaining with them.

There is an exception to the general rule that staff people lack line authority. They do have line authority over their subordinates but have only staff authority with respect to other members of the organization.

Functional Authority

Requires a high level of expertise

A special kind of staff authority, known as *functional authority*, is given to some staff people or units. Functional authority gives a staff person the right to make decisions that bind other organization members in a carefully specified area. A high degree of professional expertise is usually involved. For example, a firm's accountant normally has functional authority to define the accounts and specify the forms to be used in recording financial data. The firm's legal department usually has the right to approve or disapprove any contracts before they may be signed by corporate officers.

Some staff people and units have no functional authority. They do not need it because little is lost if their recommendations are not followed. For example, the director of training and education of an insurance company does not have the power to require that employees receive training or to demand that they take some courses and not others. He or she may, however, make training recommendations, and those with line authority usually do endorse and implement staff recommendations. In contrast, the insurer's chief counsel may have the absolute (functional) authority over the wording of policy forms.

Why is the distinction between staff and line important? The term *staff* is like a warning flag that signals the absence of line authority in a given relationship. This means, in turn, that someone must exercise more subtle forms of influence and persuasion. In addition, the role and the power of staff units are sometimes unclear. You have little leeway in complying with staff people when they have functional authority over a matter. However, you have more latitude when dealing with staff people who do not have functional authority over the matter at hand. Those exercising staff authority often seek dialogue concerning how their specialized skills may benefit your unit.

MANAGEMENT TOOLS TO COMMUNICATE EXPECTATIONS TO THE SUPERVISOR

We have discussed management's general operational expectations of unit performance, productivity, and sensitivity to profit considerations. We also pointed out that management expects the supervisor to manage the employees for whom he or she is accountable.

How do managers communicate these expectations to the supervisor? They use several vehicles, including objectives, a job or position description, and such concepts as authority and accountability.

Objectives

The term *objective* refers to the goal or desired result of a person or an organization. It is not the actions that produce that outcome. In general, the supervisor has a limited number of objectives—say, a half dozen or so—to achieve. These support such major organizational objectives as revenue, customer service, operational effectiveness, employee relations, and expense control.

Depending on their specific job and its authority level, agency and brokerage supervisors often find their objectives to be in the following areas:

1. *Commission income.* (This assumes the supervisor directly supervises the sales representatives.) The objective in this area might be to generate $4 million in commission income during 20XX. This objective, in turn, could be subdivided into objectives for commission income generated by the sales of commercial lines or personal lines. The annual objective could also be broken down into monthly (and therefore shorter) sales targets.

2. *Customer service.* Sample objective: To respond to customer inquiries or complaints within six hours (or some other specified time period) during 20XX.

3. *Operational effectiveness.* Sample objective: To process and mail commercial package policy renewals within no less than X days before the renewal date during 20XX.

4. *Employee training and development.* Sample objective: To select and begin training one customer service representative who will be considered for promotion to an outside sales position during 20XX.

5. *Expense control.* Sample objective: To hold telephone and postage expenses to no more than a 5 percent increase over the previous year during 20XX.

6. *Personal.* Sample objective: To complete a company independent-study course on letter and report writing during 20XX.

7. *Personal.* Sample objective: To complete at least one course in the Program in General Insurance of the Insurance Institute of America during 20XX.

In a large organization, such as a national or regional insurer, the supervisor's supporting objectives might focus somewhat narrowly on such areas as policyholder or agency service, productivity indices, staff effectiveness, and expense controls. One of the reasons for this difference in focus is that a larger organization can allow for a finer division of labor than a smaller organization can. In any case, the front-line supervisor should have a limited number of objectives that support key objectives in the organization.

To be considered useful, objectives should be concrete, measurable, written, and dated. In objectives 1 through 7 above, the implied target date is December 31 of the year 20XX. If this is not the intended target, a different date should be specified. For example, the objective for processing and mailing commercial package policy renewals could be targeted for March 31, June 30, or some other date.

If objectives are expressed only verbally, the supervisor and his or her manager might risk misunderstanding them, resulting in failure to achieve an objective or to achieve it adequately. To prevent this, both the supervisor and the manager should have a written copy of the objectives so that they can periodically review them.

Position Descriptions

As a supervisor, you probably need more explicit direction than objectives can provide if you are to perform the many facets of your job satisfactorily. You also should have a job or position description. A position description is a document that states the duties, responsibilities, and authority of a particular job. It is based on a careful study of the job called a *job analysis*. In some large companies, job descriptions are developed as part of an overall salary administration program. In a small organization, the supervisor and manager together or, if necessary, the supervisor alone develops a written summary of the duties, responsibilities, and authority level of the job. A typical format for a job or position description follows:

1. Heading or identifying data
2. Main objective of the job
3. Scope of the job
4. Reporting relationships
5. General authority level
6. Duties and responsibilities
7. Desirable qualifications

Let's examine each of these sections using examples.

1. Heading or Identifying Data

   Job Title: Commercial Property Underwriting Supervisor

   Location: Branch Office

   Grade Level: 14

   Job Code: 05105 (These codes can be used to identify and access job data whether they are contained in an automated or a manual information system.)

   Job Description: _____New_____Revised

   Date of Latest Revision: March 20XX

   Different or additional identifying data might be included, depending on the organization's needs and the formality of its job analysis and evaluation processes.

2. Main Objective of the Job

   "Under general supervision, to direct the production and retention of profitable commercial property insurance lines, including inland marine, within the branch."

   Notice that the general authority level of this job is set by the use of the term "under general supervision." The supervisor should receive general rather than close supervision once he or she has satisfactorily learned the job.

3. Scope of the Job

   Directs eight to ten commercial property underwriters.

   This part of the job description could also contain the annual premium dollar level that the unit is expected to process.

4. Reporting Relationships

   Reports directly to the branch underwriting manager. Eight to ten commercial property underwriters report directly to the commercial property underwriting supervisor.

5. General Authority Level

   We saw that this was defined in the description of the main objective of the job by the words "under general supervision."

   If the general authority level is not communicated in an earlier section of the job description, it can be communicated in this section.

6. Duties and Responsibilities

   A duty is a task that usually has an identifiable beginning and an end. Three examples follow:

   - Preparing the annual unit budget, including salary and non-salary items, in collaboration with the immediate manager
   - Conducting employee performance appraisals according to current job descriptions and performance standards

- Periodically reporting on unit productivity as directed

On the other hand, a responsibility is defined more broadly as continuing obligations to the firm. This could include the following ongoing processes:

- Controlling expenses within the unit
- Monitoring unit workflows and work processes and recommending revisions where appropriate

Here, the responsibilities for expense control and workflow monitoring are continuing ones.

7. Desirable Qualifications

This final section of the job description describes the desirable qualifications for the job. The following are examples:

- The candidate will have between six and eight years of progressively developing experience as a commercial property underwriter, preferably at the branch-office level.
- The candidate will possess good oral and written communication skills as well as interpersonal skills.
- The candidate will have acquired a bachelor's or an associate degree in insurance or business administration or its equivalent.

Notice that these qualifications are indicated as desirable or preferable. In a particular labor market or locale, the company or other organization may have to adjust these requirements because only a few candidates might meet them.

Authority

When we discussed the job description, we noted that each position should be given a defined limit of authority. Looking at its meaning more closely, authority is the right to give directions.

In addition to the broad granting of supervisory authority implied in such terms as "under general supervision" or "under direct supervision," the supervisor and his or her manager should spell out and periodically review the specific areas and functions for which the supervisor has authority on a day-to-day basis. Some examples follow:

- Authority to approve a homeowners insurance application up to a stated dollar amount limit of liability
- Authority to hire underwriters as direct subordinates within selection guidelines previously established by the organization
- Authority to recommend (or to approve) salary increases for direct subordinates within guidelines established by the organization
- Authority to order supplies up to a certain dollar limit without higher approval

- Authority to require that claim representative trainees attend appropriate training classes

Generally speaking, as a supervisor becomes more proficient, his or her authority level should be reviewed and accordingly enlarged.

Accountability

Accountability is another vehicle through which management communicates its expectations to the supervisor. Accountability is the obligation to answer to managers for your results and the results of your subordinates. The sample job description used earlier indicates that the branch underwriting supervisor is accountable to the branch underwriting manager for the underwriting results achieved by the unit.

The term *accountability*, rather than *responsibility*, has become popular as a way to emphasize the obligation to answer for unit results. In practice, all three terms—accountability, responsibility, and authority—are used to communicate management's expectations to the supervisor.

Written Guidelines

Guidance is provided by a variety of instructions, usually—and preferably—in writing.

Policy

A policy is a general guideline that specifies how routine matters will be handled. An operational example is an underwriting guidelines manual. Interviewing guidelines, as a further example, list questions that may or may not be asked of applicants.

Procedure

A procedure differs from a policy in that it is a more specific guide. A procedure establishes the steps to be followed in handling a routine matter. An example of a procedure in a billing and collections unit is the requirement that invoices accompanied by a check or some other payment be separated immediately from invoices not accompanied by payment. This is obviously because the processing routines for each type of invoice will differ.

Practice

A practice can be defined as a repeated or customary action. One example is a company requirement that field marketing specialists spend a minimum of two years as inside underwriters in specified lines of insurance before going out into the field.

Organizational information systems can include manuals, bulletins, memos, letters, computerized messages, and word-of-mouth communication.

In large, complex, multi-location organizations, the supervisor may use the equivalent of a small reference bookshelf when seeking guidance on operational or personnel questions. On the other hand, in a small agency, written guidance may be rare, thereby requiring the supervisor to rely more heavily on word-of-mouth communication.

WHAT EMPLOYEES EXPECT OF THE SUPERVISOR

Now let's examine what employees are likely to expect of you in your role as a supervisor. Will they expect you to never be at a loss for words? Will they expect you to have a strong personality? Will they expect you to be the unit's technical expert? Will they expect you to give them detailed, step-by-step training on what they must do? Will they expect you to deal effectively with rumors, particularly those that predict some dire happening to the unit, department, or organization?

What do you think your employees will expect of you? Take a few moments to list three or four of their major expectations. After you do this, we will compare your thoughts to those expressed in employee responses to surveys and interviews. Because such surveys and interviews identify rather long lists of characteristics and abilities expected of supervisors, only the major ones will be cited.

Research shows that employees have the following four general expectations of their supervisors:

1. Competence
2. Fairness
3. Communication skills
4. Helping attitude

How do these expectations compare with your list? You do not have to have the same words, but the basic ideas may be similar. Let's examine each more closely.

Competence

Competence here means the ability to direct the unit or department effectively. An example is the ability to perform such supervisory functions as planning or problem solving. For example, do you have a reasonable plan for the week's work, or is the unit continually in a crisis, with you asking people to work late or to come in for part of the weekend to get the work done? If you are going to implement a revised workflow, do you inform employees beforehand of its effect on them and ensure that they know how to do the revised work correctly? In addition to expecting competence in planning, employees expect you to be competent in such skills as identifying problems and decision making.

Fairness

The second major employee expectation is fairness. This means being impartial in performing your supervisory role. A fair supervisor will ensure that work assignments are equitable and that difficult, unpleasant, or hectic tasks are shared equally. Employees will often be remarkably patient with a beginning supervisor if they perceive that they are being treated fairly.

Communication Skills

In addition to expecting competence and fairness, employees expect you to possess adequate communication skills. Employees expect you to accurately and firmly represent their interests to higher management.

Helping Attitude

Employees also expect a supervisor to assist them, when possible, with reaching their goals and attaining career or job satisfaction. Employees expect you to help them with minor job problems and to be interested in helping them make career plans or qualify for promotion.

Subsequent chapters on topics such as communication, leadership, and motivation will identify other general employee expectations of a super-visor, but competence, fairness, communication skills, and a helping attitude are important foundations of which you should be aware and on which to build.

THE SUPERVISOR AS THE "PERSON IN THE MIDDLE"

You have probably witnessed many examples of supervisors trying to balance the expectations of management and those of employees. As a supervisor, you are the person in the middle, caught in the "supervisory squeeze." You have to direct the accomplishment of your unit's operational objectives within the framework of your employees' general expectations about your competence, fairness, communication skills, and willingness to help. You must represent your unit to higher management, and you must represent the expectations of higher management to your employees. These expectations can be about commission income, work processing times, customer service standards, workload requirements, and adequate cost or expense controls. Some of the ways to communicate these expectations to your employees are unit objectives, employee performance standards, meetings, performance appraisal interviews, and effective job training.

In addition to your need to balance higher-management and employee expectations, you must be aware that your supervisory role is at the meeting point of these two different worlds. These worlds are apt to be characterized by differences in language and in values. For example, higher management expects you to communicate their concerns about performance and productivity to your employees. In turn, employees expect you to communicate their concerns about fair and considerate treatment to higher management. Remember that your management role is a unique one in that you directly represent nonmanagerial employees. In contrast, higher-level executives and middle-level managers directly supervise other managers or supervisors. As a supervisor, you are a message center through which higher-management and employee communications are received, translated, and sent on.

Values are the qualities, attitudes, or ideas we consider desirable. Higher management will value a sensitivity to profit among the organization's employees and will expect you to convey this value to your staff. In turn, employees value a sensitivity to their need to be aware of the organization's plans, and they will expect you to communicate this to higher management.

In summary, as the person in the middle, you must perform two major tasks: balancing higher-management and employee expectations and serving as the meeting point between management and other employees.

SUMMARY

Perhaps you have just been offered a promotion to your first supervisory position. The excitement you feel toward this opportunity is likely to be mixed with questions and concerns about what your new role as supervisor will entail. This chapter discussed these concerns and introduced several important concepts related to supervision.

Supervision is defined as guiding the activities of people who perform the work and includes the four management or supervisory functions of planning, organizing, directing, and controlling. In addition, most supervisory positions require the critical skills of communicating, listening, counseling, motivating, leading, decision making, and training.

As is probably apparent, supervisory work differs from technical work. The nature of the job itself changes, the skills demanded of you are different, the scope of your accountability widens, and a new language must be mastered. Fortunately, effective supervision can be learned because it requires knowledge (the understanding of a subject) and skills (the ability to use one's knowledge in an expert way).

As a member of the management team, you will be responsible for meeting certain expectations of management, including unit performance, productivity, and contributions to profit. In addition, management will expect you to manage the people for whom you are accountable. The employees you manage will also expect you to be competent, fair, communicative, and helpful.

Trying to balance the expectations of these two groups, management and employees, will be one of your most difficult and most critical tasks as a supervisor.

Chapter 2

Making the Transition Into Supervision

In the first chapter, we identified several major differences between supervisory and technical work. This chapter will examine these differences in greater detail and with particular emphasis on the behavioral changes involved.

THE REALITIES OF THE SUPERVISORY ROLE

We will begin by asking you to complete a short quiz either here or on scratch paper. We will then review your answers, developing each point more completely.

1. A manager will most likely evaluate a supervisor's performance in terms of his or her interpersonal skills. *Answer: D*
    ✓ Agree_____Disagree

2. As a supervisor, you are apt to become
    _____More skilled ✓ Less skilled
    in the unit's technical or operating work.

3. Supervisory tasks are likely to be discontinuous and fragmented.
    _____Agree ✓ Disagree   *Answer A*

4. Time pressure in a supervisory position is likely to be
    ✓ Greater than _____Less than _____About the same as
    time pressure in a nonsupervisory position.

5. Change in a department or unit can affect supervisors before it affects other employees.
    ✓ Agree_____Disagree

6. The amount of education and training offered to supervisors varies widely among organizations.
    ✓ Agree_____Disagree

7. A supervisor's self-perception depends on the amount of management support he or she receives. *Answer B*
    _____Agree ✓ Disagree

Let us now review your answers. The preferred response will be given, followed by some comments for each.

1. You should have *disagreed* with this statement. As a supervisor, your manager is more likely to evaluate your performance in terms of the results your unit attains rather than on your interpersonal skills. This will be particularly true when your *span of control* (the number of employees you directly supervise) is large.

    As an example, assume you supervise ten personal lines underwriters. Your manager is apt to evaluate your overall performance primarily on the results produced by your group, such as the number of policies or applications they underwrite, the error ratio they attain, or the speed at which they respond to agents' or customers' requests for service. Your manager is likely to place less weight on how technically proficient you are as an underwriter. This is usually true even if you are handling a few special cases in addition to supervising the underwriters. He or she is also likely to place less emphasis on a direct evaluation of your supervisory skills.

    This does not mean that technical and supervisory skills are unimportant and that only results count. The point is that your manager should *first* look at unit results when appraising your performance. Your technical and supervisory skills are not likely to earn you a high evaluation if your unit is not meeting performance expectations. Furthermore, you are expected to focus on results and to obtain and use the interpersonal skills you need to help employees accomplish unit objectives.

    If your ten underwriters are to attain group results that are acceptable to your organization, you will have to concentrate on such tasks as scheduling and directing the unit's work and its people. To support these supervisory functions, you will need to use such supervisory skills as communicating, leading, and motivating.

2. Your attention and time should be concentrated on guiding employees toward the unit objectives set during the planning process. For that reason, you will become less skilled over time at performing technical tasks. Your speed and skill at doing the technical work will decline after you have left a technical position and become a supervisor. Your technical knowledge, however, will probably broaden because you will know the important tasks in all of the jobs in your unit. If, as in the previous example, you supervise ten personal lines underwriters, nearly all of your time will be consumed by performing supervisory duties—assuming that you are performing them properly. You can no longer delve into the underwriting process as before. You must leave the underwriting to the underwriters and avoid handling all of the tough applications yourself. If not, you will soon have underwriters who are dependent rather than dependable.

    Since the individual underwriters are devoting all of their time and attention to technical duties, they are or will soon grow to be more familiar than you are with underwriting standards, guidelines, and procedures.

Ironically, you may have been chosen to be supervisor because of your technical skill only to find that the demands of the new position prevent you from continuing to be the unit's outstanding technician.

3. Surveys and interviews show that supervisors and managers must adapt to the start-and-stop nature of supervisory tasks. They must meet the legitimate demands for attention from managers, employees, other supervisors, agents, policyholders, customers, or clients. As a supervisor, the interruptions *are* part of your job.

    In a single day, the activities of a busy supervisor of a dozen claim representatives can include the following:

    a. Holding a weekly staff meeting

    b. Working on a biweekly productivity report that is due the next day

    c. Notifying two claim representatives of a salary increase

    d. Interviewing one or two job applicants

    e. Approving a claim representative's enrollment in a one-week home-office training course

    f. Calling a claimant who has written a complaint about the way a claim representative handled a claim

    g. Coaching a senior employee about possible future career alternatives

    h. Meeting with his or her manager to discuss the status of the unit's expense-control objective

    i. Completing the preliminary scheduling for the coming vacation season

The supervisor can complete some of these tasks in a few minutes. For others, the best the supervisor can hope to accomplish is part of the task in one day.

4. Because you are required to deal with many people and frequent interruptions, time pressures present a significant challenge. You will almost certainly feel greater time pressure in a supervisory role than you did in a technical or an operating position. Since many of your tasks will be interrupted and must be resumed later, you will probably feel a sense of inefficiency in performing them.

5. You should have *agreed* with this statement. Some examples of change that a supervisor would logically be expected to know about and understand before the unit implements them are as follows:

    a. Changes in underwriting guidelines that increase the homeowners coverage underwriting authority for the unit's underwriters

    b. Changes in personnel guidelines, such as a new requirement that the supervisor complete a performance appraisal after a new employee has been on the job for ninety days

    c. Changes in the unit's scheduling for the coming summer months

    d. Changes in the unit's computer system or procedures

The supervisor must plan—in detail—the execution of such changes within the unit. Many of these changes will warrant a number of preparatory activities and contacts with others.

6.   You should have *agreed* with this statement. The variations among organizations can be great. For example, in some large organizations, a new supervisor will be immediately enrolled in a supervisory study course in which he or she will be coached periodically by his or her manager. Subsequently, the supervisor may attend a follow-up training course or seminar in which he or she will participate in discussion groups and workshops and do skill role-plays such as employment interviewing, performance appraising, and coaching. Still later, that same supervisor might be encouraged to enroll in other programs in knowledge and skill areas not covered in the organization's internal supervisory program.

In other organizations, particularly smaller ones, the supervisor might receive some general supervisory orientation by the manager and then be enrolled in a program such as the one you are studying. In such a case, the manager can complement the program content with training on matters specific to that company, agency, or organization. Consider also the case of organizations that give no planned or formal supervisory training; supervisors in that situation need to rely on their own skills and select readings that can help them.

We recommend that you not assume that your organization's supervisory training is all you need. Assess your own needs and take responsibility for your own supervisory education.

7.   You should have *agreed* with this statement. In a national survey of 7,000 supervisors, including those in insurance, supervisors who reported both overall job satisfaction and high self-perception as part of management received adequate support from their superiors. Such support can include a clear statement of the supervisor's responsibilities and authority; open communication; and supportive, accessible, and friendly relations with higher management.[1] Where supervisors did not perceive these elements, their self-perception as members of management and satisfaction with their jobs dropped significantly.

Although the survey cited other management actions as being important to a healthy supervisory self-perception—such as careful selection in choosing the supervisor and special sensitivity to the supervisor's first few days on the job—expressed management support can have major importance.

LEAVING THE FORMER SOCIAL SYSTEM

In addition to facing the unfamiliarity of his or her new tasks, the new supervisor must absorb the often dramatic effects of leaving the social setting in which he or she formerly worked. We can say that the new supervisor is taken away from his or her *social system*.

You are undoubtedly aware of some aspects of the social system at work; however, you probably have never looked at it carefully. The nucleus of the system is the unit or department in which you work. However, your entire social system is larger than that. It involves all of the persons with whom you have frequent contact, including the people you see regularly at work.

What does the word *social* in the term *social system* mean? It refers to the interaction between the individual and others. People are in your social system if you have relatively frequent contact with them and exchange thoughts and feelings with them.

As used in the field of management, the social system is the interaction between the individual and others within the framework of an organization. As an example, personal lines underwriter Mary Brown, a member of a Chicago metropolitan area personal lines underwriting unit, works with seven colleagues, all of whom are directed in their work by their supervisor. Mary's social system includes the other personal lines underwriters, her tablemates at lunch, a close friend in another unit, and two other employees she often sees on the commuter train. These people are important to Mary; she feels good when they have good news, and their opinions mean much to her. They constitute her unique social system.

Role of the Job in the Social System

An employee's job usually has a strong influence on his or her social system. Aspects of the job that contribute to the kind of social system that emerges include the tasks performed, the contacts required and allowed, the job location, and proximity to others. To illustrate the effects of such factors, we will describe the work of two employees. The descriptions are followed by comments on their social system and how it changes when they become supervisors.

CASE STUDY: JIM BYRNES

Jim Byrnes is a senior loss prevention engineer for a large insurer. He works out of his home in San Antonio, Texas. He conducts and reports on fire protection inspections and liability safety inspections of properties in that area. His work is entirely technical. Jim is supervised from the company's branch office in Dallas, and he is in frequent contact with his supervisor by phone and e-mail. In addition, Jim's supervisor visits him at least one day each quarter to review his job progress. Jim is also in periodic contact with other loss prevention engineers located in Texas and Oklahoma who are employees of his company.

Jim has been in San Antonio for the past four years. He has spent the last two as senior loss prevention engineer, a promotion he earned because of excellent performance. For three and a half years before that, Jim was assigned to the company's branch office in Atlanta, Georgia, doing the same type of inspection work. He was recruited into the Atlanta branch as a college-graduate engineer trainee.

Jim's unit supervisor at the Dallas branch office is planning to retire within the next nine months. The company, after reviewing the qualifications of Jim and other engineers, offered him the job, which consists of supervising ten loss prevention engineers operating in Texas and Oklahoma. Four of the ten work out of the Dallas branch office; the other six work from either small offices or from their homes, as Jim now does.

Jim Byrnes has had no prior supervisory experience or education.

Assume that Jim accepts the job offer. Take a few minutes now and identify the critical aspects of the social system Jim is leaving.

Analysis

Let's analyze your answers to the Jim Byrnes case. The exact words you used are not as important as whether you identified the general ideas or concepts involved.

The following are several of the critical aspects of the social system that Jim is leaving:

1. Jim Byrnes's work as a senior loss prevention engineer and earlier as a loss prevention engineer is highly specialized. Thus, Jim's contacts with others are mainly technical.
2. Jim interacts with a large number of people infrequently. He is accountable for conducting and reporting on fire protection inspections and liability safety inspections of properties located in San Antonio and nearby areas.
3. Jim stays in touch with his Dallas-based supervisor by phone, e-mail, and occasional face-to-face visits. His relationship with his supervisor is probably very important to him.
4. Although he is in periodic contact with other loss prevention engineers in Texas and Oklahoma, we can reasonably assume that they do not play a major role in his social system.
5. Jim does not appear to be in a small group of persons who work together and communicate constantly. In other words, he does not belong to a strong informal group.

CASE STUDY: MARIA LUMSDEN

Maria Lumsden is an experienced commercial underwriter in a large metropolitan branch office of an insurer that operates countrywide. She joined her unit of eight underwriters five years ago after graduating from a community college with an associate degree in business administration.

Since then, she has progressed well on the job, having been promoted to the senior underwriter grade. In addition, she has completed an evening school program and earned a bachelor's degree in business administration. Her present job is completely technical in that she underwrites risks submitted by twenty-five agencies in the metropolitan area. Her performance has been evaluated as above-standard by her supervisor.

One of the supervisors in another commercial underwriting unit in the same branch is being promoted to a manager's job. Maria and several other experienced underwriters are being considered for the position of supervisor. Maria is several years younger than the other candidates. The company offers her the job, which consists of supervising eight commercial underwriters and two underwriting assistants. She will also be responsible for directing the underwriting of business submitted by about 150 agencies.

Analysis

Assume that Maria accepts the promotion. Here are several of the critical aspects of the social system she is leaving.

1. Maria Lumsden's work in her present job as a senior commercial underwriter and in her earlier experience as a commercial underwriter has been specialized. Her social system comprises other underwriters and loss control specialists, and many of these interactions consist of technical discussions.
2. Maria has had many contacts with people from the twenty-five agencies she underwrites. Although not part of Maria's work group, these people have been part of her social system. She probably has developed friendships with some of them.
3. Maria no doubt communicates with the other underwriters in her unit. In fact, they probably serve as the most important group in her work life. Maria would most likely describe herself as a member of the commercial underwriter group. Her contacts with them may be largely informal and friendly, as we can reasonably assume that their desks are close together.

Characteristics of the Supervisor's Former Social System

Although there are many exceptions, the following list suggests some common characteristics of the social system most employees leave behind when they become insurance supervisors:

1. The most visible and central part of the social system is the informal work group. Most insurance employees have an opportunity to develop close ties with people they work with or near. This primary group satisfies many personal needs, such as friendship and self-expression.
2. Insurance jobs often provide opportunities for frequent contact with other organization members, particularly specialists.
3. Insurance work often involves frequent contact with people outside the organization.
4. The majority of the employee's interactions are usually with people of equal status.

ENTERING A NEW SOCIAL SYSTEM

What are some of the critical changes facing the supervisor as he or she enters a new social system? You will recall our definition of a social system as the interaction between the individual and others within the framework of an organization. For example, in Jim Byrnes's new role as a supervisor, the framework is going to include his employees; his new manager; his new peer supervisor, if any; and probably an expanded number of policyholders.

If you think back to the two cases for a moment, you will undoubtedly agree that Jim and Maria will be challenged in their new roles as supervisor of ten loss prevention engineers and supervisor of eight commercial underwriters, respectively. They will have much new knowledge and many new skills to acquire in order to master their new roles. While they learn their new roles, they must adjust to very different social systems.

Change in the Informal Group

Perhaps the greatest change in the supervisor's social system occurs in the makeup and role of the primary informal group to which he or she belongs. Informal groups of employees often center around physical proximity, work-flow contacts, and personal interests; they usually develop within the formal units of the organization. The supervisor should not try to retain membership in the informal work group to which he or she belonged before being promoted to supervisor. Supervisors need to realize that after their promotion, they are no longer "one of the gang." Although they still can remain friendly with their former peers, they can no longer have the same informal relationship with people they are now supervising.

If the new supervisor has frequent contact with other supervisors, a peer group of supervisors is likely to become the major informal group in the supervisor's social system. What about the supervisor whose contacts with other supervisors are infrequent and who spends most of his or her time within the unit? Here, the picture is less clear. In effect, the circumstances prevent the supervisor from being a full, regular member of a small group. When this is the case, the supervisor is likely to place great emphasis on the infrequent interactions with other supervisors. He or she will also tend to meet some social needs away from the job and through the relationship with his or her manager.

Greater Control Over One's Own Affairs

Supervisors can acquire relatively greater control over their own jobs, time, and social patterns than can other employees. You may recall in Jim's case that his supervisor occasionally visited him to assess his job progress. Presumably, this visit was scheduled at the mutual convenience of Jim and the supervisor. Now, as a supervisor, Jim can probably initiate the selection of dates for these personal, one-on-one visits with his employees. They can be frequent, informal, and short, or they can be infrequent, formal, and lengthy.

Similarly, he can set up guidelines with the field employees about when they can make routine calls to him. For example, he may ask the Houston engineer to call between 8:30 A.M. and 9:30 A.M., the San Antonio engineer to call between 9:30 A.M. and 10:00 A.M., and so forth. Jim can also largely initiate the subjects and the timing of the communications he has with the engineers based at the Dallas branch office.

Higher Visibility in the Organization

Another critical aspect of the new supervisory social system is the relatively higher visibility that the supervisor has within the organization. Most insurance companies, agencies, and other organizations are set up in a pyramidal organizational structure. The supervisor is known by name, and his or her performance is observed by many managers and executives.

In Maria's case, she will supervise eight commercial underwriters and two underwriting assistants. If the same ratio of supervisors to employees pertains to other parts of her metropolitan branch office, the ratio of supervisors to technical and clerical employees is about one to ten. Clearly, the small number of supervisors and managers suggests that they enjoy greater visibility within the organization.

In practice, this may either help or hinder the new supervisor. If successful in achieving some demanding unit task or assignment, he or she is more apt to receive appropriate recognition and acclaim. Similarly, failure to achieve an important result is likely to be noticed.

Higher Number of and More Complex Relationships

In addition to having greater control over their jobs and higher visibility, new supervisors are likely to find that the number and complexity of relationships often increase dramatically.

For example, Jim will be accountable for supervising the ten loss prevention engineers assigned to Texas and Oklahoma. In addition, he will report to a new boss, a manager based either at the Dallas branch office or in another location.

Jim will also assume accountability for all of the company's inspection activities within Texas and Oklahoma and will undoubtedly develop many new relationships with policyholders, clients, agents, brokers, and others.

Jim will also develop new peer relationships in the Dallas branch office and elsewhere. For example, he may be expected to coordinate activities with the supervisors of such functions as marketing, underwriting, claim processing, premium auditing, or information services.

RELATING TO MANAGERS AND EXECUTIVES

The most important of the relationships that will change as you make the transition from employee to supervisor is the one with your own manager. Before we more formally explore the dimensions of your new relationship with your manager, take a few minutes to read the following case.

Your Manager

Assume you have just been appointed as a unit supervisor by your new boss, Connie Perez, who is the office services manager in the company's Kansas City, Mo., branch office. You are going to supervise a commercial lines rating unit consisting of eight raters. The unit presently uses both manual and computerized rating techniques on their PCs.

You have worked as a rater in this same unit for the past five years. Previously, you worked in the office of a Kansas City insurance broker for six years.

In addition to managing your rating unit, Connie oversees two other units: a coding unit and a mail and office supply unit. These units are all located within your branch office. Each unit is led by a supervisor who, like you, reports directly to Connie. The supervisory spans of control vary from six to eight employees.

Connie has been in her middle management job for nearly two years. Before that, she served as the office services supervisor of the company's smaller branch office in Houston for several years. Before entering management, Connie worked as a rater in the Houston branch for four years. You estimate that Connie is in her late thirties, about eight to ten years older than you are.

Your branch office faces direct price and product competition from several sources. One is from another regional insurer that has both its home office and a large branch office in the Kansas City area. Other competitors are the branch offices of large national companies.

Naturally, your entire branch office and Connie's office services department have challenging objectives to meet. The branch objectives concern such areas as production of business balanced with an appropriate "mix" of lines; attaining a desirable loss ratio; quick, courteous service to agents and policy-holders; and expense control.

Since Connie Perez's department (through its rating, coding, and mail and supply units) serves agents, policyholders, and other departments within the branch office, Connie has departmental objectives that support those of the entire branch. Her objectives concern productivity, error ratios, timeliness, completeness of service to users, staff development, and expense control. Since it is one organizational layer down, your unit will have similar objectives that also support those of the department.

Other managers, supervisors, and employees within the branch office respect and like Connie. She tends to be pragmatic, concentrating on what is workable. She is conscientious in holding periodic meetings for unit supervisors and for the staff, meeting weekly with the supervisors and at least quarterly with the entire department staff.

Connie believes in systematic and thorough training of the staff in order to be able to meet the challenging departmental objectives. She is completing a bachelor's degree in evening school and has completed the Insurance Institute of America's Associate in Underwriting program. She has also completed the company's management education program.

During the next five months, the company plans to install several PCs in your unit for processing certain commercial lines applications. The PCs will be connected to the company's mainframe computer at the home office. Both you and Connie will need appropriate training on how to manage the system. You will also be working together to ensure its smooth installation. You will have to select several of your employees to be trained to operate the new PCs.

Using your own words, list the factors that should influence your relationship as a new supervisor with your new manager, Connie Perez.

Now consider some answers. Recognize that the various factors were intentionally presented in random order throughout the case just as they would appear to you in real life. Each factor will be followed by a brief comment.

Factors That Influence Your Relationship With Your Manager

Knowing your manager's priorities and getting agreement on how you will support them, appreciating the nature of your manager's job, and understanding your manager's experience and management style will influence your relationship with him or her.

Know Your Manager's Priorities and Get Agreement on How You Will Support Them

Not surprisingly, your Kansas City branch office is involved in vigorous price and product competition with other local, regional, and national insurers. The branch's objectives reflect this need to be price and product competitive and address the production of business, loss ratio, customer service, and expense control.

Appreciate the Nature of Your Manager's Job

The following questions might help you to be more aware of the aspects of your manager's job.

How Many Subordinates Does Your Manager Directly and Indirectly Supervise?

Connie directly supervises you and the other supervisors who head the coding and mail and supply units. In turn, each unit has a span of control of between six and eight employees.

Connie, then, has three direct subordinates and eighteen to twenty-six indirect subordinates among the three units. Because the functions the units perform are key ones such as mail and rating, they must be performed correctly, in varying volume levels, and on time.

Where Are Subordinates Located?

In Connie's case, all of the employees are at the same office location, which should make communicating, directing, and controlling somewhat easier than they might be otherwise. In contrast, recall the previous Jim Byrnes case in which Byrnes will be supervising loss prevention engineers at remote locations throughout two large states. This dispersal increases the challenge in effectively communicating with and directing employees.

Is the Management Job Line or Staff?

Connie's job would probably be considered line since most of the functions she directs are involved in generating the branch office's major products.

More than likely, Connie is in the direct chain of authority of the branch manager and reports to him or her.

What Tasks and Technologies Are Involved in the Department?

The tasks are clerical, fairly routine, and repetitious. The unit presently uses both manual and computerized rating techniques.

We can say that the department and various units within it are definitely involved in technological change, and changes are likely to continue in the years ahead.

Understand the Experience of Your Manager

Connie has been a department manager for two years and apparently does the job well. In addition, she has prior supervisory and rating experience at your company's smaller Houston branch.

You have to assume that she was capable of successfully making the transition from technical to supervisory work and from the latter to managerial work. In addition, she has made the relocation transition from Houston to Kansas City. In short, Connie seems to have a solid and successful background in both the technical and managerial side of the business.

Understand the Management Style of Your Manager

Although the subject of style, that is, the typical manner or pattern of behavior of a leader, will be described in greater detail in a subsequent chapter, we already know some useful things about Connie Perez as a manager and as a person.

We know that the following are true of Connie as a manager:

- Other managers, supervisors, and employees like and respect Connie.
- She is pragmatic, tending to concentrate on what will work.
- She is a conscientious communicator, holding periodic meetings of both supervisors and staff.
- She believes in systematic and thorough training of her employees.

We know that the following is true of Connie as a person:

- She shows ambition by completing a bachelor's degree during the evening, by having completed a designation program, and by having completed her company's management education program.

Key aspects of her managerial style include the following:

- *How does she prefer to get and give key information?* For example, does she prefer face-to-face dialogue, or does she prefer key information in writing?
- *How does she make decisions?* Does she make them alone or does she encourage input from supervisors and others?
- *How does she delegate?* Does she delegate authority to her supervisors task by task or by a prior general grant of authority once she has determined the subordinate is competent to perform the task?

The relationship you have with your immediate manager is of key importance to the success of both of your jobs. Its importance probably cannot be overemphasized. You should know your manager's priorities and determine how you can support them; appreciate the nature of your manager's job and his or her experience; and try to understand him or her as a person, including his or her management style. The items italicized above serve as a checklist for understanding your manager.

Other Managers and Executives

You should also be aware of how other managers and executives in the organization can affect the relationship between you and your manager. We will examine three facets of this effect: (1) the influence of your manager's manager, (2) the influence of your manager's peers, and (3) the organization's managerial style or climate.

The Influence of Your Manager's Manager

Just as your relationship with Connie is of critical importance, so, too, is her relationship with her boss, who is probably the manager of the Kansas City branch office. Just as you have to determine what Connie's managerial priorities are and what her management style is, she must go through the same thought processes with her manager. For example, Connie will want to know the extent and type of managerial experience her boss has had. Is her boss's managerial experience mainly in the line or operating end of the business? Has her boss had management experience at other company locations? What is her manager's functional background—marketing, underwriting, office operations? What are her manager's values and goals?

The Influence of Your Manager's Peers

Insight into the manager's role can be developed through questions such as the following:

- How many peer managers are there?
- What functions do they represent—marketing, claims, underwriting, loss prevention, office operations, accounting, information technology?
- How do these functions relate to those of Connie Perez and her department?
- Do departments operate independently, or does the work require close coordination among them?
- Do they constitute an informal group?
- If so, what are the shared values of group members?

The Influence of the Managerial Style or Climate of the Organization

Some pertinent factors include the following:

- Are managers held accountable for results?
- Is authority delegated to the lowest practical level?
- How effective are communications within the organization?

- What is the background of key executives within the organization? For example, do financial people tend to dominate the organization? Does the organization promote senior managers from within, or are these people sometimes hired from outside?
- What are the important goals and values of the organization? Does the organization tend to emphasize immediate or long-range results?
- Are changes made slowly or rapidly?

RELATING TO OTHER SUPERVISORS

In general, the organization's senior and middle managers will expect you and the other supervisors to function as a team and to cooperate with each other appropriately. In the Connie Perez case, three units were in the office services department: your rating unit and the units dealing with coding and mail and supplies. You are expected to form a team with the other supervisors who report to Connie. You are also expected to develop a broader perspective of the organization.

Teamwork

Your department manager and other managers will expect you and your supervisory peers to work as a team. This means dovetailing the work of your unit with that of other units. It may even mean sacrificing a bit of efficiency or convenience in order to help other supervisors. It may mean lending employees to help with workload peaks elsewhere and, in turn, being able to rely on other supervisors for help when you need it.

Developing a Broader Perspective of the Organization

As a supervisor, you will have to develop a broader perspective of the organization. Several facets of this perspective and a detailed description of each follows.

1. You will have to possess adequate knowledge of the work performed by other units and departments at your immediate location and elsewhere.

   In the Connie Perez case, you were the rating supervisor who reported to the manager of the office services department. Your peers were the unit supervisors for the coding and mail and office supplies units. Although you did not have to become an expert on the work these units perform, you did have to know enough about how your work product, work flows, or work processes interacted with theirs to ensure that the units worked together effectively.

   In addition, in a large branch office like the one described, you may have to know something about the work performed by other departments such as underwriting, marketing, claims, and accounting. Recall the point that your home office and its mainframe computer were located in Dallas. Once your unit has PCs that communicate with that computer, you might also need to know something about the home-office computer facility and know the key people there. You will need to know the how and *who* of unsnarling the inevitable snags in establishing and using the new data-exchangesy stem.

2. You should develop a thorough understanding of your unit's role and its support of other units in your department, its support of your department, and its support of the overall organization. This idea of developing a broader perspective builds on the previous point. You must go beyond knowing what other units do—you must have a mastery of the points at which work flows connect.

    For example, referring again to the Connie Perez case, the supervisor of the unit that distributes and collects mail has to mesh his or her operations effectively with those of other units. Schedules and activities must be adjusted so that the mail unit can handle workload peaks created by other units. Your own experience probably offers many other illustrations of the give-and-take among units whose work inputs and outputs must be harmonized.

3. You will have to develop a conviction about the importance of good communications and relations with other supervisors and develop sensitivity to lapses in effective communication.

    Recall that Connie conducted weekly meetings with her unit supervisors. This approach makes communication convenient, but the other people involved must also accept responsibility for initiating communication.

    A good technique is to have supervisors or managers periodically address the meeting on procedural and other changes within the organization. In addition to initiating this more formal, structured communication, supervisors have a continuing responsibility to communicate on a one-to-one basis and to support each other's operations as required. A key factor here is for the supervisor to periodically talk with and listen to other supervisors about how their units are progressing.

4. You should develop a sensitivity to informal influence within the organization. You may recall that this chapter discussed the effect of the background of key executives in the organization and the possible resulting emphasis on marketing, underwriting, or some other function within the organization. Although an organization should give proper attention to all of its major functions, the reality is that an organization usually emphasizes one or two functions. Indeed, some firms succeed because they excel in one or two areas.

    For example, many senior executives at the home office or managers of branch offices may have worked in the marketing department. Although such executives or managers will usually have multiple annual objectives that include tasks other than marketing, they may spend more time on marketing because they are most comfortable and familiar with that function.

    Another example of informal influence in the organization is the role of powerful employees, whether they are managers, supervisors, technicians, or clerical employees. Such people usually influence the thinking of others, especially if others view them as competent and respect them for their competence. The supervisor should be sensitive to the role influential employees play, seek their views on important issues, and use their potential to aid upward and downward communication.

In summary, the supervisor should be aware of and fulfill his or her responsibilities to be informed about the operations of other units or departments, to be able to support their supervisors effectively, and to be aware of the importance of good communications and relations with other supervisors.

RELATING TO EMPLOYEES

In addition to relating effectively to managers and to other supervisors, you are expected to have good relationships with unit employees. You may recall that, at the end of the first chapter, we discussed the supervisor's continuing challenge of balancing the expectations of higher management and employees. In general, management expects a supervisor to direct unit employees skillfully. However, employees expect you as a supervisor to be competent, fair, communicative, and helpful.

Realistically, if you are to direct your employees effectively, you will have to broaden your knowledge of how employees relate to the unit, to the department, and to the organization. In the first chapter, we discussed a variety of supervisory tools you can use to guide employees in achieving their tasks, either as a group or individually. These tools include objectives for the unit and position descriptions and performance standards for individual employees.

As Individuals

When viewing individual employees in terms of how they can be recruited, selected, trained, and developed to perform their individual tasks, you should be aware of the effects of several relevant factors. These include (1) the tasks performed, (2) the location and setting of the job (branch office, home office, working from home, travel requirements, and so on), (3) the employee's work experience, and (4) the employee's educational experience and other personal background. Let's look at each of these factors as applied to the Jim Byrnes case.

An employee performs a technical job, such as loss prevention engineer. This job requires the engineer to meet high standards of inspection and reporting because of possible future effects on the policyholder and the insurer.

The possible locations of the job included a branch office, a small field office, or working from one's home. Working from home requires one to be a self-starter, as the person must systematically plan and complete the inspection of work without the supervisor's guidance.

Work experience among the loss prevention engineers would probably vary in length, in depth, and in other factors. For example, Jim had been promoted to senior loss prevention engineer several years ago. Such a senior or an experienced employee would probably require general rather than close supervision. Conversely, a newly appointed engineer, particularly one working at a remote location, would probably require a thorough orientation before assignment and frequent personal visits from the supervisor for some time after assignment. In addition, some technical jobs in insurance require licensing or certification by a state or local agency or by some other entity. An example is a loss prevention engineer who inspects certain types of boilers and machinery. In such a case, the immediate supervisor must be aware of these requirements and, indeed, might be expected to help prepare the new engineer to take any necessary examinations.

Educational experience among the loss prevention engineers would probably also vary. Some could be college graduates in engineering, chemistry, or other fields, or they could have completed several years of study in a related field. Some have had extensive company training.

We can also apply this analysis to the Connie Perez case in which you were the supervisor of eight raters at the Kansas City branch office. In this case, we expect that you would know these raters, or some of them, reasonably well since you worked as a rater in the same unit for five years before being promoted. Having done the job that long, you should also be intimately familiar with the tasks.

Here you will be supervising your employees at one location. This should help you communicate with, train, and evaluate them.

More than likely, the raters' tasks and educational experience would vary and you will have to become sufficiently familiar with each individual's background, including which lines of insurance they can rate. This information may influence training and work assignments on the new terminals.

As a Group

As a supervisor, you should not only see employees as individuals, but also you must visualize the social system to which they belong. More critically, you must have an accurate picture of the small group or groups that are the building blocks of that social system.

As you look at the employees' social system, ask yourself several questions. Who are the leaders? When is their leadership evident? Who are the full-fledged members of the small groups? Who are occasional members? Are any employees excluded from the grapevine, coffee gatherings, lunchtime groups, off-work gatherings, and other informal activities?

Informal leaders hold a special status in the eyes of their fellow employees. You probably recognize them and treat them differently as a matter of intuition. You should make "reading" the informal organization a more deliberate process. In turn, you can tailor your actions toward its members. You can, for instance, give a measure of support to those informal leaders who support unit objectives. You can do this by consulting them, by regarding their statements as representing shared views, and by keeping them informed on matters of concern to employees.

The Jim Byrnes case illustrates an unusual situation. Because they are located in different cities, the loss prevention engineers do not constitute a strong primary group. This does not mean that they do not constitute a group, have common values, or have informal leadership roles. Because they have frequent contacts, they still constitute a group. However, in comparison to groups that have daily opportunities for face-to-face communication, the group is likely to be less cohesive, less powerful, and less important to members.

As supervisor, you should develop skill in understanding the employees in your unit. That understanding includes appreciation of their individuality and insight into their social system.

We have just examined your relationships with managers and executives, with peer supervisors, and with employees. We turn now to a discussion of how you can build a support system of people both within these groups and outside the organization.

BUILDING A SUPPORT SYSTEM

A *support system* consists of interpersonal relationships that help you to function effectively as a person and, by extension, as a supervisor. This does not mean that you concentrate on your own selfish interests and try to manipulate others to support those interests. It *does* mean that you intelligently and legitimately work within the organization and with key people and groups in a cooperative effort to meet personal needs.

Within the Organization

Your support system should include your manager, your peer supervisors, and unit employees. In addition, your support system can include members of other units that either use your work product or output as their input or vice versa.

Outside the Organization

Your support system could include policyholders, customers, clients, agents, brokers, friends, and family members. To the extent that these people meet your personal and social needs, they are part of your support system. You need not be conscious of their support to benefit from it. As mentioned before, you should ensure that you have sufficient contact with them.

Let's address the role these persons and groups play. Internally, your manager can be one of the most vital elements in your support system. He or she often controls the information you need to do your job, influences the annual objectives you set, influences your development on the job, appraises your performance, and may influence your salary.

For example, in the Connie Perez case, your manager held weekly meetings with you and the other supervisors. She believed in systematically and thoroughly training her employees, was apparently able to anticipate and absorb changes including further automation of the group's activities, and set a good example in her efforts to educate and develop herself by completing her college courses and other education. Based on what you have learned about Connie Perez, she is likely to play a vital role in your support system.

Another key part of your support system consists of your peer supervisors. These could be from your department or from other departments. An example of the former in the Perez case is peer supervisors who head the coding and the mail and supply units. As the rating unit supervisor, you could extend yourself or your staff to communicate with and support the activities of the other units, and they could reciprocate, particularly when unit work processes or workflows directly relate to each other. The same general guideline would apply to your unit's relationships to units in other departments, such as marketing, underwriting, or claims, where a provider-user relationship exists.

You are urged to build the support system you need to do your best as a supervisor. This means arranging your activities so that you have frequent contact with people you enjoy and who help you advance toward your goals.

Your Interdependence With Unit Members

Your support system contains unit employees as well as your manager. Other chapters in this book will give you ideas for developing a leadership style that helps employees meet their own needs, grow, and develop trust and respect for you. Just consider what would happen if half of your eight raters decided to restrict their production. You could not perform their work no matter how long or diligently you worked. Thus, you need the support of your employees. You can help build this support by fostering feelings of trust in you as a supervisor. Realistically, you will not develop this sense of trust overnight. It will take time, as employees observe how you act in day-to-day situations.

Other Elements in the Support System

In addition to the key roles played by your manager, other supervisors, and employees, other units or departments can play less significant roles in your support system. An example based on the Perez case is an underwriting department that uses the work product of the rating unit and other units Connie manages.

Within a small agency, an example is the support the internal clerical staff gives to the sales representatives. In a larger company or organization, other elements in the support system may be staff departments such as human resources and systems analysis. An example of the former is your consulting with a human resources specialist when there has been a change on guidelines relating to employment interviewing or to promotion. An example of the latter is consulting a systems specialist when you are considering making some changes in internal unit work processes that could have a significant effect on either "downstream" units or departments. Seeking the help of such specialists, and showing appreciation for their work, leads to their inclusion in your support system.

PROMOTION FROM WITHIN THE UNIT

Should a supervisor be promoted from within the unit? This is a classic management question. Some firms favor promotion from within a unit, while others have a policy of moving a new supervisor to another unit at the time of the promotion. Each practice has positive and negative factors connected with it. Before we discuss them, list the advantages and disadvantages connected with each practice as you see them.

Promotion From Within the Unit

Following are some key points about the question of whether a supervisor should be promoted from within his or her own unit.

Advantages:

1. The supervisor should know the various jobs in the unit and how they relate to each other.
2. The supervisor should know the employees and their major strengths and weaknesses in regard to technical skill, meeting deadlines, absenteeism, and so forth.
3. The supervisor should know the organizational climate.
4. The supervisor should understand the social system of the unit.

Disadvantages:

1. The supervisor promoted from within may have difficulty completely accepting the supervisory role. He or she may try to remain in the role of employee and "one of the group."
2. Some employees may continue to see the supervisor as a technician or clerical employee rather than as the supervisor. Some may work subtly to keep the supervisor from becoming a real boss.
3. The supervisor may not legitimately demand enough of employees in terms of productivity, quality of work, and other criteria. Such a supervisor may appear to be too apologetic when he or she asks for something.
4. The supervisor may not be honest and candid with employees, particularly in a situation in which an employee's work performance has been below par in some way. The supervisor may play favorites based on past friendships.
5. This point is the opposite of the two points immediately preceding. Some supervisors might become insensitive or arrogant in relating to employees, perhaps by demanding too much from them.
6. A final and sometimes critical factor is the possibility of a relationship problem with a disappointed competitor for the job. Other unit members, too, may have divided feelings about the selection or selection process. The new supervisor will have to respond with sensitivity to these feelings without abdicating his or her position as supervisor.

Promotion From Outside the Unit

Now consider the following advantages and disadvantages of hiring a supervisor from outside the unit or department.

Advantages:

1. The organization thought enough of the supervisor's abilities and qualities to hire him or her from outside. Since the search was broader, the new supervisor should be highly qualified for the position.
2. The supervisor brings a fresh point of view and perhaps some different skills, experiences, and expectations to the unit.
3. The supervisor starts, in effect, with a clean slate. Employees and others probably do not have any prior conceptions about him or her. Recall the point that some employees may continue to see the supervisor who is promoted from within as a peer. The supervisor promoted from outside has a relative advantage here.

Disadvantages:

1. The most obvious negative factor is that the supervisor brought in from outside has to learn a great deal about many things, often in a relatively short time. For example, the new supervisor will have to learn about the unit's jobs and how they relate to each other and to other units and departments.
2. The new supervisor will also have to build relationships with his or her manager, other supervisors, and other employees. It takes time to develop trust and easy communication.
3. The new supervisor must learn the subtleties of how the department works. These subtleties include elements previously described, such as priorities, values, and style or climate.

The new supervisor (whether promoted from within or not) must evaluate the situation. He or she cannot assume that it will be without difficulties. Some of the points made in this section will be examined from a somewhat different vantage point as we discuss reasons that some supervisors fail.

WHY SOME SUPERVISORS FAIL

Most newly promoted supervisors succeed in their new role. Surveys and interviews show that between seven and eight of ten new supervisors will succeed in one manner or another in their new jobs.

However, we want to identify why some supervisors fail so that you and your manager can avoid these causes of failure. Knowing what these causes are can help you make the transition to supervisor.

Lack of Knowledge

Not surprisingly, perhaps, lack of knowledge is the primary cause of supervisory failure. An example, to use an earlier case, is that of new supervisor Jim

Byrnes, who may not know how to conduct an annual face-to-face performance appraisal interview with each of the ten loss prevention engineers. If Jim does not know the objectives of or the recommended procedures for appraisal interviews, he is unlikely to conduct the appraisal interview properly, or he may overlook it entirely.

Lack of Skill

In the first chapter, we defined skill as the ability to use one's knowledge in an effective way. For example, a supervisor may have difficulty giving instructions when complicated procedures are involved. Despite a desire to communicate clearly, the supervisor may not be able to deliver technical instructions so that unit members readily understand them.

Lack of Motivation

A new supervisor might not want to pay the personal price in terms of effort and study necessary to master the job. Moreover, making decisions and initiating changes usually carry the risk of failure. Giving orders and correcting employees are unpleasant tasks. In all likelihood, the first months of supervising will bring many disappointments and frustrations. Some persons fail as supervisors because they allow the unpleasant aspects to become barriers to action.

Improper Selection

This and the next two causes of failure constitute managerial errors. A person who might succeed in many other supervisory positions may fail in one particular position because he or she is the wrong person for the specific job. An example is promotion of a unit's best technician to supervisor when the unit really needs a supervisor who will tighten up on expenses.

Inadequate Education and Training

For whatever reason, management may fail to provide the supervisor with adequate education and training. As a result, the supervisor may lack the necessary knowledge and not develop the skills needed to perform the job effectively. The supervisor may become demotivated when this is the case.

Inadequate Support From the Manager

Here, perhaps because of preoccupation with other things, the manager does not support the supervisor. The manager may not recognize the supervisor's need for help, or perhaps the manager sees other units or goals as being more important. Maybe the manager believes in a "sink or swim" method of supervisory training.

Personal Qualities of the Supervisor

The supervisor's ideas and feelings can undermine his or her success in the new role. For example, a new supervisor who is older and mistrusts young people would have a great deal of difficulty properly supervising a unit that contained many young people.

Wanting the Job for the Wrong Reason

If status were the only reason the new supervisor wanted the job, motivation to perform well would probably be insufficient. A new supervisor like Jim Byrnes is probably going to be on the job for forty or more hours each week with few status differences between him and the loss prevention engineers whom he supervises. The occasional gratifications of having higher rank are not likely to sustain the status-seeker through daily problems, pressures, and challenging objectives.

Dislike for Supervisory Activities

Suppose you, as the newly appointed rating supervisor in the Connie Perez case, misjudged what a supervisor actually does. Perhaps you thought that the former rating supervisor had it relatively easy since he or she did not appear to do much rating work. Once in the supervisory position, however, you could find that the job is actually difficult and demands such allegedly "soft" functions as directing and controlling. You could find yourself being constantly challenged to manage your time and to respond appropriately to the often fragmented and discontinuous nature of the supervisory job. You might find yourself under more pressure than you expected.

Your attempt to spend most of your time rating, since this is what you really like, seems to be constantly "interrupted" by employees, peer supervisors, and others who demand your attention. Once you experience this disconcerting job reality, you could face an emotional letdown if your prior perceptions of the job were greatly in error.

Failure To Obtain Satisfaction From Others' Success

Going back to the Perez case, if you, as the new rating supervisor, were so achievement-oriented that your feeling of job satisfaction came primarily from what you did as a rater, then it would be improbable that you could focus on making your employees successful. In such a situation, you might see your employees as threats to your image of yourself as the best rater in the unit. Incidentally, this is one reason promoting the best employee to supervisor sometimes has disappointing results. The person who thrives on independent, hands-on work may not make a successful transition to supervisory work.

Difficulty With the Ambiguity of Supervisory Work

As a supervisor, you are constantly balancing the often-competing demands of management and employees. In some cases, your new manager may not give you the explicit daily or weekly direction you were used to getting as a technician or clerk. Instead, the manager may tell you to "do what you think is best" or "do what you think will have the best effect on our expense picture." Such relative ambiguity in a job assignment may be frustrating and even threatening to some new supervisors.

Lack of Empathy

The new supervisor could lack the capacity for understanding another's feelings or ideas. An example is the supervisor's inability to understand feelings of fatigue and indifference after employees have worked overtime over several weeks.

Disagreement With Policy

As an example, assume that a company has a policy that underwriting supervisors should make frequent visits to the agencies in their territories. If an underwriting supervisor dislikes field visits and finds excuses for not making them, experiencing success as an underwriting supervisor in that organization is doubtful.

Failure To Separate From the Former Social System

Finally, some supervisors fail because they cannot make the necessary interpersonal adjustments. They cling to old behavior patterns and try to remain "one of the gang" with former peers. They attempt to execute the duties of a supervisor without fully fulfilling the role.

SUMMARY

In the first chapter, we identified several major differences between supervisory and technical work. This chapter examined these differences in greater detail and emphasized the behavioral changes involved.

In addition to facing the unfamiliarity of your new supervisory tasks, you must absorb the often dramatic effects of leaving the world—the social system—in which you formerly worked. Two case studies illustrated how your social system may change when you become a supervisor.

Perhaps the greatest change in your social system will occur in the makeup and role of the primary informal group to which you belong. In addition, you will gain greater control over your affairs, enjoy higher visibility within the organization, and have a higher number of and more complex relationships.

The most important of the relationships that will change as you make the transition from employee to supervisor is the one with your own manager. Actions that influence your relationship with your manager include knowing your manager's priorities and agreeing on how you will support them, appreciating the nature of your manager's job, and understanding the experience and management style of your manager.

You should also be aware of how other managers and executives in the organization can affect the relationship between you and your manager. The influence of your manager's manager, the influence of your manager's peers, and the organization's managerial style or climate were discussed. In general, the organization's senior and middle managers will expect you and other supervisors to function as a team and to develop a broader perspective of the organization.

In addition to relating effectively to managers and to other supervisors, you are expected to have good relations with unit employees both as individuals and as a group. Recall from Chapter 1 that employees expect you to be competent, fair, communicative, and helpful.

A support system is a pattern of interpersonal relationships that help you to function effectively as a person and, by extension, as a supervisor. Within the organization, your support system should include your manager, your peer supervisors, and unit employees. Outside the organization, your support system is likely to include policyholders, customers, clients, agents, brokers, friends, and family members.

This chapter also discussed the question of whether a supervisor should be promoted from within or outside the unit and gave the advantages and disadvantages of each approach.

Most newly promoted supervisors succeed in their new roles. However, knowing what causes supervisors to fail can help you and your manager avoid those causes of failure. Finally, seven reasons that some supervisors fail were explained.

CHAPTER NOTE

1. Lester R. Bittel and Jackson E. Ramsy, "Misfit Supervisors: Bad Apples in the Managerial Barrel," *Management Review*, February 1983, pp. 8–13; continued in *Management Review*, March 1983, pp. 37–43.

Chapter 3

Motivation

If you asked employees what is important to them about their jobs, you might hear answers like these: "I want to get ahead fast"; "I want to earn more money"; "I want to have more time to spend with my family." What do these comments mean to the supervisor? How can you use employee wants and needs to advance organizational goals? What can you do to get employees to perform willingly as you direct them in their duties?

These questions all relate to the subject of employee motivation. Harry Levinson, a noted industrial psychologist, wrote, "The steam engine operates at about 35 percent efficiency. People probably operate at about 10 percent of their potential. Most organizations constructively utilize even less of their potential power." If this statement can be applied to your organization, what can you, as a supervisor, do to change the situation?

Before beginning our discussion of motivation in the workplace, look at the following statements. Each one identifies a factor that has been linked to motivation. Indicate whether you agree or disagree with each statement.

_____1. Being nice to employees—complimenting them on their appearance, for example—makes them feel good and is one of the best ways to motivate them to work.

_____2. Coffee breaks and lunch gatherings of fellow employees help to raise morale and are good means of motivating employees.

_____3. Giving employees continuing opportunities to test their knowledge and abilities is the strongest factor in motivation.

_____4. Most employees are mainly interested in the paycheck and are generally not very interested in exerting extra effort for other reasons.

_____5. Lack of a challenging job will force even a well-motivated employee to be more concerned with the surroundings of the job, such as parking, office furnishings, and status symbols.

_____6. Providing employees with information on the dollar value of their benefits helps them to appreciate their jobs more fully and will also help them to realize greater job satisfaction.

_____7. Employees performing routine jobs can be motivated through frequent supervisory recognition of their *diligence* and *loyalty*.

_____8. When employees find no satisfaction in a work situation, increased use of information technology should be considered.

_____9. Strict controls, although expensive, ensure better results than leaving employees alone and imposing few restrictions on them.

_____10. An experienced employee who performs well may find all of the tasks in the unit to be routine and dull. If so, job rotation within the unit will usually maintain work motivation.

We will come back to these statements later in this chapter. As you will see, the answers are not as straightforward as you may now think. We will first define some terms and then study several theories of motivation to see how they might apply to you and your employees. Next, we will examine different ways the supervisor can affect individual motivation to increase output and employee satisfaction.

MOTIVATION, MOTIVATING, AND MOTIVES

The language of motivation, at least in the business world, is, unfortunately, inexact. Psychologists may use rather precise terminology in research on motivation, but supervisors and managers use the language of motivation far more casually. Defining the key terms used to refer to motivation should help you to see why you cannot "motivate someone."

Motivation

Motivation refers to the strength, persistence, and tenor of a person's behavior. Motivation is the energy that drives a person while he or she attempts to satisfy a need (such as hunger) or achieve a goal (such as a promotion). Motivation is the pressure that causes a person to take action.

We describe some people as being "highly motivated." This suggests commitment, persistence, and visible evidence of behavior directed toward some purpose. It does not necessarily mean that the behavior has successful results or that the purpose is achieved. This distinction is an important one for you as supervisor. A highly motivated employee does not necessarily succeed in meeting personal goals or in meeting organizational objectives. Motivation signifies only goal-directed behavior, not goal attainment.

Motivating

You will undoubtedly hear someone say that as a supervisor, you "motivate your subordinates." This is not a good way to describe reality. It follows from the definition of motivation that motivation comes from within; it is not something that one person can give to another. As a supervisor, you _influence_ employee motivation, but it is not in your power to _create_ it. You influence employee motivation to perform by providing ways for employees to satisfy their needs and wants. You can remove obstacles to the attainment of these needs and wants by providing a variety of rewards so that motivation in the right direction results in reinforcement.

You can also strengthen the link between motivated behavior and successful outcomes. You can provide resources (such as training and feedback) so that employee efforts result in effective job performance. If you choose to follow common parlance and say, "My job is to motivate my subordinates," this statement should be made with full understanding that you are overstating your power and misstating the process. Instead, you should state that "My job is to create a work atmosphere in which employees will feel motivated and satisfied."

Motives

Motives are specific, recurring patterns of motivation. The words used to identify motives usually identify the need or goal associated with the behavior. For example, we might describe a person as having motives of power, status, and affiliation. Adding to the confusion, sometimes people call such motives the *motivations* of the person. We prefer to call them motives. Seven statements about motives follow:

1. Motives direct behavior; they give rise to action. They are strong forces, but we cannot see, smell, hear, or taste them. Only the outcome, the behavior, is observable.

2. One motive may result in different behaviors. For example, an employee who wants to be liked and accepted will behave differently in the car pool, at home, in the office, or on vacation.

3. The same behavior observed in several people may stem from different motives. For instance, suppose that in a meeting, the supervisor asks whether anyone has questions about a new procedure, and no one responds. One person believes he understands and can perform the procedure, another does not want to displease the supervisor, one does not want to appear foolish in front of peers, and another is planning to leave soon and does not care about the change.

4. Motives can be estimated after repeated observations of the same behavior. Getting to know your subordinates and their wants and needs helps you to influence their behavior.

5. Motives may be in harmony or in conflict. For example, Mary Jones's motives are to earn a promotion and to increase her salary so that she will be more financially secure. These motives are in harmony, and both will tend to produce productive behavior. Bob Smith's motives are to increase his salary so that he can actively pursue his outside interests and to perform no better than the average worker in his unit so that everyone will accept him. These motives are in conflict and may cause inner conflict and contradictory behavior.

6. Motives come and go; they are dynamic. As one motive is satisfied, another surfaces. A strong motive at one time will be less strong at another time.

7. Motives are influenced by the environment and the situation. In the preceding examples, if the opportunity to advance were not available to Mary Jones, she might change her motives. Bob Smith might perform well on a team project when all of his teammates expect strong individual performance.

These axioms are intended to help you think about why employees might behave as they do. You must recognize that behavior comes from somewhere, but that "somewhere" is not always the same for an individual or for a group of individuals.

The Value of Motivation Theories[1]

A motivation theory attempts to explain how a person's behavior starts, continues, and stops. To be widely applicable, a motivation theory must fit most people. This presents a dilemma: the more general it is, the less useful a theory seems. As a supervisor, you need insight into the motivational pattern of each employee. You also need some more general models to use when you do not know a particular employee well. Fortunately, the general motivation theories help you to develop individual-by-individual understanding. As a supervisor, you should learn some motivation theories because they will help you observe and understand the behavior of others. Another reason for studying motivation theories is their popularity. You will find them again and again in supervisory and management education. They have provided buzzwords that are part of the management language.

Components of Motivation Theories

Take a moment to think about what information should be contained in a motivation theory. A common-sense expectation is that the theory should examine the individual, the job, and the organization. We know that all of these play a role in determining how diligently people work in general and in deciphering sudden changes in the apparent motivation of a given person.

Each individual has characteristics or attributes that affect motivation. Among the most important ones are the following:

- *Interests*—what the person likes to do and think about
- *Attitudes*—toward self, toward work, and toward supervision
- *Needs*—in particular, the person's need for security, friendship, and achievement

The *job* has characteristics that affect motivation. These include the nature of the work itself, the clarity of instructions, the degree of autonomy, the rewards, and the kind and amount of feedback received.

The *work environment* also influences motivation. Relevant characteristics included in a motivation theory are interactions with others, the physical environment, the kind and extent of supervision, and the social climate of the unit. Also included are organization-wide elements such as salary systems, benefits, the quality of relations among departments, the stability of the organization, and the overall organizational climate.

Limitations of Motivation Theories

To some extent, each motivation theory concentrates on one set of characteristics and de-emphasizes the role of others. Clearly, this is a limitation of the theories since the various theories offer different views and use concepts defined by the theorists. Because the theories stand separately, they do not reconcile or fit together as part of some larger model. While studying these theories, be aware of the dynamic interaction among all of the characteristics causing the behavior and performance of a given employee, supervisor, or manager.

MOTIVATION THEORIES

We have chosen four of the many motivation theories presented in popular management and supervisory texts. These four theories have achieved widespread recognition probably because they focus on work motivation rather than motivation for a broad range of life's activities.

Maslow's Needs Hierarchy

Abraham Maslow developed the **Hierarchy of Needs Theory** in the 1940s to explain what it is about a job that motivates employees to produce. He was one of the first researchers to recognize the relationship between money and other needs.

Premises

Maslow's model includes the following three premises:

1. The human being is always wanting, motivated by a desire to satisfy certain specific needs. These needs will vary in intensity. We are motivated by different needs at different times.
2. The needs that drive individuals are universal across all populations and are hierarchical; that is, once individuals have satisfied lower-order (or basic) needs, they will move up the hierarchy and attempt to satisfy higher-order needs.
3. Employees are motivated to satisfy a number of needs, and money can satisfy only some of these needs.

Five Levels

Study Exhibits 3-1 and 3-2. The starting point on the hierarchical ladder is *physiological needs*, those that must be satisfied to sustain life. The individual will concentrate on physiological needs when they are threatened. When there is no threat to life, the individual turns to meeting *safety needs*. Safety needs are concerned with protection against danger and deprivation. At work, safety needs relate to job security, benefits, and salary adequacy.

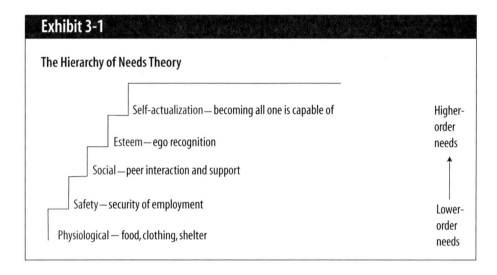

Exhibit 3-1

The Hierarchy of Needs Theory

Self-actualization — becoming all one is capable of

Esteem — ego recognition

Social — peer interaction and support

Safety — security of employment

Physiological — food, clothing, shelter

Higher-order needs

Lower-order needs

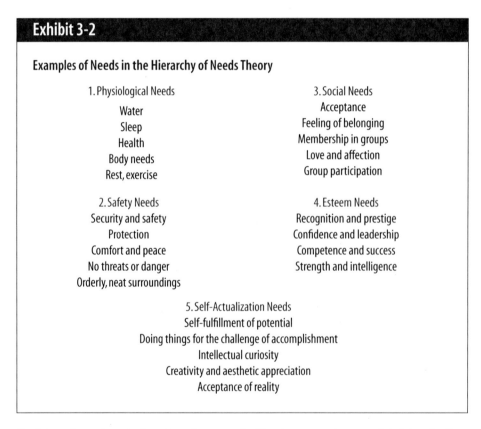

Exhibit 3-2

Examples of Needs in the Hierarchy of Needs Theory

1. Physiological Needs

Water
Sleep
Health
Body needs
Rest, exercise

2. Safety Needs

Security and safety
Protection
Comfort and peace
No threats or danger
Orderly, neat surroundings

3. Social Needs

Acceptance
Feeling of belonging
Membership in groups
Love and affection
Group participation

4. Esteem Needs

Recognition and prestige
Confidence and leadership
Competence and success
Strength and intelligence

5. Self-Actualization Needs

Self-fulfillment of potential
Doing things for the challenge of accomplishment
Intellectual curiosity
Creativity and aesthetic appreciation
Acceptance of reality

Social needs such as belonging, love, and affection constitute a third level of needs. These needs are satisfied by meaningful personal relationships and acceptance into a group. When social needs are met, the individual's *esteem needs* become more dominant. Most of us need self-respect and the esteem of others. Esteem needs demand that we achieve, be strong and confident, and gain recognition and appreciation from others. We want to feel useful and necessary. Even if all these needs are satisfied, we may still feel discontent unless we are doing what best suits us. This *self-actualization need* dictates that we strive to reach our full potential with all of our abilities and interests.

Dynamic Aspects

The Hierarchy of Needs Theory consists of more than the ladder-like arrangement of needs. The dynamic aspects—or how the needs control behavior—are equally important. The dynamic aspects are as follows:

1. The strength of an individual's need may shift as circumstances change. For example, during difficult economic times or a difficult time for your company or industry, safety and perhaps even physiological needs may dominate.

2. One level of need does not have to be entirely satisfied before the employee strives to meet higher-order needs. For example, motivation by social needs and esteem needs is possible at the same time.

3. Lower-order needs must generally be satisfied before higher-order needs become motivators. Young employees just starting families and making major expenditures for housing and appliances may place a higher priority on the lower-order safety need that salary meets.

4. A satisfied need is not a motivator of behavior. Consider our need for oxygen. Only when we are deprived of oxygen can our need for it have a motivating effect on behavior. The need for safety does not influence the daily behavior of many employees.

5. Individuals use different methods to satisfy a particular need. For example, two employees seek the approval and esteem of others. One tries to be an excellent worker and to help co-workers. The other devotes much time to community and church activities and holds a succession of offices in these organizations.

6. Money is important as a motivator because it provides lower-level satisfactions and serves as a symbol at higher levels.

7. Very few people are operating at the self-actualization level; however, many are striving toward this highest level.

Application

If you use the Hierarchy of Needs Theory, your job as supervisor is to determine the need levels of employees on an individual basis and then provide the means by which employees can satisfy these needs. You should evaluate the compensation system for its adequacy in meeting physical and safety needs. You should consider how you organize work groups and provide opportunities for developing relationships to satisfy social needs. When bringing a new person on board, you should carefully plan the newcomer's orientation to the work group. Since first impressions are important, ensure that the newcomer quickly meets everyone and is introduced in a way that highlights reasons that others should get to know him or her.

The greatest challenge to most insurance supervisors may be dealing with employees who seek to meet esteem and self-actualization needs. You should consider the extent to which praise and recognition are satisfying the esteem needs of your employees. Finally, consider what you can do to assist individuals in reaching their full potential, perhaps by granting greater autonomy and responsibility and by allowing them to integrate organizational and personal goals.

McClelland's Achievement Theory

David McClelland and J. W. Atkinson developed the *Achievement Theory* in the 1950s. McClelland continued the research, so the approach is usually attributed to him.

Three Basic Motives

Unlike Maslow, McClelland does not picture a hierarchy or ladder of needs. McClelland instead pictures the individual personality as a network of the following three basic motives or needs:

1. The need to achieve—to do something better or more efficiently than it has been done before, to excel in relation to competitive or self-established standards, and to take reasonable risks

2. The need for power—to be strong and influential, to have an effect on others, and to control the means of influencing others

3. The need for affiliation—to be liked and to have warm, friendly interpersonal relationships

Dynamic Aspects

McClelland maintains that most people have all three of these needs but that the level of intensity varies with the individual and with the situation. Accordingly, adults have the potential to behave in certain ways depending on the strength of their motives, the situation, and how they perceive the situation at a given moment.

As McClelland sees it, the individual is basically moved to action by the dominant motive(s) acquired during childhood and reinforced by childhood experiences. At work, the dominant motive will affect work behavior. It follows that such behavior will be difficult to change because it has been part of the individual for so long.

For example, an individual may have a high need for achievement, a moderate need for power, and a low need for affiliation. This individual's motivation to work will vary greatly from that of a person who has a high need for power and low needs for achievement and affiliation.

How are these needs reflected in action? People with the need for achievement tend to seek jobs that are entrepreneurial, developmental, inherently challenging, and highly active. They like situations in which they can take personal responsibility for finding solutions to problems. They receive satisfaction from achievement through personal effort and ability. They will set challenging but realistic goals and will take calculated risks, developing comprehensive plans to support goal achievement. They look for concrete feedback because they need to know the result of their actions.

People with the need for power derive satisfaction from controlling the means of influence over others. They will seek positions of influence and enjoy jobs that offer authority and power. Many politicians have a high need for power. They will work to win arguments, offer suggestions and opinions freely, and try to change others' behavior.

People with the need for affiliation seek jobs with frequent interactions; they work to maintain good relationships, to build harmony, and to pay attention to others. They are not as concerned with getting ahead as are high achievers. Many supervisors are thought to have a strong need for affiliation.

The current situation and the working environment also dictate work behavior. For example, an employee with a high need for achievement may produce sloppy or incomplete work when the tasks are routine and not challenging. Seeing little opportunity to achieve and lacking problems to solve, the employee may not pay attention to fine details or perform his or her work satisfactorily.

Achievement theory suggests that supervisors must first recognize dominating needs in themselves and in subordinates and then work to meet those needs.

Of interest, too, is McClelland's contention that most executives are highly achievement-oriented. Monetary rewards concretely reflect how well executives achieve desired results, but money as such does not motivate them to work harder or better. Money measures achievement. Perhaps executives seeking monetary rewards believe that money motivates their performance, thus perpetuating the myth that money motivates others.

Application

McClelland believes that a culture or an organization can do much to stimulate and reward the development of the need for achievement.

To arouse the motive to achieve, and the resultant work behavior, the theory suggests that you do the following:

1. Establish concrete goals for your unit.
2. Help employees set concrete goals for job performance.
3. Assist employees in understanding the standards of excellence.
4. Give feedback on how well employees are achieving goals and meeting standards; frequent and fast feedback is best.
5. Provide support to employees as they work to achieve goals and meet standards.
6. Link training to achievement of employees' current work tasks.
7. Reward achievement; focus on results rather than effort.

By identifying and learning to influence particular needs, you can strengthen and arouse achievement-oriented behavior. How might you apply this to a clerical position in which the dominant need is for affiliation? By assigning the clerk to work directly with two or three people, you provide the opportunity to develop relationships. You then work with the employee to establish production and quality standards. You and the people working with the clerk provide frequent feedback on how well the standards are being met. You recognize achievement and stress the contribution being made. In effect, you are meshing the employee's need for affiliation with your need for production.

Herzberg's Motivation-Hygiene Theory

Frederick Herzberg's **Motivation-Hygiene Theory,** developed in the 1950s, is well known among many managers and supervisors. Many consider it to be one of the most practical of the motivation theories. Herzberg focused on the situational factors that seem to be responsible for high work motivation. He found that situational factors fall into two categories, and because of this, his theory is sometimes referred to as the two-factor theory of motivation.

Two Sets of Factors That Influence Motivation

Herzberg recognized two sets of factors that influence job behavior.

1. *Hygiene or maintenance factors* relate to the *context* of the job. If these factors are missing, the employee is likely to be dissatisfied. If they are present, the employee might have low dissatisfaction but will not necessarily have high satisfaction. In other words, Herzberg argued that satisfaction and dissatisfaction are not the end points on one scale but rather are two scales.

2. *Motivation factors* relate to the *content* of the job. Their presence is associated with high satisfaction, which should result in high work motivation and superior performance.

Dynamic Aspects

Herzberg argued that dissatisfaction is not the opposite of satisfaction; rather, dissatisfaction and satisfaction are two separate variables. He contended that removing all causes for employee dissatisfaction is not enough to cause high motivation and high performance.

If an organization is to stimulate performance, it must provide the motivation factors. These motivation factors are central to the work itself and to one's experience in performing the work. The motivation factors pertain to the job rather than to its surroundings. At the risk of oversimplifying Herzberg's theory, we can say that *job content* is the source of satisfaction and motivation and *job context* is the source of dissatisfaction. In still another set of words, motivation factors are *intrinsic* to the job, while hygiene factors are *extrinsic* to the job.

Role of Money

In Herzberg's theory, money is a maintenance factor. It will not motivate an employee for more than a short period of time, but it can cause an employee to become dissatisfied. Herzberg's research shows that negative feelings are very strong when employees perceive that salary schedules are inequitable. Equitable pay does not produce strong feelings, positive or negative, and makes employees only slightly happy. When you received your last salary increase, what was your reaction? "That's nice," or "It's about time," or "I certainly deserved it." If you had a reaction similar to these, you demonstrate how Herzberg views the role of money. Increased pay rewards past efforts, not work that will be done. Nonetheless, some supervisors continue to expect a thankful reaction to pay increases and cannot understand an employee who is less responsive.

Application

Herzberg recommended that supervisors concentrate on the motivation factors to get a greater return and attention to maintenance factors so that they do not interfere with motivation. This line of reasoning led Herzberg to study job design and, specifically, efforts to improve jobs, called job enrichment.

Job Enrichment

Job enrichment means changing the job to expand responsibilities, raise authority levels, and provide opportunity for growth and recognition. To give you some idea of what this might entail, Exhibits 3-3 and 3-4 describe several principles of job enrichment and the motivation factors involved. Careful measurement and monitoring of productivity is important in job enrichment. Employees and supervisors should be able to make before-and-after comparisons and should be able to chart the progress after jobs have been enriched.

Exhibit 3-3

Principles of Job Enrichment

Principles	Motivation Factors
1. Relinquish some control while retaining accountability.	Responsibility and achievement
2. Increase accountability of individuals for own work.	Responsibility and recognition
3. Give person complete unit of work, complete task, one module.	Responsibility, achievement, recognition
4. Grant additional authority to an employee, provide freedom to make decisions.	Responsibility, achievement, recognition
5. Introduce new and more difficult tasks not previously performed.	Growth, learning
6. Assign individuals specific or specialized tasks, enabling them to become experts.	Advancement, growth

---

Ways To Enrich Jobs

To enrich jobs, the supervisor should do the following:

1. Select jobs in which motivation is poor or in which high motivation could make a difference in performance.
2. Approach these jobs with the conviction that they can be changed.
3. Brainstorm with employees about changes that might enrich the jobs.
4. Screen the suggested changes to eliminate those dealing with maintenance factors or those that would only add more of the same work.

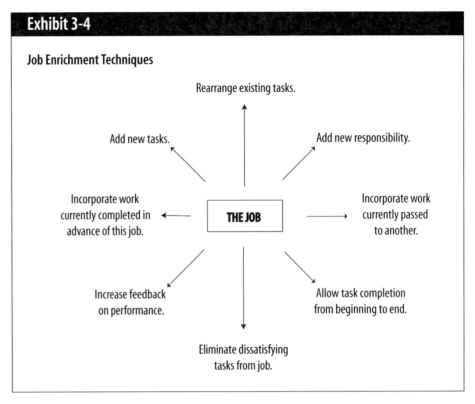

Exhibit 3-4

Job Enrichment Techniques

5. Be prepared for a temporary drop in productivity; there must be time for learning to occur.

Not all jobs can be enriched, nor should they be. Most organizations, however, are likely to find benefits in job enrichment. They will probably find that jobs have become too routine and lack meaning. Proponents of job enrichment argue that it is time to favor human aspects in job design.

The Three Theories Compared

Similarities exist between Herzberg's and Maslow's theories. Herzberg's motivation factors are related to the nature of the work itself and the rewards that flow from the performance of that work. The most potent of these factors are those that foster self-actualization. Safety and affiliation needs are related to maintenance factors and will not motivate improved performance. Exhibit 3-5 illustrates this comparison. There is also some similarity between the theories of Herzberg and McClelland in that achievement is frequently associated with the long-range factors of responsibility and the work itself. Herzberg found that when recognition is based on achievement, it provides more intense satisfaction.

Vroom's Expectancy Theory

Victor Vroom's **Expectancy Theory** was developed in the early 1960s. Its popularity reflects the fact that it treats job results and performance rewards more directly than the three motivation theories previously described.

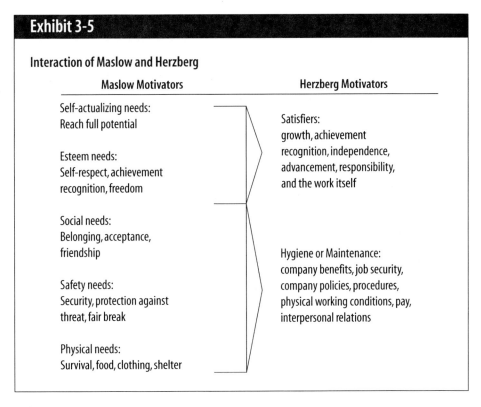

Exhibit 3-5

Interaction of Maslow and Herzberg

Maslow Motivators	Herzberg Motivators
Self-actualizing needs: Reach full potential	Satisfiers: growth, achievement recognition, independence, advancement, responsibility, and the work itself
Esteem needs: Self-respect, achievement recognition, freedom	
Social needs: Belonging, acceptance, friendship	Hygiene or Maintenance: company benefits, job security, company policies, procedures, physical working conditions, pay, interpersonal relations
Safety needs: Security, protection against threat, fair break	
Physical needs: Survival, food, clothing, shelter	

Three Variables That Affect Performance

Vroom found performance in organizational settings to be a function of at least three variables: [2]

1. Motivation level—the individual must want to perform the assigned tasks.
2. Abilities and traits—the individual must have personality traits somewhat compatible with the job and the skill to do the task.
3. Role perceptions—the individual must have an accurate understanding of the job requirements in order to perform the task efficiently.

The explanation that follows focuses on the motivation variable.

Six Elements

Exhibit 3-6 portrays Vroom's theory of motivation. It depicts a model that contains the following six elements:

1. The *effort* the individual will expend
2. The job or other *goal* to be attained through the effort
3. The *rewards* or outcomes that will follow from attaining the goal
4. The individual's estimate of the probability that the effort will result in achievement of the goal (called *expectancy*)
5. The individual's estimate of the probability that achievement of the goal will lead to the desired rewards (called *instrumentality*)
6. The degree of desirability of the rewards (called *valence*)

Vroom's model poses this as the mechanism of motivation: the degree of effort expended toward achieving a goal is determined by the individual's perceptions of the desirability of the expected rewards and of the probability that the effort will result in attaining the goal. Attaining the goal will then result in the rewards.

Dynamic Aspects

Vroom views expectancy and instrumentality as matters of degree or probability. Circumstances can affect an individual's perception that working harder will produce better results (expectancy) or his or her perception that better results will be noticed and rewarded by the organization (instrumentality). Similarly, individuals can place more or less value on expected outcomes (valence). Although expectancy, instrumentality, and valence are ultimately controlled by the individual and however he or she perceives the work situation, they may be influenced by the supervisor and the organization.

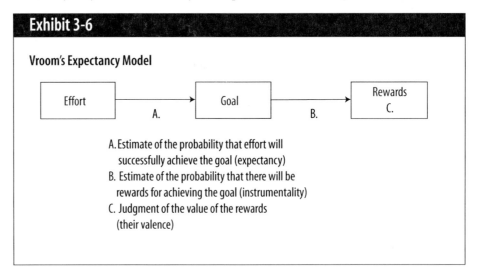

Exhibit 3-6

Vroom's Expectancy Model

A. Estimate of the probability that effort will successfully achieve the goal (expectancy)
B. Estimate of the probability that there will be rewards for achieving the goal (instrumentality)
C. Judgment of the value of the rewards (their valence)

To illustrate, you might encourage an employee to strengthen the effort-goal link by improving clerical or automated support and by giving job-related training. Similarly, you might support the perception that an employee's work on a special project will result in success (promotion, monetary benefits, etc.) by assuring him or her that you will be available to respond to questions that may arise during the project.

You might support the goal-reward instrumentality in an employee's mind by improving the performance reporting system in your unit. Frequently, you can contribute toward high instrumentality relationships by noticing good work and giving direct and immediate praise for it.

You can also contribute to employees' perceptions of how attractive rewards are (their valence). For example, you can make the position of customer service representative more attractive to employees by giving CSRs a role in making certain decisions and by increasing their opportunities to make decisions by themselves (empowerment).

Vroom has incorporated individual characteristics (needs) with job requirements and with the organizational reward system to show these variables interacting to influence individuals' work behavior. According to Vroom, motivation is based on what people believe will occur in the future; that is, on anticipated results using past experience as a guide and the value placed on those results.

Application

What can you learn from this theory to improve employee performance? Some implications include the following:

1. You should not assume that all things have the same meaning to all people. The behavior an employee exhibits depends on the behavior that is permissible in the given work environment.

2. As the supervisor, you should find out the goals and rewards that matter to each employee.

3. The expectancy that increased effort will lead to goal attainment can be positively influenced by carefully selecting, training, and directing employees and by providing necessary resources.

4. As the supervisor, you can strengthen the perception that successful performance (goal attainment) will lead to rewards by linking rewards to performance measures and by distinguishing between rewards given to good performers and those given to average or marginal performers.

5. Showing confidence in employees may heighten their perception that added effort will result in better performance.

6. Understanding why some employees are productive in a given situation may be as valuable as knowing reasons for a lack of productivity.

Guidelines for Fostering Motivation

We have considered four motivation theories—perhaps the four most popular of the many that have been proposed. Notice that there is no one, universal, generally followed motivation theory. Indeed, a major conclusion you should reach from these theories is that there is no secret, magic answer or key that grants you the power to motivate employees. Instead, each of these four theories (and others) provides some insight into human motivation and some hope for influencing it.

None of these theories says that you, as supervisor, can create employee motivation in any direct sense. You can help employees to fulfill their wants, but you cannot generate those wants. You can offer information about rewards, but you cannot force employees to seek them. You can assign job goals, but you cannot make them become the employee's own goals. You can provide information that may lead employees toward new perceptions of themselves, their work, and the outcomes of their efforts, but you cannot implant these new perceptions.

Despite their limitations, motivation theories are important because they help supervisors to think more broadly and more objectively about employees.

They help supervisors to understand that many things they do influence employee motivation. The theories encourage supervisors to search for guidelines that will help them to contribute to employee motivation. Here are the guidelines we suggest:

1. Learn as much as you can about employees—what they want, what they need, what they value, and what they hope to achieve in their careers. An opportune time to discuss these matters is during the performance appraisal. Asking employees to talk about their goals and their performance often sheds light on their motives.

2. Recognize individual differences. There can be widespread differences in the needs, goals, and aspirations of employees in identical jobs. Make a conscious effort to avoid stereotyping and seek information about every employee in your unit.

3. Examine how you and your organization give rewards. What are the rewards, both monetary and non-monetary? How do employees see the rewards as compared to those given in other organizations? Do employees see rewards as the direct results of their efforts?

4. Link rewards to individual and team performance, as appropriate. This means giving praise, recognition, and other rewards immediately after the performance to which they relate. It also means citing the performance in specific terms.

5. Analyze problem performers with the motivation theories in mind. Evaluate the job requirements and working conditions and their influence on employee behavior. Do not assume that poor performance is the result of low motivation.

6. Have a clear picture of yourself—your strengths, limitations, expectations, goals, values, and needs. Seek feedback from peers and managers and, in appropriate ways, from subordinates.

7. Praise in public but punish in private. When giving critical feedback, focus on the employee's behavior and its results, not on the employee's personality.

8. Distinguish among outstanding, competent, marginal, and unacceptable performance. Develop ways to measure individual and team performance. Include both quantity and quality measurements. Periodically check with employees to verify that they accept the measurement procedures. If necessary, revise the measurements; employee acceptance of standards and measurements is critical.

9. Periodically evaluate the design of tasks and workflows.

10. When revising jobs, focus on enriching them rather than merely expanding them (more challenging work as opposed to simply more work).

11. Pay attention to your approachability. If necessary, spend time each day in employee work areas to emphasize your accessibility and interest. Discipline yourself to set other matters aside so that you can give undivided attention to an employee's problem.

12. Request (if necessary, fight for) equipment, staff, and other resources needed to support the mission of your unit.

13. Provide the "big picture" to employees. Help them to see how their work contributes to the mission of the department and the organization.

14. Seek employee input when making decisions. Being consulted is in itself an important reward. Employee participation typically has two results: you make better decisions and employees show greater acceptance of those decisions.

MONEY AS A MOTIVATOR

Throughout this chapter, we have touched on the topic of money as a motivator. Is money the sole motivator of performance? Little evidence exists to support the view that it is. As you have seen, the leading theorists treat pay as *one of several factors* that govern work motivation.

Based on the four theories you have studied, the following ideas summarize the role of money:

1. Money is important, more so in difficult economic times. An income is crucial to an individual's well-being—in addition to paying for other essentials, it pays the mortgage or rent and pays for food, helping to satisfy needs at the lower levels of Maslow's needs hierarchy.

2. Work is a contract exchanging effort for pay. Pay is the most tangible form of recognition for this effort. To make salary adjustments effective, they should be consistent with performance, and employees should clearly understand how performance objectives and rewards are linked.

3. How much money is enough? Each person has expectations concerning the type and amount of reward for services given. To avoid dissatisfaction, salary should be comparable to pay elsewhere in the industry and in the locale.

4. You must evaluate what money represents to the individual to determine its role as a motivator.

Money is a motivator when it is perceived as a means for satisfaction or as a means for obtaining things to satisfy needs. If money is only one of several motivators, why have American business and industry held to the belief that it is the primary motivator for so long? The following are three good reasons:

1. Society equates earnings with success when there are no better indicators of success. This is partly true of most people and may be completely true of some people. This is exemplified by entrepreneurs and salespeople.

2. Increased productivity might occur after a pay raise, which would lead to the conclusion that money motivates. But other factors may also be at play, such as the performance appraisal process or a change in responsibilities. Saying that more money leads to higher output is too simple a conclusion.

3. For a supervisor, pay is the easiest reward to manipulate. It is also the most obvious reward the employer can give, and therefore, there is the tendency to believe that it must motivate.

We cannot conclude that money makes little or no difference, but we do not know what the difference really is. Money as a motivator must be considered in context with all of the other factors discussed in this chapter.

Remember the short quiz you took at the beginning of this chapter? Go back now and review your answers. Would you change any of them?

Some questions do not have a single right answer, but following are our reasons for selecting one answer over another.

- Statements 1 and 2 deal with the need for affiliation. We would disagree with both statements, following Herzberg's thoughts that these are really maintenance factors. If they did not exist, that would create dissatisfaction. When they do exist, they do not truly motivate.

- We agree with Statement 3. Opportunity to achieve motivates and builds esteem. Personal growth and striving for self-actualization motivates strongly. If you disagreed because of the word "strongest," you may be right in the sense that what motivates one may not motivate another as strongly.

- We disagree with Statement 4. An employee can be interested in exerting extra effort for other reasons.

- We disagree with statements 6, 7, 9, and 10. The existence of benefits and how well they are understood reduces dissatisfaction. Supervisory recognition for diligence and loyalty also reduces dissatisfaction; however, neither of these factors is in itself motivating. They do not generate the desire to do better. Supervisory recognition of performance results would increase motivation. People generally want responsibility and some self-control; imposing controls can lead to demotivation and deterioration in performance. Finally, task rotation to break up the routine may or may not maintain motivation. Job enrichment, which includes expanding job responsibilities, is a better alternative.

- We agree with statements 5 and 8. Individual characteristics, job requirements, and working conditions are interrelated. If the job requirements do not motivate, the individual will look to other variables. According to Herzberg, if the work itself is not a motivator, the organization and the supervisor should consider job enrichment or look for ways to combine the job with another.

This quiz underscores the complexity of your challenge in influencing the motivation of the people who work in your unit. Despite this complexity, the rewards for you—and for them—have lasting significance.

SUMMARY

This chapter dealt with the subject of employee motivation, which refers to the strength, persistence, and tenor of employee behavior. Motivation is the energy that drives employees while they attempt to satisfy their needs or achieve their goals.

As a supervisor, you *influence* employee motivation, but it is not in your power to create it. You influence employee motivation by providing ways for employees to satisfy their needs or attain their wants. These ways include removing obstacles, providing rewards, and strengthening the link between motivated behavior and successful outcomes. Fourteen guidelines for fostering motivation were provided in this chapter.

Also discussed were four of the most popular motivation theories: Maslow's Hierarchy of Needs Theory, McClelland's Achievement Theory, Herzberg's Motivation-Hygiene Theory, and Vroom's Expectancy Theory. Although motivation theories cannot create employee motivation in any direct sense, they will enable you to think more broadly and more objectively about employees.

This chapter also discussed the topic of money as a motivator. Although little evidence exists to support the view that money is the sole motivator of performance, pay is certainly one of several factors that govern work motivation.

CHAPTER NOTES

1. This chapter draws from many sources in summarizing selected motivation theories. Most principles of management and organizational behavior texts provide descriptions and analyses of the major motivation theories. The following are suggested:

    Ricky W. Griffin, *Management*, 3d ed. (Boston: Houghton Mifflin Company, 1990).

    John M. Ivancevich and Michael T. Matteson, *Organizational Behavior and Management* (Plano, TX: Business Publications, Inc., 1987).

    Robert Kreitner and Angelo Kinicki, *Organizational Behavior* (Homewood, IL: Richard D. Irwin, Inc., 1989).

    John R. Schermerhorn, Jr., *Management for Productivity*, 3d ed. (New York: John Wiley & Sons, 1989).

    Donald D. White and David A. Bednar, *Organizational Behavior: Understanding and Managing People at Work* (Boston: Allyn and Bacon, Inc., 1986).

2. Victor H. Vroom, "An Outline of a Cognitive Model" from an article in Richard M. Masters and Lyman W. Porter, *Motivation and Work Behavior* (New York: McGraw-Hill, 1975), p. 187.

Chapter 4

Leadership

In Chapter 1, leadership was defined as the ability to achieve desired results through others and, at the same time, to win their confidence, cooperation, and loyalty. The process of leadership is linked to motivation. Motivation drives people to do well in general. Leadership channels employee motivation toward specific goals. It may stimulate employees to set—and attain—higher objectives than they would otherwise. Good leadership may lead to higher motivation.

Two general types of leaders exist in a work unit or situation. One is the *task leader*; the other is the *social leader*. We are concerned primarily with exploring the ramifications of your role as the task (or formal) leader of the unit.

LEADERSHIP DEFINED

Alternative definitions of leadership emphasize facets or nuances of the process that are somewhat different from those of the definition we are using. Nevertheless, these are worth a quick review.

1. The dictionary simply defines leadership as "the office or position of a leader; or the quality of a leader; that is, the capacity to lead."

2. A book on organizational behavior states that most management writers agree that leadership is "the process of influencing the activities of an individual or a group in efforts toward goal achievement in a given situation."[1]

3. A book for insurance supervisors defines leadership as "the ability of a supervisor to inspire employees to work hard to achieve the goals of the company or organization."[2] This definition is accompanied by the observation that we can usually recognize the results of leadership, even if we cannot always recognize the quality itself. We can often measure the achievement of unit goals by employees more easily than we can identify leadership traits in their supervisor.

Let's divide the definition of leadership into its key ideas and expand on them.

Key Idea	*Comment*
1. The ability of the supervisor or manager. . .	In this context we can define ability as competence in doing something.
2. . . .to achieve some type of desirable group result or goals. . .	The emphasis here is on a collective rather than an individual result.
3. . . .through the efforts of employees. . .	The focus is on the efforts of others rather than on the leader's own individual efforts.
4. . . .and at the same time, positively influence employees and win their confidence, cooperation, and loyalty.	This connotes that the employees are responding to positive factors in their perception of the supervisor and not solely to negative factors such as fear of punishment.

The terms *leader* and *manager* are often used interchangeably in everyday conversation. We do not do so here, for we want to concentrate on the special quality of leadership. Some managers are known as good leaders; others are not. When we think of leaders, we think of people who have committed, willing followers. When we think of managers, we mainly think of the four major management functions mentioned in Chapter 1 and decision making.

Management scholars and practitioners have debated for a long time whether leadership is an inherited characteristic or an acquired one. Are leaders born or made? No evidence seems to exist to support the proposition that leadership is an innate ability; that is, that a person is a leader throughout his or her career and in all situations. Despite that lack of evidence, many cling to the notion that leaders are born with special gifts.

Since the ability to lead is not innate, we conclude that leaders can be made. Successful leaders generally are perceptive enough to identify their leadership knowledge and skill needs and to go about meeting them.

CHARACTERISTICS OF EFFECTIVE LEADERS

We will introduce the topic of characteristics of effective leaders by asking you to complete a short quiz either here or on scratch paper. You should be aware that no single leader or supervisor is going to possess all of these characteristics.

1. The effective leader's intelligence is

_____Greater Than _____Less Than_____About the Same as

that of his or her followers.

2. The effective leader is more perceptive than the ineffective leader.

_____Agree_____Disagree

3. The possession and display of enthusiasm tends to be restricted to certain personality types.

_____Agree_____Disagree

4. The effective leader

_____Is_____Is Not

influenced by his or her followers.

5. The effective leader has a high capacity to understand the ideas and feelings of others.

_____Agree_____Disagree

6. Effective leaders tend to

_____Be Self Centered

_____Accept Responsibility for the Welfare of Others

7. The judgment of an effective leader is

_____Greater Than _____Less Than_____About the Same As

the judgment of an ineffective leader.

8. The effective leader would rather

_____Be the Outstanding Individual Achiever

_____Influence Others

_____Be One of the Crowd

9. Good verbal facility

_____Is_____Is Not

associated with effective leadership.

10. The effective leader's initiative is

_____Greater Than _____Less Than_____About the Same as

his or her followers'.

11. Effective leaders project greater self-confidence than do ineffective leaders.

_____Agree_____Disagree

12. Effective leaders tend to derive satisfaction from

_____Their Own Individual Achievement

_____Subordinates' or Employees' Achievements

13. The effective leader should first learn to be a good follower.

_____Agree_____Disagree

14. The effective leader must have integrity.

_____Agree_____Disagree

Let's now review your answers. The preferred answer will be given along with some comments for each point.

1. To be effective, the leader should appear to possess the same general intelligence level as the followers. The supervisor who is not as bright as the subordinates could lose their respect. However, the leader or supervisor who consistently tries to appear to be much brighter than the followers might seem to have little understanding or patience about why employees cannot do a task or cannot learn it quickly. In some instances, a highly intelligent leader might not be as effective as one of lesser intelligence.

2. Being perceptive refers to the ability to observe and understand. According to research, effective leaders tend to possess this characteristic in good measure. In particular, effective leaders do well at distinguishing between their best employees and those who are less valuable.

3. Many effective leaders, particularly in business, have to commit themselves to the accomplishment of some group task such as increased sales, improved customer service, or greater teamwork. This commitment requires the leader to communicate the task to followers and others enthusiastically. Some good supervisors are outgoing; others are more reserved. Each supervisor or leader can possess and display enthusiasm in his or her own way.

4. Various studies show that followers or employees can have a major effect on the leader's accomplishment of the group's tasks. An example is a unit of ten telephone claim representatives, four of whom are trainees. This staff composition will affect the supervisor's or leader's expectations of the group. The supervisor should not expect this group to be as productive as an experienced group, and he or she should not treat all employees equally with regard to the need for direct supervision.

5. Effective leaders should possess the characteristic of *empathy*, the capacity for understanding another's feelings or ideas. An example is a supervisor's interest in the participation of his or her underwriters in a professional designation program. An empathetic leader would be sensitive to the work involved in regular study and knows, without prompting, to show concern and support as the examination nears and anxiety mounts.

6. The United States Department of Commerce, commenting on research on the characteristics of effective business managers and supervisors, points out that such people are generally respected by customers, peers, employees, and the community because their conduct reflects their willingness to assume responsibility for the well-being of others.

7. Judgment in this context refers to one's capacity to discern. An effective leader tends to be a better judge of people, situations, and decision alternatives than an ineffective leader.

8. Effective leaders want to lead rather than perform alone or be part of a crowd. An outstanding individual achiever, whether a salesperson, technician, or clerk, is not likely to be the best supervisor. Such people tend to concentrate on the technical aspects of the job to the exclusion of other considerations, such as the necessity to communicate instructions to others.

This does not mean that an organization should promote mediocre employees to supervisory positions. The organization should select supervisors from able employees who can adapt to the specific demands of the supervisory role.

9. Effective leaders tend to have good verbal skills because leadership demands it. This does not mean that effective leaders are glib or clever. Instead, it means that they are good communicators.

10. Effective leaders display initiative. Initiative relates, at least in part, to several other characteristics discussed here. It relates, for instance, to the leader's ability to become committed to the accomplishment of some group task and to communicate enthusiasm to others.

11. Because of the need to project self-confidence, some people urge new supervisors to "fake it until you make it." They think that supervisors should make a deliberate effort to show confidence in themselves, in employees, and in the organization. Employees can hardly be expected to follow a person who appears uncertain.

12. Effective leaders gain satisfaction from the achievements of their employees and in no way feel threatened by them. Good leaders take pride in their ability to obtain such a collective result.

13. Fortunately, most supervisors or managers begin their careers as technical or clerical employees. They should therefore be able to empathize with how employees think, feel, and want to be treated. Furthermore, most leaders have bosses; they are also subordinates. The leader's own behavior as a follower is observed and frequently copied by his or her followers.

14. Some leaders achieve results through questionable means, such as "bending the truth." Long-term leadership success is hardly ever achieved with such tactics. The effective leader displays honesty and integrity or adherence to ethical values. An ethical person habitually does what is right and does not bend the rules or distort the truth in order to look good or to achieve some immediate goal.

CHARACTERISTICS OF THE SUPERVISOR'S JOB AFFECTING LEADERSHIP

The effective leader finely tunes his or her behavior to the situation. Generally speaking, the characteristics of the supervisor's job affecting leadership include the nature of the job; unit objectives; the requirements for performance, productivity, and quality; complex interpersonal relationships; and the pace of change.

Nature of the Supervisor's Job

To study the influence of the supervisor's job on leadership, read each of the following cases and identify the major differences you see between the jobs of Larry Richman and Dorothy Belasco.

Case Study: Larry Richman

Larry supervises a technical claim unit consisting of seven telephone claim representatives and two outside claim representatives. The unit is located in a branch office of a large national insurer and processes private passenger automobile and homeowners claims. The two outside claim representatives handle the more complex claims and those that require personal contact.

Before Larry was appointed to the supervisory position three years ago, he had been an outside claim representative and a telephone claim representative in a different claim office of the company for a total of six years.

The nine employees who report to Larry possess a considerable range of claim-processing experience. For example, one of the outside claim representatives has worked in claims for the company for fifteen years. The two newest telephone claim representatives have, respectively, nine months and six months of claim-processing experience.

New telephone claim representatives in the office first complete a two-week independent-study course interspersed with coaching sessions with either their supervisors or senior telephone claim representatives. This is followed by a period of on-the-job training. After having been on the job for three months, trainees attend a one-week technical training course at the company's home office. This course is followed, in turn, by more on-the-job training.

Three months before Larry was appointed to the supervisory job, he enrolled in an independent-study course on supervision. Within several weeks of being appointed a supervisor, Larry attended a one-week supervisory training seminar at the company's home office.

Case Study: Dorothy Belasco

Dorothy is the underwriting manager of the Dallas branch office of an insurer with branches in Dallas, Atlanta, Kansas City, and Chicago. The commercial property, commercial liability, miscellaneous commercial lines, and personal lines underwriting managers report to Dorothy. The experience of these underwriters ranges from ten to twenty years.

Dorothy has been in her present job for five years. Before that, she held other underwriting management and supervisory positions for a total of seven years. She has completed her company's management development program, which consists of a series of independent-study courses and a one-week seminar at the company's home office.

Contrasts

Review the major differences you identified between the jobs of Larry Richman and Dorothy Belasco. We have deliberately contrasted a supervisor and a manager. Of course, you do not have to use our exact words as you identify some of the key differences.

1. Larry Richman, like any other first-line supervisor, supervises the people who do the work. In contrast, Dorothy Belasco, as an underwriting manager, directs other managers. Larry Richman has the special challenge of translating the company's objectives into terms that are meaningful to nonsupervisory employees.

2. Larry's span of control is larger than Dorothy's. He directly supervises nine technicians, whereas she oversees four subordinate managers. For cost-effectiveness, the span of control of the front-line supervisor is usually as large as possible, as long as adequate attention can be given to each employee.

   On a related point, as the supervisory span expands in order to be more economical, the nature of the supervisor's job changes; the supervisor may spend relatively more or less time on each of the major functions of leading, organizing, planning, and controlling.

3. The range of technical experience of Larry's nine employees is from six months to fifteen years. In contrast, Dorothy is dealing with a more homogeneous group; the underwriting management experience of her subordinates ranges from ten to twenty years.

A key characteristic of the supervisor's role that affects leadership is the requirement in many supervisory jobs of a high level of sensitivity to technical matters. As an example, we learned that Larry Richman supervises nine claim representatives, seven of whom are telephone claim representatives and two of whom work outside. Because of his supervisory duties, it seems doubtful that Larry can maintain his former technical expertise in claims. The technical expert is probably the outside claim representative who has worked for the company for fifteen years. However, Larry will often be called on to evaluate, at least in a general way, matters such as adequacy of the claim reserve established or the value of further investigation. Since Larry is a supervisor, his area of technical competence may be larger, yet he is likely to lose his finer skill in performing specific procedures within some of the jobs.

Larry's position as a front-line supervisor probably requires more familiarity with technical matters than Dorothy Belasco, the middle-level manager, needs. As a branch-office underwriting manager, she could certainly make some occasional technical decisions such as recommending acceptance of a large, complex risk. Dorothy would probably already have received recommendations from her subordinate managers. Therefore, her final decisions would often be ratifications of alternatives someone else already developed. Larry checks on the technical adequacy of work, and Dorothy checks on the soundness of subordinate decisions.

We have contrasted the jobs of Larry and Dorothy in detail in order to make this point: Good leaders have a clear picture of their organizational roles. They know what is expected of them—by management, by subordinates, and by others. The more closely their behavior fits these expectations, the more likely they will be to demonstrate leadership.

Unit Objectives

Many supervisors are required to play two roles, supervisory and technical. The supervisor must integrate the differing objectives involved in these roles. To illustrate this idea, consider the following case.

Case Study: John Piasecki

John is a supervisor in a small branch office in metropolitan Los Angeles. His company, a regional insurer with strong agency representation in the Southeast and in Texas, entered the southern California commercial property-liability market about seven years ago.

Although the branch's premium volume has grown steadily, the company management has conservatively directed that the staff be kept as lean as possible, consistent with good service. Consequently, John supervises two commercial underwriters, a rater, and a clerk, in addition to working as an underwriter himself. John's underwriting responsibility, in terms of the number of applications handled, is about two-thirds that of the other two underwriters. The unit employs rating software on a PC. Everyone in the unit is expected to be able to use the PC.

John was promoted to the position of supervisor four years ago. Before that, he worked full-time as a commercial lines underwriter in the branch since its inception. Before his promotion, he received formal training in supervision and in commercial lines underwriting at the company's home office.

John estimates that he spends approximately 65 to 70 percent of his time on technical tasks, with the remainder spent on supervision. In the last several months, he has spent considerable time planning and training the underwriters and the rater in coverage and rating features of a new commercial package policy. As part of the training, he used training handbooks and software developed by the company's home-office education department.

John is accountable for achieving a half-dozen objectives that support those of his branch manager. John's objectives include attaining a target loss ratio, productivity, expense control, turnaround time, and staff development. He is further expected to hold periodic staff meetings, to appraise the performance of each employee, and to oversee the development efforts of unit members.

John's manager has also asked him to review and recommend possible revisions in the performance standards for all jobs in the unit, including that of the supervisor.

Dual Responsibilities

Here, then, is an example of a common situation in which, for good reason, the supervisor is expected to be proficient in both the supervisory and technical roles. This dual responsibility will affect the supervisor's leadership effectiveness. John will be required to switch hats often—to shift from fellow worker to superior and back again. If he misreads his role, he is likely to seem either too bossy or too weak as a leader.

Performance Standards

Another aspect of the supervisor's job that affects leadership is the challenge of meeting standards of performance, particularly those of productivity and quality. These demands are not always reconcilable, and organizations often tolerate a degree of conflict between the two.

Low productivity in office work is a recognized problem; some regard it as a major national problem. Studies show that office workers perform at 50 or 60 percent of their capacity. Output per worker rises significantly—and sometimes doubles—when jobs and work flow are carefully studied, improvements are made, performance feedback is installed, rewards are linked to performance, and employees are given time to reach their highest performance levels.

We have no reason to believe that insurance office workers are more productive than office workers in general. Many large insurance firms openly acknowledge productivity improvement as a major goal, and many insurance supervisors have productivity as one of their most important objectives.

Although productivity improvement may be a clear goal, its measurement is often difficult. Insurance output is often measured in terms such as numbers of policies handled, transactions completed, sales calls made, claim files closed, and premium volume per employee. There are wide variations in the work required to process transactions. For instance, some endorsements take hours to process; others are done in a few minutes. Hence, productivity is difficult to measure, and employees may question the validity of the yardsticks in use.

Posed against the productivity challenge is the need for high quality. Quality, visibly important in insurance work, is often measured in such terms as turn-around time, error counts, and items missing. We do not mean to ignore other demands on the supervisor in highlighting the central goals of productivity and quality. We consider the quantity/quality relationship to be crucial. In many situations, there is an apparent tradeoff: doing better in one may mean a loss in the other. The clarity with which the supervisor conveys his or her expectations for productivity and quality may have a great bearing on his or her ability to lead.

Interlaced with the challenges management presents to the supervisor are the general expectations that the employees have of the supervisor. Employees expect the supervisor to be competent, fair, communicative, and helpful.

Numerous and Complex Interpersonal Relationships

Another characteristic of the supervisor's job that affects leadership is the increase in number and the growing complexity of relationships compared with those of the technical or clerical employee. Larry Richman has relationships with his manager, department members, insureds, and claimants. He might also have relationships with agents, attorneys, auto repair firms, home-builders, contractors, and mortgagees. Depending on the size of his company,

Larry could have other relationships, both line and staff, with supervisors and members of various departments and functional areas.

Most insurance workers are knowledge workers. They have access to vast fields of information and communicate directly with many people outside the work unit. As a result, many see little need for close supervision. The supervisor who understands employee expectations and reflects them in his or her behavior is likely to be regarded as an effective leader. This does not mean allowing employees to define your supervisory role; it means that an understanding of their expectations is an essential ingredient in the recipe for your success as a leader.

The Pace of Change

The final characteristic of the supervisor's job that affects leadership is the introduction of change into the department or unit. The supervisor is concerned with effectively anticipating and absorbing change. The supervisor is usually at the lead point in introducing change into the unit or department.

Change comes in many varieties and at different speeds. Some changes—new equipment or revised procedures—are internally generated. Other changes—new legal requirements or a shift in the insurance market—may come from outside your unit or organization. With some change, you have considerable leeway in how fast you respond and what actions you take. With other changes, you may feel that your hands are tied. Some changes come without warning, while others give you ample lead time. In brief, the way you handle change weighs heavily on your effectiveness as a leader.

We have not tried to examine all of the elements that affect the ability to lead others. We consider some to be paramount: the nature of your job, its objectives, the challenges of productivity and quality, your relationships with others, and the pace of change. Your ability to lead is based frequently on your response to the forces at play in a given situation. The *way* you do things is often as important as *what* you do. Effective leadership cannot be found in having a single style or approach or an unchanging manner.

If there is a single word to associate with leadership, it is *flexibility*. Strong leaders assess each situation and respond with behavior that fits the circumstances. At its best, this behavior is a marvelous integration of diverse forces. We now want to examine some theories of leadership. These theories emphasize the need for flexibility in your leadership.

SELECTED THEORIES OF LEADERSHIP

Although many theories of leadership exist, we are going to restrict ourselves to examining five of them. The benefits of examining these theories include the following:

1. You will have an opportunity to study illustrations of effective and ineffective leadership using the theories as a framework.

2. You will have an opportunity to assess your own leadership posture and effectiveness in the context of the theories.

3. This self-assessment, in turn, can prepare you to become a more effective leader.

Situational Theory of Leadership

Can one leadership style be effective all of the time? Common sense gives this answer: "No, it depends on the situation." How are we to identify which elements of the situation are the important ones? Fred E. Fiedler's work seems to provide the most useful answers.

Three Variables

Fiedler identified three major variables that affect leadership effectiveness.[3] Fiedler's theory is sometimes called the *contingency theory* to emphasize that it shows that the desired leadership style is contingent on the following three variables in a given situation.

1. *Leader-member relations*. These include the degree of confidence in the leader, mutual trust, loyalty shown to the leader, and how likable the leader is in the eyes of the followers.

2. *Task structure*. This variable refers to the degree of definition and structure in the tasks of the followers. Are the job procedures and expected results clearly spelled out, or are they vague and shifting?

3. *Position power*. This deals with the formal authority and legitimate power of the leader's position. Does the leader have the right to make important decisions such as salary increases?

Let's illustrate Fiedler's theory by contrasting two leadership situations. In the first situation, the supervisor of a premium auditing unit is well respected and trusted by unit members. They have confidence in him and feel free to approach him with problems (good leader-member relations). The exacting work of premium auditing is highly structured, and procedures are well established (task is highly structured). The supervisor operates with considerable autonomy and authority (position power is strong).

For contrast, imagine the situation of a person picked to lead a college alumni fund drive. Many of the people who have agreed to help with the fund drive barely know the leader (leader-member relations are poor). Although the goal is clear (raise money), the methods to be used are not specified in much detail (task is unstructured). The leader lacks the power to sanction those who falter or to reward those who obtain large contributions (weak position power).

It is not possible to say what kind of leadership would work best in each of these two situations until we define styles or patterns of leadership behavior.

Two Styles

Fiedler developed two styles of leadership behavior:

1. *Task-oriented leaders* focus on the work and pay close attention to results, backlogs, and workflow problems. They provide active, controlling, structuringl eadership.
2. *Relationship-oriented leaders* concentrate on people and their feelings. They provide more passive, considerate leadership.

These styles should be viewed as the end points on a scale, with variations in between. The distinction between task-oriented and relationship-oriented leadership is a matter of emphasis, but the outcomes can be of sweeping importance.

What kind of leadership do you think would work best in each of the two situations, the premium auditing unit and the fund drive? Fiedler's research indicates that task-oriented leadership is likely to be effective in both instances. Exhibit 4-1 summarizes these findings.

Exhibit 4-1

Fiedler's Leadership Model

Leader-Member Relations	Task Structure	Position Power	Preferred Leadership Style
Good	High	Strong	Task-oriented
Good	High	Weak	Task-oriented
Good	Low	Strong	Task-oriented
Good	Low	Weak	Relationship-oriented
Poor	High	Strong	Relationship-oriented
Poor	High	Weak	Relationship-oriented
Poor	Low	Strong	Relationship-oriented
Poor	Low	Weak	Task-oriented

Following is a case to which you can apply the Fiedler model.

Illustration: The Automated Rating Case

A large, national, multiple-lines insurer has converted from manual to automated rating for major commercial property and liability lines. In its St. Louis branch, the third of twenty-one branches to convert, a new rating unit has been formed and, following the new procedure, is located in the information technology area rather than in the underwriting department.

The new supervisor, Maria Norcross, comes to the job with seven years of commercial rating experience. The unit consists of six raters who operate PCs that connect with the company's server located in its home office. Of these six raters, two come from the old manual rating unit, now charged with rating several commercial specialty lines. These two people worked with Maria there and like and respect her. The other four are relatively new to Maria and she, to them. They were drawn from such units as policywriting and personal auto rating.

Maria and the six raters were trained by information technology experts during a four-week period at the St. Louis branch. The training included a combination of independent-study and "hands-on" experience with the new computer hardware and specialized training software. The new unit is set to begin processing "live" data.

Maria is also new to her boss, Roger White, who is the branch operations manager. White is known to give general rather than close supervision. Maria has a draft position guide for her job and for that of her raters. She and the employees also have some tentative performance standards for their major responsibilities.

Take a few minutes to evaluate Maria's position in terms of Fiedler's contingency approach.

- *Leader-member relations*. Two of the six employees previously worked with Maria in the manual rating unit, like her, and apparently have confidence in her. Presumably, they will be loyal to her. The other four people are new to Maria, and she will have to work at developing good relations with them to earn their confidence and loyalty. Overall, we regard the leader-member relations as poor.

- *Task structure*. Allowing commercial rating software to make decisions is a relatively new venture for the company, since this was only the third branch to be converted. Nonetheless, position guides and performance standards are available, and training was substantial. We regard the task as highly structured.

- *Position power*. We have little to go on but regard Maria's position as strong. Her boss is known to favor general supervision, and she has unique knowledge of the new operation.

Managerial Grid Theory of Leadership

The Managerial Grid Theory, developed by Robert S. Blake and Jane S. Mouton, two behavioral scientists, is widely used in management development programs. Their theory, like Fiedler's theory, is based on research.

Blake and Mouton have graphed leadership styles on a two-dimensional grid, shown in Exhibit 4-2.

Five leadership styles, only a few of the many possible ones, are shown on the grid. The five styles are based on a concern for production (similar to task-oriented leadership) and a concern for people (similar to relationship-oriented leadership). Concern for production and concern for people are plotted on the horizontal and vertical axes of the grid, respectively.

Movement along the horizontal axis means that production is of greater concern to the leader. A rating of nine describes a leader whose concern with production is maximum. The leader's concern for people is plotted on the vertical axis. A nine on the vertical axis shows that the leader has intense concern for people.

The point on the horizontal axis should be read first. The grid positions and nicknames of the five leadership styles are as follows:

1,1—Impoverished Leadership. The leader exerts minimal effort to accomplish the task or to build relationships with followers. The coordinates reflect indifference to both production and people.

9,1—Task Leadership. The leader concentrates on task efficiency but shows little regard for the human element.

1,9—Country Club Leadership. The leader focuses on being considerate to followers and is minimally concerned with task efficiency. Such a pattern is the opposite of Task Leadership.

5,5—Middle of the Road Leadership. The leader seeks a balance between task efficiency and group morale. The (5,5) leader typically seeks to compromise task and human aspects.

9,9—Team Leadership. The leader maximizes concern for both production and people. Rather than seeking compromise, the (9,9) leader strives for solutions that meet both task and human demands.

Exhibit 4-2

Managerial Grid*

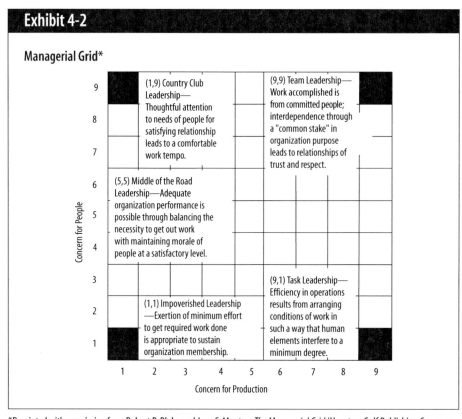

*Reprinted with permission from Robert R. Blake and Jane S. Mouton, *The Managerial Grid* (Houston: Gulf Publishing Company, 1964), p. 10.

Blake and Mouton contend that the (9,9) or team leader has the most effective leadership style on the grid.[4] Trying to define such a leader for the many individual types of managerial and supervisory jobs is undoubtedly a challenge. The two behavioral scientists address this point by implying that a multi-phased developmental program can help leaders to acquire a (9,9) style. They believe that the training experience will help the manager or supervisor to achieve skill in showing concern for others and to develop expertise in achieving maximum production. The management development program includes these phases: (1) small group meetings to learn about oneself, (2) team development, (3) meetings with other groups, and (4) organizational goal setting.[5] The grid concept is the unifying theme in this formal program of development, serving as the language and framework for learning.

You will now have an opportunity to apply the grid concept. Which of the five major leadership styles is exemplified by each of the following statements? Write the style you select—for instance (5,5) or (1,9)—next to each statement or on scratch paper. We will then review the preferred answers.

_____ A. "I know that I am not going to be popular with you statisticians, but please, I have got to have your agency loss ratio reports this afternoon. You remember, they were due yesterday morning."

_____ B. "I always come out of those supervisory meetings charged up to increase the number of policies processed, but once I hear how the staff feels about it, I realize that I have to compromise the two viewpoints."

_____ C. "What do you mean, do my programmers work hard? They had better work hard, or they won't be around here long. I've got enough problems already, so I will not put up with unmotivated employees."

_____ D. "We have good people and the secret is to try not to get in their way. They are professional underwriters and would resent close supervision."

_____ E. "I'm proud of our rating unit. We continually exceed our production goal, and our error ratio is one of the best around. Maybe it's because I try to get the raters' ideas about how to do things, even when some of their thoughts are different from mine. They have never disappointed me. In fact, sometimes their enthusiasm is greater than mine."

Let's now look at the answers preferred by supervisors and managers in various seminars. Each answer will be followed by a comment. In this exercise, you should be as concerned with the reasons for your answer as with the answer itself.

For statement A, you should have selected (1,9), the Country Club leader. The supervisor is apparently quite considerate of the statisticians' feelings, but is almost apologetic about being concerned with productivity or task efficiency.

For statement B, the preferred answer is (5,5), the Middle of the Road style. If you graphed this supervisor's attitude immediately after he or she came out of the supervisory meeting, it might measure, say, (7,3), with a relatively higher concern for productivity. After hearing from the staff, however, the supervisor's attitude apparently changes in the direction of a lower concern for productivity.

For statement C, you should have selected (9,1), the Task Leader. The supervisor focuses almost completely on task efficiency, with little regard for the welfare of the programmers.

For statement D, the preferred answer is (1,1), Impoverished Leadership. The supervisor shows minimal concern for either production or the underwriters. You might speculate whether a mature employee with this attitude should have been made a supervisor in the first place.

For statement E, you should have selected (9,9), the Team Leader style. The supervisor exhibits a maximum concern for both production and people. According to Blake and Mouton, this supervisor would be using the most effective of the major leadership styles depicted on the grid.

Where would your leadership style appear on the grid? Does your organization have a preferred style? What can you do to change your style? Addressing these questions can help you become a better leader.

Authoritarian, Consultative, and Participative Styles

The three words you are most likely to hear in discussions of leadership styles are these:

1. Authoritarian style—The leader tends to be commanding, gives directions a great deal, and makes decisions without consulting subordinates.
   - Example—Jones supervises a unit characterized by high turnover in low-skilled, repetitive jobs in a large agency. Faced with a continuing training problem, Jones gives work assignments and reassigns employees as he considers best without allowing employees to take part in the decisions.
2. Consultative style—The leader asks followers or employees for their recommendations or opinions. The leader then makes the decision.
   - Example—Willoughby, who supervises a personal lines underwriting unit in a company branch office, solicits employee opinions before reorganizing underwriting territories.
3. Participative style—The leader asks followers or employees for their recommendations and openly allows the responses to influence his or her decision.
   - Example—Chadwick, a marketing supervisor in the regional office of an insurance company, asks unit members to define the criteria for allocating projects. He is committed to using their criteria unless the criteria violate company rules.

These three styles can be viewed as points on a continuum of participation. You may encounter simpler, two-point analyses that refer only to authoritarian and participative leadership. We recognize that participation occurs in degrees. The authoritarian, consultative, and participative styles represent no, some, and extensive sharing of decision making with subordinates.

Theory X and Theory Y

What you believe about employees—their very nature—affects your selection of a leadership style. Let us consider a famous comparison developed by Douglas McGregor.[6]

McGregor thought that the traditional, hierarchically layered organization tended to assert close control over decision making and work assignments. He believed that this approach reflected certain assumptions about human behavior. He labeled them Theory X.

In essence, Theory X asserts the following: *Authoritarian style*

1. The average person inherently dislikes work and will avoid it if possible.
2. Because of this dislike, most people must be coerced, controlled, directed, or threatened with punishment to get them to put forth adequate effort toward the achievement of organizational objectives.
3. The average person prefers to be directed, wishes to avoid responsibility, has relatively little ambition, and wants security above all.

These assumptions also suggest that workers tend to respond positively to pay and benefits and negatively to the threat of punishment or the loss of job security.

Once McGregor described these characteristics of Theory X, he asked whether its implied perception of human behavior in the work context was correct. He went on to question whether managerial or supervisory actions flowing from these relatively pessimistic assumptions about people are practical in the work world. For example, he saw a contradiction between the Theory X approach to supervision and the notion that people are expected to participate as intelligent, informed, mature members of a democracy. Another possible contradiction is the fact that many people are educated, both generally and vocationally or professionally. They prefer to make decisions about their work and do not want to be closely controlled. McGregor concluded that Theory X inaccurately perceived human work behavior and, consequently, was inadequate as a theoretical foundation for how to manage people.

McGregor formulated Theory Y as an alternative, more optimistic theory of work-oriented human behavior.[7] Theory Y's assumptions about people include the following:

1. *The expenditure of physical and mental effort in work is as natural as play or rest.* The average human being does not inherently dislike work. Depending on controllable conditions, work may be a source of satisfaction (and will be performed voluntarily) or a source of displeasure (and will be avoided if possible).
2. *External control and the threat of punishment are not the only means for bringing about effort toward organizational objectives.* People will exercise self-direction and self-control in the service of objectives to which they are committed.

3. *Commitment to objectives is a function of the rewards associated with their achievement.* The most significant of such rewards, that is, the satisfaction of ego and self-fulfillment needs, can be direct products of effort directed toward organizational objectives.

4. *The average human being learns, under proper conditions, not only to accept but also to seek responsibility.* Avoidance of responsibility, lack of ambition, and emphasis on security are generally consequences of experience, not inherent human characteristics.

5. *The capacity to exercise a relatively high degree of imagination, ingenuity, and creativity in the solution of organizational problems is widely, not narrowly, distributed in the population.*

6. *Under the conditions of modern industrial life, the intellectual potentialities of the average human being are only partially used.*

McGregor admitted that the relatively optimistic assumptions of Theory Y have not been conclusively validated; however, he believed them to be more consistent with the findings of behavioral science than are those of Theory X. He believed that more and more managers hold views that resemble those of Theory Y.

Perhaps McGregor's most important message is a plea that you examine your beliefs about people. Do not adopt a style or practice that conflicts with your assumptions about the nature of employees. If you believe they must be directed, watched, and occasionally threatened with punishment, participative tactics are likely to fail in your hands.

As a practical matter, a supervisor or manager must recognize the possibility of the occasional discrepancy between formally espousing Theory Y assumptions and actually supervising in a participative manner. As with the managerial grid, Theory X and Theory Y assumptions are essentially an aspect of supervisory attitude.

Sometimes a supervisor can mistakenly conclude that Theory X or Theory Y assumptions are always undesirable and the contrary assumptions are always preferred.[8] Such a conclusion ignores McGregor's implication that most people can *potentially* exercise self-control, seek additional responsibility, and motivate themselves. In day-to-day reality, not all employees will display motivation and maturity all the time. Consequently, sometimes a supervisor who usually has a Theory Y attitude has to supervise in a relatively controlling, Theory X manner. An organization facing a survival threat may shift toward more authoritarian supervision (consistent with Theory X) until the threat has been overcome.

Supervisor's Decision-Making Style

Robert H. Tannenbaum and Warren A. Schmidt, two behavioral scientists, drew attention to the decision-making style of leaders. They present a broad range of possible delegating and decision-making styles. See Exhibit 4-3.[9]

Tannenbaum and Schmidt show leadership behavior as a broad continuum. Seven positions are shown on the continuum, ranging from the authoritarian leadership style on the left to the fully participative style depicted at the right. A moment's reflection reveals that the Tannenbaum/Schmidt seven-step model addresses the same aspects as the three-step authoritarian-consultative-participative framework, but with greater precision.

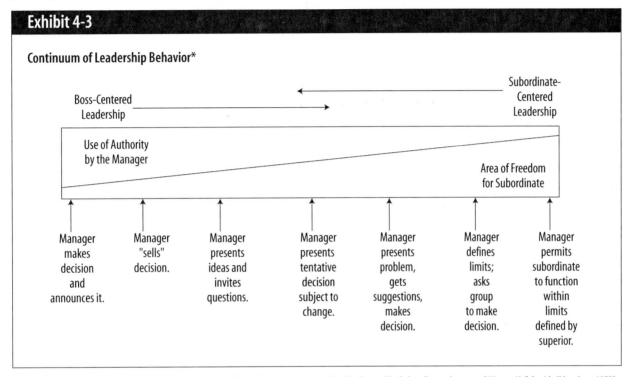

Exhibit 4-3

Continuum of Leadership Behavior*

*Reprinted by permission of *Harvard Business Review*. Exhibit from "How to Choose a Leadership Pattern" by Robert Tannenbaum and Warren H. Schmidt (May-June 1973). Copyright 1973 by the President and Fellows of Harvard College; all rights reserved.

As you study the seven Tannenbaum/Schmidt levels of participation, recognize their use in communicating with employees. What happens when employees misunderstand the degree of participation being granted in a given circumstance? Disappointment, mistrust, and anger may result when employees find they were given a smaller role in a decision than they initially thought. Inferior decisions may be the result of the opposite situation, wherein employees do not understand the degree of participation they were intended to have. In short, you must proceed carefully when telling employees exactly how great a participative role is being established each time you invite their contributions to a decision. We suspect that mixed signals about participation are a common and costly event.

AN INTEGRATIVE QUIZ

Let us now analyze the authoritarian, consultative, and participative leadership styles in more detail. These three styles focus attention on the critical leadership process of sharing decision making.

In order to analyze the three styles, we will ask you to complete a quiz. The quiz should help you (1) identify the characteristics of each style; (2) give examples of each style in terms of the Managerial Grid, Theory X or Theory Y, and the Tannenbaum/Schmidt continuum; and (3) explain the advantages and disadvantages of each style.

Write your answers on the quiz itself or on scratch paper. After you complete the quiz, you will have an opportunity to review the preferred answers along with a comment on each.

1. Of the three popular leadership styles, the one that seems most distrustful of employee attitudes and abilities is the

   _____Authoritarian Style_____Consultative Style

   _____Participative Style

2. One of the benefits of the _____ and _____ leadership styles is that they can appeal to skilled employees' need for involvement.

3. On the Tannenbaum/Schmidt leadership behavior continuum (Exhibit 4-3), a supervisor who defines limits and asks the work unit or group to make the decision is using a relatively consultative leadership style.

   _____Agree _____Disagree

4. The leadership style that is most likely to create employee resentment over the long run is the _____style.

5. The leadership style that balances speed of decision making with employee participation is the

   _____Authoritarian Style_____Consultative Style

   _____Participative Style

6. A benefit of the _____leadership style is that it seems best suited for use in a crisis situation.

7. The most authoritarian attitude would be depicted on the Managerial Grid as

   _____(5,5) _____(9,1) _____(1,9)

8. On the Tannenbaum/Schmidt continuum, a supervisor who presents a tentative decision to employees, subject to change, would be using the

   _____Authoritarian Style _____Consultative Style

   _____Participative Style

9. The consultative style usually requires the supervisor to accept some mistakes as employees learn to live with the style.

   _____Agree _____Disagree

10. On the Tannenbaum/Schmidt continuum, a supervisor who makes a decision alone and then tries to "sell" it to the staff is using the _____ __leadership style.

11. The most participative attitude on the Managerial Grid is

    _____(5,5) _____(9,9) _____(1,1)

12. Of the three styles, the one that can usually be established most quickly is the

    _____Authoritarian Style _____Consultative Style

    _____Participative Style

Let us now review the preferred answers, followed by a comment on each answer.

1. The leadership style that seems most distrustful of employee attitudes and abilities is the *authoritarian* style. A supervisor who often uses an authoritarian style tends to hold onto authority and to make decisions alone. This approach can indicate a lack of confidence in employee abilities and employee maturity.

   An authoritarian leader will probably argue that "experience proves that employees cannot be trusted," and may tell "war stories" to support this sad conclusion. Do you agree? This view may have some support in fact, but one wonders if the mistrust came first and poor employee behavior followed.

2. Skilled employees presumably have the knowledge and experience to affect the unit's productivity. Both the *participative* and *consultative* leadership styles can tap such knowledge by sharing authority with employees and allowing them to influence decisions. Would you agree, from your experience, that most employees show a desire (need) to have a say in decisions?

3. You should have *disagreed* with this statement. The continuum places this action toward the participative end of the spectrum. The supervisor limits his or her use of authority and, simultaneously, enlarges the area of freedom for the employees since they will make the decision.

4. The *authoritarian* leadership style may be necessary for speedy decisions or when the organization is in a crisis, but over the long term, research shows that employee resentment, particularly among skilled workers, can develop.

5. Under *consultative* leadership, the supervisor seeks employee opinions or recommendations. The supervisor then makes the decision. This will usually take less time than the participative approach. Consultative leadership is a strong style because it combines speed with employee involvement.

6. Crises call for drastic action. They often require hard choices and unpleasant assignments. The *authoritarian* style is appropriate for crises. For example, a company or an agency may find itself in a poor competitive position because its expenses are too high. Some authoritarian decisions may have to be made to reduce expenses. It is unwise to have employees decide the persons or functions to be eliminated.

7. You should have checked the (9,1) or task style as your answer to this question. The (9,1) supervisor concentrates on task efficiency but shows little regard for the human factor.

8. The *consultative* style allows the supervisor to take this middle-of-the-road approach. He or she moderates the use of authority and leaves the door open to a possible change in the decision.

9. We disagree that *consultative* leadership requires the supervisor to accept mistakes as employees learn the style. Because the consultative style reserves the supervisor's right to make decisions, the likelihood of poor decisions is limited.

10. "Selling" a decision to subordinates is a hallmark of *authoritarian* leadership.

11. The (9,9) or team style indicates that the supervisor maximizes concern for both production and people by aiming at maximum productivity through the efforts of a committed staff.

12. Since the *authoritarian* style restricts the power to make decisions to the supervisor, it can be established more quickly than the other two styles. Employees should not take long to "read" the supervisor's style and to recognize the behavior expected of them.

The three leadership styles, with their hallmarks, disadvantages, benefits, challenges, and relation to other theories, are shown in Exhibit 4-4.

SELECTING YOUR LEADERSHIP STYLE

Our discussion so far has made clear that there is no one ideal leadership style. How should you go about evaluating your own style or deciding what style to adopt?

Three Major Factors

Tannenbaum and Schmidt provide a now-classic guide to choosing a leadership pattern.[10] They recommend that you consider three general factors:

1. You
2. The employees
3. The situation

You

Your assumptions about people and why they work are of paramount importance in selecting a leadership style. McGregor provided Theory X and Theory Y as two patterns of assumptions but cautioned that there can be many more. If you believe the assumptions of Theory X, a highly participative style is not likely to work for you. Your leadership style must be consistent with your beliefs about people and the reasons they work.

Your background is of obvious importance in choosing a leadership style. What knowledge and skills do you have? How have you been supervised? What supervisory styles have been successful in your observations? What supervisory behaviors have worked for you? Which have failed?

What do you understand about your own motivation? How do you see yourself in terms of the Maslow needs hierarchy, the McClelland need-for-achievement model, and the Vroom model?

The Employees

The experience, knowledge, and skill of employees play a major role in determining the style of supervision they consider appropriate. Are the

Exhibit 4-4

Leadership Styles Compared

Name of Style	Hallmark(s)	Relation to Other Theories	Disadvantages or Benefits	Challenges
Authoritarian	1. Holds onto authority	1. Tends to Theory X assumptions	1. Is quick	1. Productivity may not last
	2. Makes decisions alone	2. Depicted at (9,1) on the grid	2. Can be useful in a crisis	2. Can create employee resentment over the long term
	3. Distrustful of employees' abilities and attitudes	3. At left end of Tannenbaum/Schmidt continuum	3. Can be useful with trainees or beginners	
Consultative	1. Seeks employee recommendations or opinions but makes decisions	1. Could have both Theory X and Theory Y assumptions	1. Can combine decision speed with employee participation	1. Some employees might resent not being more actively involved in the final decision
		2. Tends to mid-point on the continuum	2. Can be helpful when working with new procedure or technology	
		3. Near (5,5) on Managerial Grid		
Participative	1. Allows employees to influence decisions	1. Tends to Theory Y assumptions	1. Appeals to skilled employees' sense of involvement	1. Takes longer to implement since employees have to be trained and coached to make recommendations and use increased authority
	2. Shares authority with employees	2. Depicted at (9,9) on the grid	2. Productivity of high quality should be sustained	2. Supervisor has to accept some employee mistakes as employees learn to live with this style
	3. Is optimistic about employees' abilities	3. At the right end of the T-S continuum		

employees similar, or do they vary widely in their competencies? What do you know about their motivation? What are their career goals and expectations? What styles of supervision have they experienced? Most importantly, what style do they expect and/or prefer you to exhibit?

The Situation

Task design, work flow, and technology are among the most important situational elements affecting the appropriateness of a leadership style. Are these elements stable, or do they change often and greatly? Are there clear performance measures and standards? How does the unit fit into the larger organization, and what demands are placed on it by outside organizations? What is the culture of the larger organization and what is its dominant management style?

We have hit only major points in discussing factors to consider when analyzing yourself, your subordinates, and the situation. Many others might apply. In a given situation, you might place considerable weight on factors not mentioned above. You should complete a thorough and sensitive analysis of the elements under each heading before you select a leadership style.

Primary and Secondary Leadership Styles

Leaders typically have a primary leadership style and a secondary style. The primary style is the style they believe is most effective and with which they are most comfortable. The secondary style is the one they are likely to use when the primary style is unsuccessful. Leaders may resort to the secondary style when a crisis arises or when things simply seem to be going wrong. Rather than perform a careful analysis and search for a new style, leaders typically resort to a backup or secondary style.

In identifying your secondary style, ask yourself what changes could cause you to shift your supervisory style? What evidence would convince you that your leadership pattern is no longer effective? What style would you adopt, and why do you favor that style? Does your secondary style echo your experience or imitate that of someone you admire?

Style Flexibility

Flexibility of style is widely regarded as a hallmark of an effective leader. A good leader seems to select a style that fits the particular circumstances. In effect, a good leader has a number of styles readily available and is not limited to a primary and secondary style. For instance, the leader may give close, active supervision to inexperienced employees while others in the same unit receive passive, more general supervision. He or she may depart from the style normally used when overseeing a given project. Are we saying that good leaders are inconsistent? In a sense, we are. Good leaders select the pattern of behavior appropriate in each leadership situation. They seem to be able to adjust their behavior to circumstances without much conscious effort. They reflect on their own behavior and have perfected their listening skills.

Developing style flexibility is not easy. One reason is because most of us are influenced by images of leadership from television, motion pictures, and fiction. These images usually show leaders as firm, consistent, and forceful.

Another reason flexibility is hard to develop is that we tend to repeat behavior that is rewarded. A supervisor tends to repeat the behavior associated with early supervisory successes. He or she may rely on convenient shortcuts such as applying past solutions to current problems. Take time to evaluate each situation and guard against shortcut answers from the past.

SUMMARY

To be a good supervisor, you must be a good leader. This chapter examined the topic of leadership as it relates to your role as the task (or formal) leader of the unit.

Leadership is the ability to achieve desired results through others and, at the same time, to win their confidence, cooperation, and loyalty. Management scholars and practitioners have debated for a long time whether leadership is an inherited characteristic or an acquired one. No evidence seems to exist to support the idea that leadership is an innate ability, so we can conclude that leaders are made.

Effective leaders finely tune their behavior to the situation. Among the qualities effective leaders possess are perception, commitment to accomplishing group tasks, empathy, self-confidence, honesty, and flexibility. Generally speaking, the characteristics of the supervisor's job that affect leadership include the nature of the job; unit objectives; the requirements for performance, productivity, and quality; complex interpersonal relationships; and the pace of change.

In examining leadership behavior, this chapter discussed the results of five scholarly efforts aimed at unlocking the secrets of leadership: Fiedler's Situational Theory of Leadership; Blake and Mouton's Managerial Grid Theory of Leadership; the authoritarian, consultative, and participative styles of leadership; McGregor's Theory X and Theory Y; and Tannenbaum and Schmidt's seven-step model of decision-making styles.

Although there is no one ideal leadership style, Tannenbaum and Schmidt provide a guide to choosing a leadership style based on three factors: you, the employees, and the situation.

Leaders typically have a primary leadership style and a secondary style. The primary style is the style they believe is most effective and with which they are most comfortable. The secondary style is the one they are most likely to use when the primary style is unsuccessful. A good leader, however, has a number of styles readily available and is not limited to just a primary and a secondary style.

CHAPTER NOTES

1. Paul Hersey and Kenneth Blanchard, *Management of Organizational Behavior: Utilizing Human Resources*, 3d ed. (Englewood Cliffs, NJ: Prentice Hall, Inc., 1977), p. 84.

2. Martin M. Broadwell and William F. Simpson, CPCU, *The New Insurance Supervisor* (Reading, MA: Addison Wesley Publishing Co., 1981), p. 58.

3. Stephen P. Robbins, *Organizational Behavior*, 2d ed. (Englewood Cliffs, NJ: Prentice Hall, Inc., 1983), pp. 294-297.

4. James H. Donnelly, Jr., James L. Gibson, and John M. Ivancevich, *Fundamentals of Management: Functions, Behaviors, Models*, revised ed. (Dallas, TX: Business Publications, Inc., 1975), p. 225.

5. Donnelly, Gibson, and Ivancevich, pp. 221 and 222.

6. Douglas McGregor, *The Human Side of Enterprise* (New York: McGraw-Hill Book Company, 1960), pp. 33-35.

7. McGregor, pp. 47-49.

8. Hersey and Blanchard, p. 56.

9. Robert Tannenbaum and Warren E. Schmidt, "How to Choose a Leadership Pattern," *Harvard Business Review*, March-April 1957, pp. 95-101.

10. Tannenbaum and Schmidt, pp. 95-101.

Chapter 5

Understanding Others

Each of us experiences the world subjectively. Everything we encounter by means of our five senses is interpreted in a way that is unique to the individual. Three people observing the same incident will each perceive it differently, at times very differently. Consider the following situation:

John Sparks, marketing manager, enters his unit's area at 9 A.M. Two marketing representatives and John's assistant are already at their desks. John looks straight ahead, frowning and silent. His hair is somewhat disheveled, his cheeks are flushed, and his tie is slightly askew. He goes straight into his office, sits down at his desk, and reaches for the phone.

Marketing Rep #1: I guess we'd better be careful today. It looks as if John had a bad night last night. I know how it is to have a fight with your wife.

Marketing Rep #2: He had a breakfast meeting scheduled with our agent, Harry Moffitt. Harry gives everyone a rough time. I bet John got a real earful because we turned down a risk.

Assistant: You're both reading more into John's behavior than you need to. Neither of you is in the office enough to see how he looks every day. In about an hour, after three or four cups of coffee, he'll be his usual, jovial self. I do wish just once in a while he'd say hello and make me feel I have some value around here.

As you can see, each of the three people in the office interpreted John's behavior in a different way. Let's now look at what was going through John's mind as he entered the office.

John: Mary and I need to go out more often. I think I'll take her to the restaurant that Harry mentioned this morning. He certainly was in a stormy mood, but I think I finally helped him see our point of view about that risk. He seemed pleased with my suggestions about how to place the risk elsewhere. Well, everyone is here this morning. I think I'll take the opportunity to get them all together and tell them what a great job they've been doing lately. First, I'd better call Mary to arrange our dinner plans.

Not one of the people observing John was able to interpret his behavior correctly. The messages he was sending out through the visual clues and body language misled even the assistant who works with him every day and feels she knows him well. Understanding others is a complex and difficult undertaking, as this example demonstrates. Understanding oneself, a parallel skill, is just as difficult—John Sparks would probably be surprised by the impression he makes on his co-workers.

As a supervisor, you are responsible for understanding employees and for guiding and influencing them toward behavior that will contribute to the achievement of your organization's goals. This chapter will aid you in increasing the depth of your understanding of yourself and others. After looking at the process of perception and the factors affecting an individual's way of perceiving the environment, we will discuss some of the barriers to understanding that are frequently encountered in the workplace and examine ways to overcome them.

FACTORS AFFECTING PERCEPTION

Perception is the process of selecting, organizing, and interpreting what we see, hear, taste, touch, and feel. It affects our response to other people and our behavior. The factors that shape an individual's perception should be studied in order to reach an understanding of that person. Six of the most important factors are discussed below.

Individual Needs

What a person sees and hears depends greatly on what that person *needs* to see or hear. An employee will select from a particular conversation only the things he or she has a need to hear and may either misinterpret or not even hear the rest. For instance, a supervisor tells a unit member, "You've done a good job this month, Tom. Your work shows much improvement over last month. Keep it up!" If Tom is a person with a great need for esteem, he may hear only the part of the conversation in which he was praised and disregard or not hear the part referring to his inferior performance the previous month. If the supervisor's intention was to communicate both satisfaction with current performance and dissatisfaction with previous work, only half of the message got through. As a supervisor, you must try to keep in mind what you know about a person's needs in order to determine what he or she may perceive in any given situation.

Experience

What we perceive is often a result of what we have seen before in similar situations. Evidence is interpreted in light of our past experiences. For example, if your manager tends to call you into his or her office only to point out errors or discuss problems, you will come to expect that he or she will have no other reason for doing so. Recalling the example in the previous section, suppose your manager calls you in and says, "Your unit has done a good job this month. There has been a big improvement in productivity over last month. Keep up the good work!" If you have been conditioned by previous experiences to expect only criticism from your manager, you may interpret his statement as a criticism of last month's performance or even as a threat that if you don't keep up the good work, you'll be in serious trouble.

Values and Attitudes

Values and attitudes affect our perceptions by serving as the basis of how we evaluate what we experience. Our *values*—that is, our beliefs in the relative worth of what is around us—differ according to background, experience, and character. A person raised in a strict, religious farm community will probably have very different values from one raised in a crowded urban center. People raised in similar environments but in different generations will also have different values. *Attitudes* define our position toward other people and their ideas. They are more specific and are more changeable than values. For example, a person who places great value on honesty would, in most cases, be unlikely to alter this value easily; however, an employee with a cautious attitude toward working with attorneys may easily change that attitude after having a positive experience with an attorney.

Knowing the values and attitudes of your subordinates can help you to deal effectively with them and to influence their behavior on the job. You must remember, however, that your job as supervisor means focusing on behavior, not values or attitudes.

Self-Concept

The way we perceive others and situations depends on the image we have of ourselves. Four components compose the self-concept:

1. The way you see yourself—For example, you may think of yourself as sincere, personable, and outgoing.
2. The way you would like to be—For example, you may wish you were brave, resourceful, and brilliant.
3. The way you think others see you—You can, for the most part, only estimate this.
4. The way you are—the "real" you.

The more similar these four components are, the clearer the self-concept will be. The more they conflict, the more likely we are to feel confused or to seem confusing to others. We tend to hear and remember what supports our self-concept and reject or become defensive when presented with information that conflicts with it. A receptionist who sees himself as adept at dealing with irate phone calls may reject outright any suggestion that he needs to improve his phone manner.

Structural Cues

Structural cues refer to concrete, external, and objective elements. The clothes people wear, the cars they drive, and the pictures they hang on their office or cubicle walls are all interpreted by us on the basis of our own values and attitudes. You should avoid placing heavy emphasis on these factors in your perceptions of others.

Expectations

What we perceive is colored by what we expect to perceive. Suppose you observe a person clearly dominating a discussion. You may perceive the person as friendly and helpful if told he is an executive or as aggressive and overbearing if told he is a newcomer. Others may expect you as a supervisor to possess skills and competencies of a particular kind and level and will perceive you in terms of how well you fulfill their expectations of your role. In addition to your meeting the formal role demands of your job, your employees may expect you to meet informal role demands, such as being the first to arrive and the last to leave the office, even if this is not office policy.

BARRIERS TO UNDERSTANDING OTHERS

Understanding the behavior of others should be easy because we do it—or try to do it—every day. Nonetheless, understanding others is anything but easy. Human beings are complex and often unpredictable, and our language abounds with clichés to prove it. Chances are, you are above average at understanding the persons around you. You are not likely to have been selected as a supervisor if you demonstrate difficulty in seeing others as individuals and in relating to them in ways that reflect their uniqueness. Nonetheless, your supervisory responsibilities require you to be highly sensitive to others, especially employees. A deliberate effort to sharpen your skill in understanding others should bear fruit throughout your supervisory career. We begin by considering some of the barriers to understanding others.

Perception

The preceding discussion of the perceptual process underscores the conclusion that perceptual distortion is normal. Put another way, the human body is an imperfect machine for data gathering. Because physical reality is filtered through needs, values, attitudes, experience, the self-concept, structural cues, and expectations, the perceived image is rarely exactly the same as the thing being perceived. The message we receive is seldom exactly the same as the message the sender intended.

Making Judgments

People have a natural tendency to make judgments in order to facilitate learning and conversing. These judgments often work against fully understanding what someone is trying to communicate and may even change what the person says or how it is said.

Perhaps this is best seen by example. Suppose a member of your unit, Paul, complains to you about the "noisy conversations" in his work area and argues that the noise is keeping him from doing his best work. Paul has complained about co-workers before, and you know he has no close friends within the unit. If you make a quick judgment that "This is just another one of Paul's old complaints," you are not likely to understand all that he is trying to tell you. If your face, your body language, or your words communicate this judgment to Paul, he may feel rejected and decide that there is little hope of getting through to you. Maybe the general noise level *has* increased, or other employees *are* talking more frequently than before, or a recently developed workflow problem has made Paul more sensitive to conversations around him. Perhaps Paul's complaint is unjustified and one you should eventually ignore. The point is that you will block a portion of Paul's communication if you rush to judge him and his message.

Judgments about what is morally right and wrong often raise insurmountable barriers to understanding others. Suppose, for example, that an employee in your unit develops the problem of alcohol dependence. If you see alcoholism as something evil or as a sign of innate character weakness (rather than as a progressive disease), you are not likely to hear the employee's requests for help or to assist the employee once he or she is in recovery.

Insufficient Information

The lack of adequate information is another major barrier to understanding others. While interacting with others, you have your own need to proceed with other things. So do they. There never seems to be enough time to get or give complete information. You are often asked to give your immediate attention to a matter whenever someone needs a quick answer. To make matters worse, our culture places a high value on decisiveness by managers and interprets slow action as a sign of weakness. Repeated and conscious efforts on your part may be necessary to make sure you gather full information about the people you seek to understand.

Defensiveness

Just as perceptual distortion is normal, so is the need to defend one's self-concept. A natural reaction is to explain or justify your actions when they are criticized. Supervisors often "read into" an employee complaint and hear the message that they are being blamed for the matter. If your image of yourself as a competent supervisor is attacked by a unit member, you raise defenses automatically. You can, through conscious effort, develop the habit of withholding your defensive responses and encouraging the other person to explain his or her thoughts.

Lack of Listening Skills

As you may have observed, some overlap exists among these barriers to understanding others. The final barrier, *lack of listening skills*, seems to overlap with the others yet emphasizes the supervisor's power to overcome them. Few people are born good listeners. Most supervisors and managers become good listeners by working at it. They develop the skill of *active listening*. A recommended method for active listening is discussed in Chapter 7.

IMPROVING YOUR UNDERSTANDING OF OTHERS

We will examine eight techniques to control the effects of the preceding barriers and to improve your skill in understanding others. The techniques are discussed in the context of an interaction between supervisor and employee.

1. *Have an open, accepting mind.* You must be amenable to change where justified. The ideas of others should be given weight equal to that given to your own ideas. A willingness to be questioned and challenged helps you to evaluate yourself and to expand your knowledge and skills. Seek the ideas and opinions of others. Although the open-door policy is a cliche of the business world, you should ask yourself, Is my door open or shut? Is my mind open or shut? An "open" door does not generate heavy foot traffic when the mind is closed.

2. *Show and feel genuine respect for others.* False respect is easily identifiable as insincere behavior. Employees bring their competencies, their experiences, and their perceptions to the workplace. These must be respected for what they offer to you, your unit, and your product. Concentrate on the positive contributions of employees even when things are going poorly. If you show honest respect, employees will express themselves more readily, and, in turn, you will know more about them.

3. *Be objective,* carefully inspecting your ideas and the facts. Be aware of your assumptions and your expectations. Take time to reflect. Ask others for negative views or evidence that does not support your idea. Discriminate between personal impressions and facts.

   The following conversations between supervisor and subordinate illustrate these techniques at work.

Conversation #1

Jim Jones, a first-year underwriter, approaches Emily Scott, his supervisor, with an office building renewal and says: "I think we should decline this renewal." Emily recognizes the account and the agent who submitted it. She says: "No way, I underwrote it myself two years ago, and it's a good risk. We are getting a good premium and we don't want to anger the agent. The building owner is his personal friend. Sign off and send it to rating right away!"

Is Emily's mind open and accepting? Is there genuine respect? Is Emily being objective, inspecting today's facts? What is the effect on the underwriter? Jim is probably learning to be far more cautious about questioning any risk Emily underwrote before her promotion, realizing that he had better not challenge her. He is likely to spend extra time documenting the file to protect himself.

How many conversations do we have every day that effectively teach our subordinates the door is open but the mind is not, or that the supervisor knows more than the subordinates do?

Conversation #2

Jim enters Emily's office saying he has a risk he wants to decline. Emily, looking at the file, says: "Oh? I remember when I looked at that risk two years ago. I thought it was pretty good then. Jim, tell me why you want to decline it."

Jim: The neighborhood has deteriorated, and four reported occurrences of theft and vandalism have taken place in the last six months. There is a new owner, and he is not a good credit risk according to D&B; in fact, he went through bankruptcy several years ago. There is also a high vacancy factor since the bank on the ground floor moved out last month and three other floors are only partially leased.

Emily: I see. What does our agent think?

Jim: He suggested we surcharge the premium. I get the feeling that he really doesn't care, since he and the new owner haven't done business before.

Emily: O.K., Jim. I'll support your declination. Your reasons are good. Thank you for checking it out with me first. I appreciate that.

Although Emily is busy, she took the time to question Jim. A difference of three minutes has obviously led to a better decision and should enhance the relationship between Jim and Emily.

Other techniques to improve understanding include recognizing hidden agendas, separating facts from feelings, identifying behavior patterns, having patience and confidence, and listening actively.

4. *Recognize hidden agendas.* A *hidden agenda* is what one individual involved in an interaction really wants to accomplish but hides from

the others involved. Often, the agenda is very different from the stated objective. The individual may even be unaware that he or she has a hidden agenda or, if aware of it, may not be fully aware of its importance. Each person involved in a meeting can have a hidden agenda, complicating matters even more. If you suspect a hidden agenda, ask the person involved to air his or her thoughts. This helps the person to explore his or her own understanding of the subject and tends to bring out any hidden agendas. The more one expresses knowledge and feelings about a subject, the clearer knowledge and feelings usually become to the speaker and to others. Listeners can help an individual develop knowledge by asking questions that explore the subject from various angles and in depth.

Before entering into a discussion with a subordinate, you should search for any hidden agenda of your own. Do you have one? What is it? How can you bring it into the open? If you want positive action to result from your discussions with subordinates, you should state your objectives explicitly.

5. *Separate facts from feelings.* During your interactions with others, mentally list the key points and, as you do so, separate facts from feelings. Is there a central theme with supporting facts? Feelings are expressed not only in words but also in behavior. Look for "body language." Watch a person's eyes and facial expressions to see whether these support or contradict the words.

In any interaction, feelings are part of the message. How a person feels about a subject may be more important to you than the details of the subject. At times, an individual may feel guilty because his or her feelings are so strong. The more you acknowledge that feelings have their place and that you accept them, the more likely you are to get the information you need. If you are accepting of others' feelings, subordinates will be less likely to "cover them up." "Covering up" takes concentrated effort on the part of the employee and diminishes your ability to understand what is going on in a particular situation.

6. *Identify patterns.* People usually behave in a consistent way. You should identify the behavior patterns of employees. Knowing each individual's background, values, attitudes, and opinions; the group with whom he or she associates; and his or her information sources helps you to see a pattern in feelings and behavior, to understand how facts are presented, and to realize the nature of the subordinate's relationship with you.

7. *Be patient and confident.* For successful interaction to occur, you must exercise a great deal of patience. People need time to formulate and express thoughts, to question in pursuit of facts, and to uncover possible hidden agendas. Your patience will be rewarded if you keep your goals for the interaction in mind: better understanding of the subordinate and information gathering to enhance your decisions. You also need to exercise confidence, trusting that your subordinates want to perform well and that any criticism you may receive from

them is well intentioned. Indeed, if your mind is open to challenge and criticism, your skills grow and your decisions improve.

8. *Listen actively.* Underlying all of these techniques is the need to be an active listener. In short, this means listening without interruption, withholding judgment, being patient and open-minded, and not arguing or defending. Active listening means paying attention to the content and the intent—that is, what lies beyond the words. Every opportunity you have to *hear* your subordinates is an opportunity to acquire a greater understanding of them and, in turn, to gain their best efforts. Chapter 7 will explain the process of active listening in greater detail.

EMOTIONAL BEHAVIOR

Strong or persistent feelings are often called *emotions*. To understand others we must understand their emotions. Exploring what emotions are or are not, we can say the following:

1. Emotions are not chosen. They cannot be selected, added, or discarded at will; however, we do try to control their expression.

2. Emotions are displaceable. They can be concealed even from ourselves. We tend to shift emotions to something external of ourselves. (For example, someone spills coffee on a policy and turns to a neighbor, saying, "Can't you be quiet? You disturbed me and look at what I've done!")

3. Emotions vary in intensity depending on the underlying cause. A burst of anger over a spilled cup of coffee suggests that something far more disturbing than this trivial incident is going on.

4. Emotions are internal but can be triggered internally or externally. This means that we generate our own emotions. To illustrate an internally generated emotion, think about the occasions when you have awakened excited, feeling alive and happy for no apparent reason. Carrying that happy feeling to work, you may find after an hour or two of facing a series of problems created by others' errors that frustration and anger at people have replaced those happy feelings. Your frustration is caused by the external situation.

5. Emotions are not usually predictable in a specific situation. Two people in the same situation may have two entirely different emotional reactions. A person will not always react with the same feelings each time a recurring event takes place.

The following example illustrates these elements at work. You, as supervisor, announce to the unit members that the unit will soon have a new method for accessing outside databases. Mary and Jane will be trained in the new procedures. Over the next few days, Mary appears to be angry, slamming things around, complaining about the work, and heaving deep sighs whenever you make a request. Jane comes to you complaining that Mary is not carrying her share of the work and that she is tired of Mary's behavior. Jane is looking forward to having the new methods because she sees how much more often she'll be able to access a greater variety of information. She hopes you won't change your mind just because Mary is behaving badly. You talk with Mary. Indeed, she is angry about your decision. She expresses doubt that she will be able to learn how to use the new methods quickly and thinks you will discover you need only one person. Since she thinks she might not do the job as well as Jane, Mary fears she may be fired. Mary's emotions include *anger*, directed at the supervisor and at her perceived competitor, Jane; and *fear* of her own lack of abilities, of the unknown, and of the possible loss of job security. Jane's emotions include *frustration* and *anger*, directed at Mary, and *anxiety* over possibly not getting something she wants.

Neither Mary nor Jane can select how she feels. Mary has displaced her emotions—she appears to be unhappy about the work you are giving her rather than about the new procedures. Mary's emotions are internally generated by self-doubt. They seem quite strong and proportionate to the threat that she perceives as real. Jane's emotions reflect the situation, particularly Mary's response to your announcement. Both employees face the same change, but their reactions are totally different. As supervisor, you have ample evidence that the behaviors of Mary and Jane are presently dominated by their feelings.

HANDLING EMOTIONAL SITUATIONS ON THE JOB

As part of this brief overview of emotions, let's turn to handling emotions on the job. Emotions are often repressed at work, presumably because the organization's culture dictates the amount of permitted emotional expression, which is based on the fairly uniform perception that society frowns on showing emotion. Even if an organization allows the open expression of some feelings, most individuals continue to believe that the display of strong negative feelings is politically unwise.

We learn very early when it is "proper" to express emotions. In school, teachers tell us to behave ourselves and to contain our emotions. Children tease one another for displaying their feelings. We carry what we have learned about showing our feelings into the workplace.

The best way of coping with our emotions is to find a friendly ear and express how we feel. Denying or withholding an emotion is, in effect, not coping with it and it can lead to an accumulation of internal tension, which must eventually explode. Faced with joy or positive feelings, supervisors usually listen attentively, letting the person talk it out and get back to business. However, supervisors often respond to negative emotions by being logical and reassuring; the supervisor does the talking in an attempt to help the individual control his or her emotion.

A typical conversation might sound like this:

Charlie: I am really angry at what went on in that meeting.

Supervisor: Calm down; let's talk about it. There is a reason for everything. Let me share our rationale so you can understand why we want to go in this new direction.

Charlie is not going to be receptive to reason and logic at this stage; in fact, such assurances could heighten and reinforce his emotions. What Charlie needs is an outlet for his feelings. When the feelings are related to work, the most appropriate place to vent them is with the supervisor. The individual can expect the supervisor to have empathy and can trust that the conversation will remain confidential.

Far from trying to stifle emotions, your goal as supervisor should be to encourage the expression of emotions that affect work so that the individual can begin to resolve the issues in question.

As supervisor, you should practice the following:

1. Encourage expression to allow release of the emotions and enable the individual to cope with them.
2. Accept emotion without criticism or judgment.
3. Recognize that the individual, in coming to you, has given you a vote of trust and confidence.
4. Help the individual become aware of emotions he or she is repressing based on your observations of behavior.
5. Decide what, if anything, has to be done in relation to the cause of the emotion.

A caution should be noted: as supervisor, you must use judgment in deciding whether to help an employee express an emotion. Some emotions are too intense and potentially disturbing. You should never assume you know what feeling is being withheld and pry. You should instead use active-listening techniques to encourage the expression of feelings. You must not push the person; you can only show your willingness to listen to whatever he or she wants to disclose.

Once the emotion has been openly expressed, the individual will usually return to normal. He or she may then, alone or with you, explore ways to control or avoid what caused the emotional reaction.

Although you may feel very uncomfortable around an emotional display and feel inadequate at "handling" it, you should encourage such a display in the privacy of your office. Help the individual begin to cope with what caused the emotional reaction, and work together to identify actions that can resolve the situation. That way, you are really not "handling" the emotion but instead are facilitating the expression of the emotion so that the individual can handle it. You cannot be responsible for other people's emotional reactions, but you are responsible for their work output. If they are tied up emotionally, their work suffers. Without playing psychologist, you can encourage the venting of pressure and the expression of emotions so that an upset employee can become calm and resume productivity.

DEFENSE MECHANISMS

Each of us strives to know and deal with reality and, at the same time, to avoid pain or psychological discomfort. When feelings of anxiety over potential or real criticism are aroused, both of these drives come into play. We seek to understand the criticism, to weigh its merit, and, perhaps, to change. We also want to avert anxiety and protect ourselves against the hurt inherent in any negative criticism. Many of the protections we habitually use are called *defense mechanisms*. If the criticism is perceived to be mild, we may not activate any defenses. If it is perceived to be harsh, defense mechanisms automatically spring into action. Operating unconsciously, these mechanisms allow us to change what we hear, what it means, or how we handle it, and to reduce the pain we feel. At the extreme, they can completely block an unpleasant message so that we do not hear or see it.

The use of defense mechanisms is normal; we all use them when we need to. They protect us from pain or limit the pain to a tolerable level. They help us to grow by enabling us to handle anxiety. If things are going well, we are less likely to use them and more open to disruptive messages. If our self-concept is shaky at the moment or we have suffered recent criticism, our defenses rise to protect us.

As noted earlier, being *defensive* is a barrier to understanding others. Defensiveness means giving an explanation or justification. It is a direct "It wasn't my fault" response. In contrast, defense mechanisms are more indirect reactions that seem to displace or repress the response.

Types of Defense Mechanisms

Although there are dozens of defensive behaviors, following are some of the more common ones encountered at work.

Withdrawal

By withdrawing from the situation or person causing the anxiety, an individual can avoid feeling, seeing, or hearing the conflict. A tendered resignation, absence, a request to skip meetings, and a request to move to another location or to drop a project are all examples of withdrawal. An individual may walk out of the room, take an unscheduled coffee break, or claim sudden illness when needing to withdraw temporarily.

Repression

By repressing frustration, an individual can exclude anxious feelings from his or her consciousness. The individual does not think about the conflict and will deny it exists if asked. For example, two people in a meeting argue different approaches to a task. Observers see that a deeper conflict exists between them. When asked about what is going on, the two people sincerely deny any personal conflict and stress that it is their responsibility to the company and its goals to stand up for what they believe is the right approach.

Regression

An individual may revert to less mature behavior when frustrated. This defense mechanism is usually used when others don't sufficiently still the anxieties. Childlike outbursts and stewing are examples.

Aggression

Aggressive behavior is often injurious. The energy created by the anxiety needs to be discharged. Fighting verbally or physically, destroying materials, or participating in competitive sports are examples of aggressive behavior.

Compensation

Compensation is exhibited when an individual exerts an unusual amount of energy on an activity to make up for a deficiency in another area. To illustrate, an individual becomes extremely active in his company's social activities, assuming a leadership role to compensate for his failure to be promoted.

Projection

Projection is attributing one's own feelings or motives to someone else. For example, an employee who wants a promotion to a supervisory position, obtains it, but then proves unable to handle the new job may gossip about the "incompetence" of another supervisor. The employee projects his or her sense of inadequacy on another.

Fantasy

Wish fulfillment, an escape from reality through daydreaming or some other form of imagery, is fantasy. An employee who distorts a contribution on a project by envisioning his or her role, knowledge, and skills as being most critical to the project's success is engaging in a fantasy.

Rationalization

To rationalize is to give logical and reasonable explanations for attitudes, actions, or behavior in order to mask the true reason, which, if recognized, would produce anxiety. It is frequently used to explain events such as not getting promoted or not being recommended to work on a project. A typical rationalization is: "I'm glad I'm not on the committee; it would have taken too much time."

Reaction Formation

In reaction formation, certain actions unacceptable to the individual consciousness are repressed, resulting in the individual's acting in a way that contradicts his or her real feelings and doing so with considerable force. For example, an individual who has a deep need to be liked by peers may forcefully say, "I don't care" when he or she is excluded from group discussions. A subordinate's extreme obedience to a supervisor's request is another example.

When dealing with your subordinates, you need to be aware of these defense mechanisms and their effect on your communication, particularly when you are taking corrective action.

Identifying Defense Mechanisms

To practice identifying defense mechanisms, decide which defense mechanism is in use in each of the following examples.

1. The underwriter pores over every shoe-store application and most often turns down these risks because the first one he wrote had a huge loss.
2. The claim technician insists that the defense attorney encouraged the out-of-court settlement of the claim, which resulted in overpayment to the claimant.
3. The accountant goes to the racquetball club every day at noon and pounds the ball against the wall, exhausting his opponents.
4. The secretary tells her friend how she personally talked the president into making a major investment in computer equipment.
5. The marketing representative who isn't making quota tells his supervisor that many of his personal lines agents prefer another company's interface and therefore give that company all the business they can.

The defense mechanisms involved in these examples are (1) reaction formation, (2) projection, (3) aggression, (4) fantasy, and (5) rationalization.

As a supervisor, you will want to examine what subordinate behaviors you reward, attempt to correct, or punish. Answering the following three questions will help you to deal with an employee who is using a defense mechanism.

1. Was the initial behavior the result of an unclear job description or role? Improper behavior may arise because the subordinate does not clearly understand what is expected, the authority level on a project, or how a procedure works. In such cases, clarification, not correction, is needed.
2. Does the individual think you are ignoring his or her position, opinion, or values? This question, too, is directed at you and, specifically, at

your ability to listen actively. Are you being aggressive and creating a defensive atmosphere?

3. Why does the individual feel a threat? Why has the anxiety risen to such a level that a defense mechanism is needed? Could it be misperception—he or she read more into your actions than you intended? Or did he or she perceive things accurately but react with emotion? Perhaps your behavior touched a sore spot or triggered old anger. In any event, you need to get more information from the individual before proceeding.

At work, unproductive defenses often arise when the organization's management imposes unreasonable goals. Managers and other employees are sometimes pushed to give better performance and criticized for failure. Managers may respond with such tactics as building slack into the budget, underestimating sales, and overestimating staff needs and expenses. They arm themselves with "objective data" to explain any failure to meet goals. The creation of tension and resulting failure situations does not usually result in productive behavior.

RESISTANCE TO CHANGE

Change is an integral part of organization life. Emotions and defense mechanisms are often aroused by change. After all, change means the individual must revise behavior and perceptions. The announcement that a major change is coming also usually arouses fear. This is equally true for managers, supervisors, and other employees.

Responses to Change

Any change in the work environment will produce one of three responses:

1. Acceptance and positive support
2. Compliance and minimal support
3. Resistance

When planning for change, you can anticipate that human reactions will vary widely. Persons comfortable with the present situation may resist change because they do not know whether things will be as pleasant as they are now. Some will resist because they dislike or fear change in general. Some employees may be eager for the change, perhaps seeing potential growth opportunities, variety, and challenge. Others will support the change because they dislike the current situation. We tend to accept changes that we think will benefit us, changes with which we agree, or changes we had a part in making happen. We tend to resist changes that have no perceived benefit, changes with which we disagree (especially if we argued against them), and changes we had no role in making. Thus, a given change may trigger all three responses within a unit.

Uncertainty characterizes all change. The future will be different, but we can never be sure how or to what extent. We also cannot be sure the change will make things work better. This uncertainty intensifies resistance.

Reasons for Resistance

Employees realize that change will affect their lives in many ways and will probably disrupt their routines. Even though individuals may not be able to pinpoint its effects, they are aware that change may do the following:

1. Disrupt their routines
2. Threaten their safety and comfort
3. Shake up or revise their psychological world
4. Have an economic effect
5. Threaten their status and role in employee groups

Individuals will wonder: Can I do it? Will I fail? Will I be as good as a supervisor as I was as a regular employee? Will it be as pleasant a position as my previous job? Whom will I be working with? Will I lose contact with my friends?

Supervisors who are aware of coming changes should anticipate resistance and prepare their units and each employee to accommodate the changes. Any observed resistance is a warning signal to supervisors, and it must be dealt with if organizational objectives are to be met.

One major change in the insurance business is the use of information technology in rating and policy writing. The following case study illustrates some potential responses to change in a typical rating unit. Useful supervisory techniques for overcoming resistance will be applied to the case.

Case Study: Zavier Agency

The staff of the Zavier Agency consisted of five producers, seven customer service representatives, and six clerical employees. Henry Davis, manager of the agency, informed the staff that the agency would soon implement the use of the Internet with three of the companies that the agency represented.

The agency already had interactive interface with a number of companies. Under interactive interface, an agency employee, usually a customer service representative, sat at a personal computer or dumb terminal and responded to instructions on the screen in order to exchange data with a company computer. The system was programmed to recognize some types of data-entry errors. It rejected certain incorrect entries and immediately notified the CSR that corrections were needed.

In the initial phase, the CSRs would send completed data files to the companies via the companies' Web sites. The data would be loaded into the individual company's system at night, and Zavier would receive an error report highlighting any inaccurate or missing data.

At a staff meeting, Henry Davis announced that the changeover would take place next month and that training would begin in two weeks. He further suggested that vacation plans for this time period should be changed. He invited all agency employees to talk with him individually about their concerns.

Here are the employees' responses (some shared with Henry, some privately thought, and some discussed with other employees).

Janet, Lisa, and Dottie, clerical support employees, each with several years' experience, discussed the change over coffee.

Janet: I don't like it. Every morning we'll be greeted by a list of data-entry errors that we will have to correct. We're bound to look bad.

Lisa: I bet we end up doing work that the CSRs now do. What bothers me most is that we'll be blamed for all the mistakes even if we didn't make them. I've never liked entering a lot of data all at once—it's boring.

Dottie: You know what always happens with these computer changes? Productivity goes down and service slips. Just when we have things under control, something new comes along that is bound to hurt our performance. I don't think Henry has ever seen us at our best.

Doris and Don, customer service representatives, sought out Henry Davis and told him the following.

Doris: I'm looking forward to having batch interface. It should eventually bring down the cost of interfacing with the companies.

Don: If I can do anything to help train the others, I'll be glad to help. But I do have one concern. The new error report will draw attention to our individual errors and make them public knowledge. You know that sometimes we enter endorsements and other things while the customer is on the telephone. We're bound to make some little mistakes in the process.

Pam and several others kept their thoughts to themselves. Here is what they were thinking.

Pam: I'll have to change my vacation plans again. How I wish I weren't the junior CSR, always getting the short end. Darn this agency, always something new, just to keep things jumbled.

Charlie: Henry hasn't gotten all the bugs out of the present interface, and here we go again. I'll bet we're the guinea pigs on this installation.

Susan: I wonder if they'll pay more. They should. After all, we're doing more of the company's work.

George: I've heard that it's difficult to remember all of the codes and commands. If they don't give us all that stuff in writing, I know I'll have trouble remembering. I'll bet they find out it's a mistake and change back again.

Henry Davis faced the challenge of preparing his subordinates for the change and overcoming the resistance that existed in order to make the change most productive for the unit and the company.

Forms of Resistance

Henry Davis, or any other supervisor, should first identify who is resisting and determine why. In the case study, only those who are pleased with the change have directly told Henry their feelings of acceptance. The problem Henry faces is finding out how the others feel and working with anyone who has resistance to overcome it.

Resistance can take many forms, as the preceding comments suggest:

1. The person complies but does not accept. This might be the case with Susan and George, who were concerned with salary compensation and remembering codes. Henry's approach can be to test their commitment to the change. He can acknowledge that, over time, salaries will be adjusted to reflect performance and output. He can ask for George's ideas about how to master the codes. If he is encouraged to make some suggestions, such as taping a list to the terminal, George may become more committed to the change. The absence of suggestions is an indication of "compliant" resistance.

2. The person argues and resists. Henry could question Pam and quickly learn about her vacation plans. After letting her vent her frustration, he could work with her to outline the pros and cons of rearranging her vacation. Henry's goal will be to persuade Pam to accept the change. He wants her to identify the benefits to her of learning the new process at the time the training is offered and to see how the change itself will provide her with important benefits.

3. The person gives rational reasons for resistance. Henry must evaluate the reasons, looking at their merit, and then present a superior case with greater merit for the company's decision. One rational reason Dottie gave was the lack of productivity when learning a new procedure. Henry must accept the validity of this point and recognize the implied need for reassurance that a drop in productivity is expected and allowable.

4. The most difficult form of resistance to handle involves reasons that are hidden. The person may rationalize why he or she dislikes the change and cite irrelevant issues. Janet and Lisa did this; their concerns make one suspect that they have self-doubts. Listening to each of them, Henry should express understanding of their feelings even though he does not agree with them. He must make them aware that they are resisting and request that they examine the pros and cons of the change. He must attempt to move them from resisting for

resistance's sake to identifying objectively what they like and don't like. They need to explore what they can get from the change and what they perceive they can lose.

Ways To Overcome Resistance

Once you and employees understand what form resistance is taking and why, there are several methods you as a supervisor can use to prevent or overcome resistance.

1. Communicate. Share as much information as you have about a coming change and its potential benefits to employees, the unit, and the company. Answer questions, be available, and ask for reactions.

2. Conduct participative goal-setting on an individual or a group basis. Since changes will occur in expected behavior, you need to help employees clearly understand their role, what is expected of them, what the new behaviors are, what the goals are, and how all of this differs from the unit's previous routine. As supervisor, you should share your expectation of success, explaining that each goal is feasible and that training and support will be available. Identify for unit members how you will measure goal achievement and what kind of feedback will be provided. Set target dates for changes in the productivity rate and help individuals establish controls to measure how well they are doing.

3. Use your knowledge of group dynamics and proper leadership in meetings, the latter of which is discussed in Chapter 7. If most members of the unit accept the change, use their enthusiasm to convince any resisting individuals. For example, in a group meeting, you can ask several accepting individuals to report the benefits as they see them. You can also suggest to a person who is doing well that he or she spend time with someone who needs help.

4. Construct an Assets/Liabilities Account with a resisting individual or group. List all of the assets (the gains resulting from the change) and all of the liabilities (losses) so that you have a balance sheet of sorts. As you go through this exercise, explore how to minimize losses and maximize gains. There should be gains and losses for the company, the unit, and individual employees.

5. Use the informal structure that exists in the work group: consider passing information about unacceptable resistance through the group's informal leader or closest co-worker.

To conclude this section, let's return to the case study of the Zavier Agency and see how these methods might work.

Henry has talked with everyone and has discovered, to the extent that he can, how they feel and the forms of resistance that exist. To implement the preceding methods, he does the following:

1. He sets up a fifteen-minute unit meeting every Friday between now and the week of change. At each meeting, he shares all of the information

he has about what will happen, the goals of the change, and the benefits he sees for the group and each individual. He encourages questions and is available to anyone who wants to discuss with him any aspect of the change.

2. Once the switchover has been made and the initial training has been conducted, Henry plans to meet with each employee for a participative goal-setting session. They will examine in detail how the job has changed and what additional training and support the individual needs. They will set production goals, allowing time for the learning curve, and identify ways the employee can gauge whether he or she is meeting the goals.

3. Henry plans to schedule training for employees according to their needs, as well as to talk frequently with each employee to give feedback and recognition.

4. He will continue the Friday morning staff meetings after installation and training, encouraging the group to discuss problems and work together on solutions.

The effect of changes on the group and on individuals will naturally vary. In this particular case, Henry recognized that a new procedure was a major change and would have a profound influence on his unit's performance. He invested his time and theirs to make it work as smoothly as possible.

Other changes may require minimal time and perhaps involve only one or two individuals. In any event, a change is likely to cause resistance somewhere, and anticipating that resistance, planning how to overcome or prevent it, and carrying out that plan are what make the change either work or fail to work in your unit.

SUMMARY

As a supervisor, you are responsible for understanding employees and for guiding and influencing them toward behavior that will contribute to the achievement of your organization's goals. This chapter focused on increasing your understanding of yourself and others.

Perception is the process of selecting, organizing, and interpreting what we see, hear, taste, touch, and feel. It affects our responses to and understanding of other people. Six of the most important factors affecting perception—individual needs, experience, values and attitudes, self-concept, structural cues, and expectations—were discussed.

Your supervisory responsibilities require you to be highly sensitive to others, especially your employees. Having a distorted perception, making judgments, relying on insufficient information, being defensive, and lacking listening skills are all barriers to understanding others. We also reviewed eight different techniques that can be used to minimize or control the effects of these barriers.

Strong or persistent feelings are often called emotions. To understand others, you must understand their emotions. Your goal as supervisor should be to encourage the expression of emotions that affect work performance.

Defense mechanisms allow us to avert anxiety and to protect ourselves against the hurt inherent in negative criticism. Although being defensive reduces the pain we feel, it also serves as a barrier to understanding others. This chapter discussed the more common defense mechanisms encountered at work: withdrawal, repression, regression, aggression, compensation, projection, fantasy, rationalization, and reaction formation.

Change, an integral part of organization life, is likely to cause one of three responses: acceptance and positive support, compliance and minimal support, or resistance. A case study of the Zavier Agency illustrated some potential responses to change in a typical rating unit. Finally, we discussed useful supervisory techniques that can be used to overcome resistance to change.

Chapter 6

Coaching

As a supervisor, you are evaluated largely by what unit members achieve, not by the technical work you do. Your job is to influence, direct, and motivate employees to do a good job. Supervision can be relatively easy when employees know what you expect, know when to consult you, take responsibility, and cooperate with co-workers. These things do not just happen by themselves. Employees need to be coached. Coaching is what the supervisor does in daily interaction to encourage employee development.

All employees need coaching:

1. An unsatisfactory performer needs to be coached to bring performance up to standard.
2. A trainee needs to be coached to do his or her present job better.
3. An experienced employee who is a good performer, but who is not interested in or capable of advancement, needs to be coached to sustain performance and to grow and develop in the present job.
4. An upwardly mobile employee needs to be coached to prepare for new responsibilities.

Coaching means improving performance through day-to-day communications between supervisor and employee. Opportunities for day-to-day coaching include the following:

1. Giving directions and monitoring performance to keep employees on target
2. Helping employees handle work problems
3. Helping employees see how they fit into the larger picture of the organization
4. Helping employees monitor their performance and guiding them to improvement
5. Reinforcing and recognizing good performance
6. Assisting employees in identifying learning needs so that they can prepare themselves for future responsibilities

Many supervisors and managers believe that coaching is a once-a-year activity, achieved through conducting performance appraisals for all employees and career-planning sessions for employees who are being groomed for advancement. However, an annual activity will not develop employees. The success of formal appraisals and career-planning sessions hinges on the day-to-day coaching and development that must go on all year.

The formal appraisal procedure will be discussed in *Supervisory Skills*, the text for the second course in this program. In this chapter we will discuss the following:

1. Steps in the coaching process
2. Qualities required for coaching
3. Coaching to improve performance of unsatisfactory performers
4. Coaching to maintain improved performance
5. Coaching for development
6. Developing your coaching abilities

THE COACHING PROCESS

To be an effective coach, you must recognize each employee's growth potential, determine where he or she is now, and then assist and guide the employee toward desired development outcomes. Coaching on a day-to-day basis can be defined by these three phases:

1. Observing performance and behavior
2. Giving and eliciting feedback
3. Guiding development

Observing Performance and Behavior

Many of us think of ourselves as good judges of people. We believe that we can sense potential. This assumption can unfortunately stand in the way of making accurate observations and realistic evaluations. The process of perception, discussed in Chapter 5, also poses barriers to the objective observation of performance.

Common Problems in Observing Behavior

You should be aware of the special difficulties involved in observing the behavior of employees for whom you are responsible.

Self-Fulfilling Prophecy

Your perception of an employee's competence often becomes a *self-fulfilling prophecy*; that is, the prediction itself causes the result. If employees believe you expect them to perform satisfactorily, they work hard to live up to this expectation. If employees believe you do not see them as having potential to grow and develop, they may figure "What's the use?"

Is it enough for you to show positive, high expectations? Unfortunately, unrealistic expectations, either negative or positive, can get you and employees into trouble. Here are two extreme examples.

(Handwritten margin note: coaching on a day-to-day basis consists of 1) observing performance and behavior 2) Giving and eliciting feedback 3) Guiding development)

1. John Wright's supervisor saw him as highly competent and capable of growing into one of the best employees in the department. He gave John additional responsibilities and challenging work assignments. He waited and waited for actual performance to meet his expectations. After a couple of years, the supervisor finally had to admit that John had some serious deficiencies. The supervisor felt somehow betrayed. John noticed the obvious change in his supervisor's manner, and he felt frustrated and resentful. The unfortunate thing is that if the supervisor had identified John's deficiencies early, he might have been able to help John remedy them.

2. Jim Black's supervisor saw him as an unmotivated and irresponsible employee, so he closely supervised Jim. Jim grew increasingly cautious and afraid to make a decision on his own. After a year, Jim requested and received a transfer to another department, where he became an excellent performer.

Expecting employees to do a good job should increase their motivation. Having and voicing *realistic* expectations can also provide continuing motivation because such expectations will be reinforced by what occurs for both the supervisor and the employee. The problem with unrealistic expectations is that we tend to evaluate the whole person and generalize. Generalizations often open the door to the "halo" or "horns" effect.

Example of the Halo Effect

George's supervisor likes him. George always meets deadlines, has a pleasant personality, and appears to be confident about his work. The supervisor therefore infers that George's work is competent and on time. This positive generalization obscures any deficiencies. The supervisor simply does not see or rationalizes away George's problems. To this supervisor, George is top-notch and always has been.

Example of the Horns Effect

Gordon's supervisor does not particularly like him. Gordon often makes arithmetic errors. The supervisor therefore infers that he is incompetent and makes other mistakes. The supervisor always sees the "horns," or the errors, and this becomes his overall image of Gordon. This negative generalization discounts positive performance and achievements. The supervisor does not see or believe any indications that Gordon does some tasks very well.

Generalizations can also be discriminatory. For example, Mary's supervisor believes that older people always have a more difficult time adjusting to change than do younger people. She was concerned that Mary, who was fifty, would not be able to master new computer equipment as easily as would three younger employees. As it turned out, Mary learned to operate the equipment first and then trained all of the younger employees. What the supervisor did not know was that Mary's family was involved in computers. Mary not only had background knowledge but also was eager to share it.

Increasing Objectivity

To avoid making harmful or unproductive generalizations, observe specific performance and behavior, suspend judgment, and be prepared to reevaluate based on new information. You should expect to be continually surprised by new insights and observations.

Measure Performance

Performance can be evaluated by the quantity and quality of completed work in a given amount of time. How much work does an individual complete in a day, a week, or a month? How does he or she compare to other employees in your unit? How much does a trained employee produce or complete when working under normal conditions? What do you expect of a trainee? What do you expect of a senior, experienced person? Your judgment and good record-keeping are at the heart of an inescapable supervisory responsibility—knowing how much an employee should be able to do.

Similar questions can be raised to determine the quality of work. How often do you review each employee's work? What feedback do you receive in the form of complaints from other departments, agents, or policyholders? What is a reasonable number of errors for a trainee, an experienced employee, or a senior employee?

Maintaining objectivity requires self-discipline. You must not allow one incident to color your evaluation permanently. One missed target date or one irate customer does not necessarily mean the employee has a deficiency any more than one incident of superior performance indicates high overall competence. You are most likely to make too much of an employee's error when you are embarrassed or inconvenienced by it. Notice performance daily or weekly. Even if you do not keep detailed records, be aware and notice the little things that go on in the unit. In short, *measure* performance, don't "eyeball" it.

Distinguish Performance From Behavior and Attitude

We have a natural tendency to generalize based on observations of other people. The English language contains thousands of words that describe the characteristics and idiosyncrasies of people. To illustrate: How long would it take you to list five words that apply to each of the people in your unit? Most of the words you would use would be words that describe behavior patterns or, at a higher level of abstraction, personality traits.

To assess performance accurately, you must overcome this natural inclination to think in terms of behavior patterns, attitudes, and personality traits. You must instead focus on job results. You must concentrate on indications of the quantity, the quality, the timeliness, and the value of the work accomplished by the employee. Job results are *facts*, whereas behavior patterns and personal traits are *perceptions*. An employee may have a minor quarrel with the facts about his or her performance, but he or she is still far more likely to accept evidence about performance than your perceptions of him or her as a person.

Discuss Performance, Not Attitude or Personality

To gain a full understanding of an employee's performance, you must usually discuss job results and obstacles with the employee. This discussion should concentrate on the performance and not on attitudes or personality traits. You should discuss *facts* (about performance, measured as carefully as possible) rather than *your opinions* about why performance is unsatisfactory. If you criticize the employee as a person, the likely response is denial, aggression, or other defense mechanisms. Triggering an emotional reaction or a defense mechanism only hinders your efforts to gather information about performance and about the obstacles to better performance as the employee sees them.

Consider three simplified ways of telling an employee that he or she was a week late in completing a report that your manager requested: (1) "The report was a week late," (2) "You can't seem to meet deadlines," and (3) "You don't seem to care about getting work done on time." The first message reports a fact in a nonthreatening way. It gives the employee maximum leeway to explain what happened. The second message conveys a generalization about the employee's work, draws attention away from the immediate incident, and is likely to elicit a defensive response. The third message places the focus on the employee as a person; it constitutes an attack on the individual and will probably cause a strong emotional response. If you seek to understand why the report was late, the three messages are, respectively, desirable, dangerous, and disastrous.

Giving and Eliciting Feedback

Two types of feedback are essential for coaching: feedback from the supervisor to the employee and feedback from the employee to the supervisor. None of us can learn or grow in a vacuum. Employees need to know whether their supervisor believes they are doing well and how they can improve.

Employees often excuse lack of effort by saying to each other, "What difference does it make whether we do a good job? The supervisor never notices." Even employees who are initially motivated tend to become discouraged and do not expend extra effort if they feel no one really cares. In surveys, 70 to 80 percent of the employees questioned stated that they could be more productive than they are. Is this caused by the need for a little feedback on a regular basis?

Job Expectation Technique

Frequent two-way feedback gives both the supervisor and the employee an opportunity to clarify expectations. You might try the following job expectation technique:

1. List all of the employee's responsibilities in one column on a piece of paper. Make two copies.
2. List what performance you expect from the employee in the second column on your copy.

Job Expectation
2 column chart
shareasing responsibilities

3. Give the employee a copy of the list of responsibilities and ask him or her to fill in the performance expectations in the second column.
4. Compare the two copies, discuss them, and come to an agreement on performance expectations.
5. Ask the employee what he or she would like you to do to help him or her meet these expectations.

Incident-Feedback Technique

The following is a good technique for investigating potential problems or checking your perception of performance:

1. Identify a specific performance or behavioral incident involving the employee.
2. Describe the incident to the employee and ask the employee to give his or her views of the incident. Use open-ended questions. Ask for clarification and explanation as the employee answers your questions.
3. After hearing the employee's views, state your own perception and assumptions.
4. Listen to the employee's reaction to your perception.
5. Come to an agreement on what should be done.

For example, when Steve Squires was promoted to a supervisory position, he assumed that his good friend and co-worker, Wayne Craig, was capable of working on his own without much direction. Steve felt that Wayne was as knowledgeable as he was and therefore needed little supervision. Steve assigned Wayne a difficult project, giving him the objectives and target date. Two months later when Steve checked, he found that Wayne had done almost nothing on the report.

Steve: Wayne, I'm puzzled. For two months' work, I have only five pages of copy. I thought you would be more than halfway through with the report. What happened? (open-ended question)

Wayne: Well, I don't like to rewrite and redo work.

Steve: Why do you think you would have to redo the report? (asking for clarification)

Wayne: Because I don't know what you want.

Steve: What kind of additional information would you like? (open-ended question)

Wayne: I'd like resource material and statistics. I'd like to know exactly what you want in the report.

Steve: I thought you knew where to go to get the information. (perception checking)

Wayne: You never told me.

Steve: How did you get information for reports before I became your supervisor? (open-ended question)

Wayne: Mike always gave me the information. (Mike was the supervisor before Steve.)

Steve: In other words, Mike always gave you the details of what he wanted? (perception checking)

Wayne: Yes. Once I knew exactly what he wanted, I would give it to him.

Now that Steve has identified what Wayne expects of him, he will have to revise his assumption that Wayne can do all of his work without close supervision.

So far, we have been looking at two phases of coaching: (1) observing performance and behavior and (2) giving and eliciting feedback. With the third phase, guiding development, the attention shifts to future growth.

Guiding Development

Three key steps in guiding development are (1) setting an objective and devising a plan to meet the objective, (2) implementing the plan, and (3) monitoring results.

Setting an Objective

In many formal appraisal systems, supervisors and employees formulate one or more developmental objectives and set plans to meet them. Other developmental needs may surface at any time. Effective supervision requires that these developmental needs or *performance improvement* needs should be addressed immediately and not postponed until the scheduled appraisal. For example, what should Steve do about Wayne in the preceding example? Steve's options include the following:

1. Closely supervise Wayne as the former supervisor did
2. Formulate an objective to develop Wayne's ability to research reports and become more self-sufficient
3. Do nothing on the grounds that Wayne has now gotten the message

Say that Steve decides to set a developmental objective. Steve must first discuss this objective with Wayne and gain his agreement. There might be some negotiation, perhaps about the timetable for change and measurement of progress. The purpose of a developmental objective is to define the desired change in behavior or performance. The objective should be specific, measurable, and time-bounded—the characteristics of any good objective. For example, Steve and Wayne agreed on four objectives.

Wayne will be responsible for the following:

-   Identifying what information is needed for the assigned report
-   Making personal contacts to obtain the information

- Deciding on the statistics and graphs to be included
- Submitting a completed report by the fifteenth of next month

Implementing the Plan

Setting a developmental objective is not enough. Wayne needs guidance and help from his supervisor. Before he can provide this guidance and help, Steve first has to make some determinations:

1. What is Wayne expected to do on his own?
2. What assistance and guidance will he as Wayne's supervisor provide?

In this situation, Steve might decide to hold a project planning meeting with Wayne. The purpose of the meeting would be to agree on whom Wayne must contact for the information in preparing the next report. Steve does not tell Wayne what to do but rather asks him to describe his plans for performing these tasks.

Monitoring Results

Steve must review progress regularly, take corrective action when needed, and recognize and acknowledge signs of success. This kind of follow-up is essential if the plan is to result in achieving the objectives. If progress is not monitored, Wayne is likely to believe that his supervisor is not serious or that the developmental objective "isn't all that important." Many developmental plans fail because the supervisor neglects to or becomes too busy to follow up on them. The supervisor can communicate that the project is important and that he or she is available to help if a snag occurs simply by asking something like, "How's the report coming along?"

COACHING TECHNIQUES

To become an effective coach, you must do the following:

1. Be helpful and supportive.
2. Challenge employees to grow and develop.
3. Build a climate of mutual trust.

Be Helpful and Supportive

The way employees perceive you may depend largely on the extent to which you are helpful and supportive. This perception is generally based on a number of supervisory practices, especially the following.

Be Willing To Listen

You must be willing to listen and encourage employees to express their opinions and ideas, even if they contradict what you expect or would like to hear. The preceding chapter described the importance and skills of communication.

Refrain From Giving Advice

Giving advice is not coaching or development. If you tell an employee what to do, you have no assurance that the employee will be able to perform the task without specific directions in the future. Your job as a coach is to help the employee think through a situation and develop a plan of action.

When an employee asks you for advice, suggest two or more options from which the employee might choose. This approach forces the employee to take responsibility for making the final decision.

Do Not Act as the Expert

Since you are often more knowledgeable than the employee, you can easily fall into the role of the expert. This can be very irritating to some people, and it also denies employees the opportunity to learn how to tackle difficult situations on their own. A better approach is for you to share the individual's experiences and feelings, as the following example illustrates:

Supervisor: Yes, I know how difficult some of them can be to get along with. I still remember Joe McCall, who was the most abrasive agent I have ever had to deal with. He gave me plenty of trouble.

Employee: How did you handle him without losing your temper?

Although the supervisor's experience with Joe may not be exactly like the employee's present problem, the account of how the supervisor attempted to cope helps the employee gain insight into his own situation. The employee learns that such trying situations are not unusual and that other people have learned to deal with them effectively. This technique of sharing experiences is particularly important for young employees who have limited work experience and do not know what to expect. Sharing experiences also defines the kind of behavior the supervisor expects from an employee and allows the employee to view the supervisor as a person.

The employee will not only be able to learn more easily from the sharing of an actual experience but also will assign greater credibility to what the supervisor is saying.

Do Not Allow the Employee To Become Boss-Dependent

Support and help should not lead to dependency. An effective coach gradually shifts responsibility to the employee by giving the employee greater freedom to act without first consulting the supervisor.

Challenge Employees To Grow and Develop

An effective coach challenges employees by doing the following:

1. *Setting high expectations and standards.* Most people will push themselves to meet the expectations and standards set by their parents, teachers, and supervisors. You do a disservice to employees by setting unit or individual performance standards that are easily achieved. At the opposite extreme,

a standard that is unreachable is also harmful. Performance expectations, quality, and other standards should be moving targets. They should help employees to surpass their previous accomplishments.

2. *Taking immediate corrective action when needed.* Give feedback on a performance or behavioral problem immediately after discovering the problem. Focus the feedback on the specific details of the problem. Feedback that is delayed or couched in generalities is rarely as effective as immediate, fact-based feedback.

3. *Encouraging innovation and risk taking.* Praise employees for their new ideas and for their attempts to improve work methods.

Build Mutual Trust

To build mutual trust between you and each employee, it is important for you to first become the role model. What are the characteristics of people we trust? Supervisors, managers, and technical employees who have been questioned in workshops report giving trust to the person who can do the following:

1. Develop credibility
2. Keep confidences
3. Keep commitments

Develop Credibility

When participants in the workshops were asked to further define *credibility*, they focused on two important factors.

Handle Information Carefully

The person who is seen as credible is one who develops opinions and ideas based on observable facts. He or she checks the accuracy of information before sharing it and presents ideas honestly and straightforwardly.

The person who has credibility is willing to consider the opinions of others with an open mind. He or she is accessible to employees when they need to talk about problems or make recommendations.

The credible supervisor explains to employees, when possible, why he or she made a decision. This way, employees know when their ideas and recommendations have been considered and why other recommendations were rejected.

Exhibit Responsibility

Accept responsibility for all decisions. Do not announce decisions as coming from higher management with the implication that you want to be dissociated from them. Use "we" instead of "they" when communicating instructions and changes. Explain the reasons for a decision as honestly and accurately as you can. If the reasons are confidential, say so.

Keep Confidences

Keeping confidences is a prerequisite to maintaining an effective relationship, especially supervisor/employee relationships. You expect employees to identify problems and pinpoint their own performance shortcomings, development needs, and career goals. To be an effective coach, you cannot betray this trust without damaging the relationship and the coaching process. To build and maintain confidence, you must adhere to the following practices:

1. When you must correct someone or identify problems, do it privately so that co-workers cannot hear.

2. Do not discuss one employee's problems with another employee, no matter how much you trust the other person.

3. If one employee reveals a performance or work behavior problem of another employee, listen and then tell the complaining employee you will handle the situation. Do not reveal the source of the information when taking action. If an employee reports another personal (not performance or job behavior) problem, you should indicate that his concern over another employee's personal affairs may be well-intentioned but is improper nonetheless.

4. Keep personnel files confidential.

5. If an employee reveals a personal problem to you, treat the disclosure as confidential, even if you suspect that others know about it.

Whom can a supervisor confide in without betraying employees' confidences? If you must discuss a problem employee, go to your human resources staff or to your manager. Some insurance organizations have a Personal Assistance Counselor or obtain counseling services from an outside organization. If you have access to counseling services, you can usually discuss an employee's problem with the appropriate professional without violating confidentiality.

As a member of management, you will have access to information that should not be revealed. What do you do if a subordinate asks you a direct question and you know the answer but cannot reveal the information? You might respond, "Your question will be answered later," "A memo will go out to all staff members," "I can't answer your questions at this time," or "The matter is confidential at this time."

Explaining your views on confidentiality can preclude problems, since matters of confidentiality are delicate and involve value judgments.

Keep Commitments

One manager in a workshop defined this quality in a brief but powerful way, saying that the person who keeps commitments is one who identifies, promises, delivers, and follows up. The manager said this was also his definition of integrity. The process of identifying, promising, delivering, and following up is an integrated series of actions.

Why do supervisors sometimes fail to keep their commitments? Some problems just fade away as attention goes to newer problems. A commitment to help an employee may fade with the circumstances that brought it into being. Perhaps an employee may show progress toward a development objective. The supervisor, seeing improvement, loses sight of the agreed-on goal or assumes the employee can achieve it without further assistance. Development objectives rarely clamor for attention the way operational objectives do.

Keeping commitments provides reinforcement and recognizes improvement. An employee who is recognized for improving is more likely to continue to improve than is one whose improvements go unnoticed.

So far we have discussed the process of coaching and the qualities of an effective coach. Coaching is the process of (1) observing performance and behavior, (2) giving and eliciting feedback, and (3) guiding development. It works best when the supervisor (1) is helpful and supportive, (2) challenges employees to grow and develop, and (3) builds a climate of mutual trust.

We will now show this process and these qualities in practice by discussing how to do the following:

1. Coach unsatisfactory performers
2. Coach competent performers
3. Coach for development

COACHING UNSATISFACTORY PERFORMERS

As a supervisor, you can expect to deal with unsatisfactory performers occasionally. The majority of these employees can reach a satisfactory level through effective coaching. If coaching does not take place immediately, the unsatisfactory performer may degenerate into a problem employee. Problem employees not only lower productivity but also make life miserable for you and for co-workers.

Identifying Performance Problems

As a supervisor, you must continually observe and judge performance. You must know what constitutes a good day's work (a moving target sometimes). You also need to fight against the natural tendency to cling to outdated assessments resulting from the "halo" or "horns" effect.

Warning Signs

There are some early warning signs that indicate that a performance problem may be developing. Warning signs that should be noticed and discussed with employees include the following:

1. Decline in quantity of work. A sudden drop in output always warrants investigation.
2. Decline in quality of work. A problem is signaled if an employee's work contains more errors than that of other employees.

3. Missed target dates.

4. Interpersonal conflicts. If an employee has difficulty relating to customers, co-workers, or employees from other departments, this can create problems for your unit. Generally, supervisors become aware of conflicts through complaints from other people who have been affected by the employee's abrasive remarks or unwillingness to cooperate. You should proceed slowly, gathering objective facts, such as observed actions, and avoiding such intangibles as attitude.

5. Absences. If absences increase above an acceptable level or if absences take on a pattern that causes suspicion, inquiry is necessary.

Possible Causes of Poor Performance

You will need to tell the employee about your observations and gain feedback before you can determine a cause. Causes of poor performance may include any one of or a combination of the following factors:

1. The employee does not know how to do the job or part of the job and needs additional training.

2. The employee does not know what you expect.

3. The employee has poor work habits—he or she has absenteeism and tardiness problems, sets incorrect priorities, is inaccurate and inattentive to details, and/or procrastinates and wastes time.

4. The employee has personal or family problems that are interfering with job performance.

5. The employee is in the wrong job.

6. The employee has become complacent because of a lack of challenge or direction or sees no negative consequences to performing poorly.

Coaching for Performance Problems

Once you have identified a potential performance problem, you will need to conduct a coaching session to determine whether a problem exists and, if so, to ascertain the cause of the problem. A plan for correcting it must then be formulated. Following is a format for this kind of coaching session:

1. Describe your observations and level with the employee.

2. Elicit feedback from the employee.

3. Develop and gain agreement on a performance improvement plan.

4. Provide follow-up.

Describe Your Observations: Leveling

The techniques used to gather evidence about performance, described earlier in this chapter, are the basis of the approach recommended for confronting employees about poor performance. Describe the specific performance or behavior you have observed: "There were four missed target dates in the last month." Or define a specific behavior: "I overheard you yelling at Jane a few minutes ago."

Frame your comments in "I" messages instead of "you" messages: "I want to talk with you about missed deadlines. In the last month you missed four target dates. I become very concerned when important deadlines are missed." Stating your feelings honestly in this way is known as *leveling*.

Identify any negative effects that the employee's behavior or performance has had on the unit: "When you are absent, other employees have to do your work."

By carefully selecting your words and defining only observable performance and behavior, you give the employee little reason to be defensive. He or she is then more likely to hear what you are saying.

Leveling is difficult for many supervisors. Many people do not like confrontation. Experienced supervisors, even those who would prefer to avoid conflict, say that it is better to level when problems are developing than to wait. Minor, uncorrected problems have a way of growing into serious problems. Most performance problems do not correct themselves, but the majority are correctable if the supervisor is willing to confront the issue. Guidelines for leveling are given in Exhibit 6-1.

Exhibit 6-1

Guidelines for Leveling

The guidelines for leveling are:

1. Describe the specific behavior or performance that concerns you.
2. Explain its negative effects on performance or behavior.
3. Send "I" messages whenever possible instead of "you" messages.
4. Admit your feelings.
5. Do not discuss what you think the employee's attitude may be.
6. Do not generalize or suggest causes of the poor performance or unacceptable behavior.
7. Do not make judgmental statements.
8. Speak in a calm, unemotional voice.

Obtain Feedback

After you have leveled, the employee will probably give a response that sheds light on the problem. If he or she says nothing, ask open-ended questions. Use nondirective communication techniques to encourage the employee to talk and to analyze the situation. For example, Steve Squires has just been transferred to the commercial underwriting unit as supervisor. One of Steve's senior employees, Ralph Blandina, is just not getting the work done. The work Ralph does is of high quality, but he is always behind. Although he appears to work hard, other departments and agents complain that he is not giving them the material they need on time. In a coaching session, Steve levels with Ralph.

Steve: In the last month I have had seven complaints from agents that you haven't given them quotes on time, and as a result, they lost the business. I am concerned because the agents said that our price was the lowest and we could have had the business. (leveling)

Ralph: I'm sorry, but there are just so many hours in the day. I had so many things to do, I couldn't get to the quotes.

Steve: What other things? (asking for clarification)

Ralph: Regular work. Underwriting files. Rating the policies. Getting information to loss control. Attending meetings with Sales.

Steve: You believe you have too much work to do? (perception checking)

Ralph: Yes, I do. I'm expected to rate my own business because the rating department can't rate special policies. I put in my own loss control reports. Anything to do with our new Total Commercial Package is dumped on my desk.

Steve: Why can't rating give you support? (open-ended question)

Ralph: Because no one has trained them to rate the Total Package.

Steve: No one has been trained? (reflecting)

Ralph: Last month I took time to try to train one of the raters.

Steve: Try to train? (reflecting)

Ralph: Yes. But Marty just doesn't know all the commercial coverages.

Steve: You don't feel Marty can do the job? (perception checking)

Ralph: Not unless he has more training, and I just don't have the time.

Steve: Ralph, we really do need to solve this problem so that you will have time to get your work done. What would you recommend?

Ralph: There is one experienced rater, Annie. She could learn with minimal training. Get the rating supervisor to assign her to the Total Commercial Package.

As this example illustrates, the purposes of eliciting feedback are as follows:

- To check your perceptions and assumptions
- To obtain additional information from the employee
- To elicit at least one recommendation from the employee as to how the problem might be solved

Set Performance Improvement Objectives

After getting feedback, the supervisor should evaluate the situation by combining what he thinks and what the employee has said. For example, Steve Squires believes that Ralph's problems may have two parts:

Steve: Let's try to identify all the problems. First, you need someone to do the rating for you.

Ralph: Someone I can train in a short amount of time.

Steve: Second, you need to gain control over your time so that you can get high-priority items done on time.

Ralph: I know, but I need help.

Steve: Here's what I propose. I'll talk to the rating supervisor. I think he'll release Annie to do your rating. Now, here's what I want you to do. Set up a schedule for training Annie and for doing the rest of your work. Also, keep a log of the time you actually spend doing each task. In two weeks, we will review the schedule and time log and see where we are.

Steve shifted to a more directive communication approach and defined what he was willing to do and what he expected Ralph to do.

Follow Up

For the coaching to be effective, Steve must follow up in two weeks as he promised. If continuing problems are identified, he will need to go through the coaching session again and perhaps set new performance-improvement objectives.

Behavioral Guidelines for Dealing With an Unsatisfactory Performer

Many experienced supervisors say that the most difficult task they had to learn was how to deal with an unsatisfactory performer: the coaching sessions, the guiding, and, occasionally, the involuntary termination. They agree on one point—the earlier the supervisor levels and starts to deal with the problem, the easier the process is for everyone.

Three qualities are necessary for coaching an unsatisfactory performer:

1. Assertiveness
2. Tolerance
3. Detachment

Be Assertive

In most instances, you must initiate the action. The unsatisfactory performer is not going to come to you and say, "I have a problem." He or she is not likely to be sensitive to feedback on performance and may even deny having a problem. Many problem performers have difficulty admitting they might be wrong, even to themselves. Others may recognize a problem, but they do not know how to correct it.

As the supervisor, you must learn to be assertive, which often entails risking conflict and disagreements. Because the first step, leveling, is difficult, many supervisors script what they are going to say before the coaching session.

You might find it helpful to prepare a one-minute opening statement that defines exactly what you want to discuss and why. Then prepare a plan. Think what you are about to say and carefully hear the words you have chosen. Imagine what the person's response might be, and formulate an answer. This mental preparation helps you to visualize a realistic situation and allows you to picture yourself succeeding.

Be Tolerant

Tolerance means accepting the person the way he or she is. It does not mean that you accept below-par performance or unacceptable behavior. You must separate the person from the performance problem.

Tolerance means being fair even when you are angry and frustrated. The employee depends on you to give an opportunity to solve his or her problem. When you use nondirective techniques to encourage the employee to express ideas and feelings, when you listen and check to make certain you understand the message, you are demonstrating respect and tolerance.

Be Detached

Avoid taking the employee's remarks personally or over-identifying with the employee. Either of these responses can create problems for you and be detrimental to the employee's chances for improvement. You should show empathy (an understanding of the employee's feelings) without taking responsibility for those feelings. You must not get your own emotions caught up in the employee's problem.

Do Not Take Remarks Personally

Problem employees may have had their problems in one form or another before you met them. They may have developed certain defense mechanisms and games that they use whenever they feel threatened. When they react to you, they may be following the lines in an old script.

Avoid Game-Playing

When Steve Squires was coaching another employee, Colette, he offered what he thought was an excellent suggestion. Colette answered with, "Yes, but I can't do that." Steve continued to make suggestions and Colette continued to answer, "Yes, but..." until Steve felt frustrated and defeated.

When you think you are getting hooked into playing a win/lose game, break the pattern of discussion and try a different approach. For example, Steve could say, "Colette, I have stated I believe you have a performance problem. What do you think you should do about it?"

Steve has sensed Colette's game by noticing its repetitive quality. Even if Colette has no immediate suggestions, Steve can say, "I recommend you think about the problem and find a solution" or "Here is what I suggest you consider doing about it."

Coaching for Behavior Problems

At times an employee's behavior, rather than his or her performance, constitutes a problem that requires you to take supervisory action. Our concern here is with problems that meet two requirements: (1) the employee's performance is acceptable overall but (2) the employee's behavior causes *identifiable problems* within the organization.

Difficult Behaviors

Consider some of the words commonly used to describe unusual behavior: we say that a person is different, difficult, odd, strange, or weird. Consider some examples of behavior that may constitute a problem in the office. An employee may dress in poor taste or wear unconventional clothing. An employee may surround his or her work area with pictures and objects that seem, to most people, to be out of place in an office. An employee may speak repeatedly about subjects in which no one else has any interest. An employee's sense of humor or manner of speaking may seem strange and perhaps annoy others. An employee may be extremely aggressive or overly silent or may voice the same complaints again and again. Such behaviors may be difficult to accept and may at times be irritating, but they are not supervisory problems in their own right. They become supervisory problems when they affect the work results of the unit. There is a temptation to call some interpersonal conflicts "personality clashes" and to regard them as impossible to influence. Exhibit 6-2 presents an argument that you should use coaching techniques when employees seem unable to get along with each other.

Exhibit 6-2

Personality Clashes

Do you think that some employees squabble because of a personality clash? Is there really such a thing as a personality clash? Can two persons simply dislike each other regardless of the activity or circumstance that brings them together?

Real personality clashes are probably quite rare. True, we have all seen situations in which two persons simply cannot get along, and the efforts of peacemakers are fruitless. However, we have also seen apparent enemies suddenly become friends. This may happen because they join to fight a common enemy, respond to a crisis together, or realize that cooperation will achieve their individual aims. Less dramatically, antagonism usually melts when two persons simply spend time together and get to know each other's goals, values, and hopes.

You should be slow to call a conflict a personality conflict. Doing so offers you an easy way out. Although outright personality conflicts may occasionally occur, chances are that most of the interpersonal conflicts you observe will be of a milder sort and can be influenced through coaching.

"Unusual" behavior is acceptable unless it clearly affects performance. Unacceptable consequences, rather than unusual behavior, provide the justification and basis for your supervisory intervention. Your responsibility as supervisor is to establish a clear connection between an employee's behavior and its harmful consequences within the unit or elsewhere in the organization.

Harmful Consequences

What are the kinds of consequences that justify your asking an employee to change his or her behavior? These are some possibilities:

- Other employees do not trust the employee's work and check it needlessly.
- Other employees do not provide information or resources to the employee.
- Customers avoid contact with the employee or take their business elsewhere.
- Teamwork suffers in identifiable ways.
- Creativity and problem solving are reduced when the employee is involved.
- The performance of other employees suffers because of difficulties in collaborating with the employee.
- Employee time and energy are diverted from work and instead are spent trying to change the employee's behavior.

These harmful consequences have the common element of employee behavior that disrupts or at least fails to contribute positively to the attainment of organizational goals. They illustrate the delicacy of the problem that exists when an employee's individual performance is satisfactory, but his or her behavior has harmful effects that show up elsewhere in the unit. These negative effects are often subtle and difficult to document.

Discuss Consequences, Not Personality

A previous recommendation from this chapter also applies here: if you want to change behavior, focus on results rather than on personality. The likelihood of success in seeking a change in behavior is much higher if you confront the employee with evidence of the consequences of that behavior rather than address the employee's personality or attitudes or the behavior itself. Since the employee's individual performance is adequate, you will not have an easy time convincing him or her that changes are necessary. Your success may depend on the amount and strength of the evidence you present.

What Happens When Performance or Behavior Does Not Improve?

Coaching may have a short-lived effect. You may conduct a coaching session after which the employee's performance or behavior improves, but it then declines. You may conduct another coaching session after which performance improves, then declines. One supervisor described this cycle by saying, "I feel as if I'm on a roller coaster."

Transfer is a valid solution if the employee is in the wrong job. Proceed cautiously, since trying to transfer your problems to other supervisors is likely to damage your relationships with them. If you think a transfer is the best remedy, you should confer with your manager, the human resources manager, and the other supervisor. Through this joint effort, selection of the employee's new job and the new supervisor's developmental plans should form a clear program to help the employee toward a new behavior.

However, a transfer is not always possible. If you have coached an employee and given a reasonable amount of time for improvement to take place, and it does not occur, then the best solution may be termination. Keeping a below-par performer on staff not only lowers productivity but can also create morale problems. Co-workers know the employee is not performing, and they can come to resent the employee's presence in the unit. In addition, you may be spending so much time with the problem employee that you are paying inadequate attention to other employees.

Unfortunately, some problem performers are allowed to drift through their careers until they are approaching retirement, at which time management decides to "live with the problem a little longer." If the employee had been fired when the problem surfaced, maybe today he or she would have a job he or she likes and can perform well.

Before firing an employee, check your firm's human resources policies and procedures. Discuss your decision with a personnel representative in your organization and confer with your manager. Chapters 8 and 9 discuss legal aspects of personnel decisions.

Referring Employees for Professional Help

When you coach, you encourage employees to open up and talk. Consequently, they may sometimes reveal serious personal problems: marital difficulties, financial problems, alcoholism, or many other problems of modern living.

As the supervisor, you are rarely qualified to counsel employees on these issues, but you can encourage them to seek professional help. If your organization has an employee personal assistance program, refer the troubled employee to a personal assistance counselor.

This point bears repeating: UNLESS YOU ARE PROFESSIONALLY TRAINED AS A COUNSELOR, DO NOT DEAL WITH THE SERIOUS PERSONAL PROBLEMS OF EMPLOYEES. No matter how good your intentions, your amateur efforts may reinforce, prolong, or even intensify a problem.

If your organization does not have a counseling program, help the employee find professional help elsewhere. A physician may be able to give suggestions. Your local telephone directory may have a guide to human services. Make a few calls and do other research to find out what kind of help is available. Once you have identified sources of professional help, write the names and telephone numbers on a piece of paper and give it to the employee. This action is often necessary because the troubled person might have difficulty taking this first, critical step.

Organizations with employee personal assistance programs usually advise supervisors to avoid getting personally involved and to urge employees to seek professional help. Sometimes troubled employees delude themselves into thinking, "If my supervisor understands, I'll buy time until things work out." You can get caught in the same trap if you lead yourself to believe that you will be the rescuer by giving time and relieving pressure from the employee.

In situations in which the employee has shown enough trust to reveal personal problems, you are bound to confidentiality, except for dealing with a personal assistance counselor. On occasion, you may have to talk to your manager under the condition of confidentiality. Your focus should be on the employee's performance and its improvement, not on the personal problem.

COACHING COMPETENT PERFORMERS

Coaching is more than a technique to raise the performance level of sub-par employees. Satisfactory and good performers need coaching and guidance if they are to maintain performance, grow and develop in their present jobs, and avoid complacency.

Complacency may occur because of the supervisor's benign neglect rather than because of some lack of motivation or problem of the employee. Here is an example: Rose Cahill was always evaluated as a good performer. Her supervisor, P. J. Halverson, felt she could always count on Rose to get the work done. Rose was experienced, and when any problems developed, she always took the initiative to investigate and solve the problem without requiring assistance from P. J., who was aware of this and grateful for it. Rose was very easy to supervise and P. J. assumed that Rose did not need or want much direction from her.

How does Rose feel about the situation? "I like P. J. She never gives me any hassle like some supervisors I have heard about. I get an annual performance appraisal and a raise every year. I like my job. I'm comfortable in it. It's routine and not very challenging. I must be doing what P. J. wants, but I'm not always certain. I could be more productive. I do see things that could be changed. Sometimes, I'd like more challenge and the opportunity to try new things. But P. J. is always so busy."

If Rose remains in the job much longer without any guidance or challenge, she will become a complacent performer, doing only what is required of her.

Recall the discussion of motivation in Chapter 3. If an employee's needs are unmet, he or she may look beyond the workplace for greater challenge. For example, Frank has been doing the same work year after year. Although he is considered an adequate performer, he shows little interest in or enthusiasm for his job. Frank's supervisor concludes, "He's good in his present job but shows little potential." The supervisor is amazed to learn that Frank is the president of a local organization, serves on the board of his school district, and is considered one of the best fund raisers in the community. "Why doesn't he show that kind of initiative and dedication at work?" his supervisor wonders.

Did any of Frank's supervisors take time to develop and challenge him? Were they too busy, or did they think Frank did not need guidance? Frank's current supervisor may have to overcome the effects of his predecessors.

Some employees slip into serious performance problems rather than complacency. Even though all development is, at root, self-development, many employees still need encouragement, reward, and direction to point them toward development opportunities.

Employee Needs Addressed

Experienced, competent performers need the following day-to-day coaching:

1. Periodic clarification of expectations
2. Informal feedback on performance
3. Occasional help with solving problems
4. Opportunity to make recommendations
5. Opportunities for teamwork
6. Challenge and opportunity for growth

Let's consider an example of coaching in action.

A commercial lines underwriting supervisor, Ann, has set up a two-week schedule for coaching each of her employees. She has four underwriters, and each week she meets with two of them—one on Tuesday and one on Thursday. Sessions last from a half hour to a maximum of two hours depending on what the employees want to discuss. Typical subjects of discussion include the following:

1. Review of one underwriting file. Each employee selects a file that required judgment, was an exception to the rule, or was in some other way unique. This allows Ann to see how each underwriter thinks and decides. It offers her an opportunity to provide guidance by making suggestions or assuring the underwriter that the decision was good.
2. Report on trends. This forces the underwriters to think and analyze, and it provides Ann with valuable information.
3. Report the problems and opportunities of agents they call on or talk with on the phone. This gives Ann an opportunity to see how the underwriters relate to the agents and to learn what is happening in the field.

Benefits

The benefits of scheduling coaching sessions with competent employees include the following:

1. Coaching and development receive priority attention.

2. Employees tend to gather questions rather than interrupt the supervisor repeatedly, thus saving time in the long run.

3. The supervisor is kept informed and can spot trends and potential problems developing.

4. Communication breakdowns are less likely to occur.

5. Supervisor and employees tend to pay more attention to priorities among tasks.

6. If all employees receive coaching, there is less embarrassment for those being coached for performance problems.

Coaching sessions with competent employees differ from other discussion sessions in that the employees have the primary responsibility for bringing up subjects and identifying areas for discussion. Competent, experienced employees generally know where they need help and guidance.

In summary, be careful not to ignore the satisfactory and good performers. They need coaching and guidance, too! After all, many of these employees are likely to work with you the longest. Most can be even more productive and cooperative with continuing encouragement from you.

COACHING FOR DEVELOPMENT

Coaching for development involves helping employees to identify short-term and long-term career goals and to plan ways to reach those goals. Some organizations call this kind of coaching career planning, while others call it development planning. Career or development planning is sometime integrated with the formal performance appraisal, and sometimes it is done in a separate coaching session. Organizations may treat career or development planning formally or informally. Whatever it is called and whenever it is done, the steps and the concepts are similar.

Who Needs Coaching for Development?

All employees, even those who do not appear to want promotions, need your help via development coaching. The only exception should be those who have serious performance problems. They require coaching for performance improvement. Employees have to understand that performance problems must be corrected before you will talk about their career plans.

Employees who do not appear to be ambitious or who have stated that they do not desire to progress beyond their present positions still need career planning and development. Every employee has a career even if he or she remains in the same position for the duration of that career. Helping an employee to think in terms of a career, rather than "just a job," is an important goal of coaching. The effort invested in a career is different from the effort an employee is willing to invest in a job.

Agencies and insurance companies are changing so rapidly that the positions many employees will hold five or ten years from now may not exist today. As a supervisor, you must help employees plan, develop, and grow so that they can adapt to the business environment of tomorrow.

Understanding Today's Employees

Understanding today's employees involves understanding contemporary attitudes toward work and recent career patterns.

Evolving Attitudes Toward Work

"What happened to the 'old' work ethic?" Some people say that the desire to do a good job is gone forever. Others say it has merely changed. People today expect more from work, just as they expect more from their lives overall. When people see the possibilities of achieving more, their career aspirations rise. The following can be said about employees who share contemporary work values:

1. They have less tolerance for authoritarianism and arbitrary organizational restraints.
2. They question management decisions and want the right to influence decisions that affect them.
3. They seek self-fulfillment in their work.
4. They expect open communication, opportunities to voice opinions and grievances, and the right to criticize the company and its management without repercussions.
5. They have a tendency to hold back and bargain harder in exchange for good performance.
6. They seek a lifestyle of leisure and self-expression outside of work.

Career Changes

The time when an employee stayed with an organization for twenty or thirty years is fading. Young employees tend to look at career goals, not just in terms of their present employer, but in terms of the broader job market. Dramatic career changes are not uncommon, even for people in their fifties. Retirement often means a second career, at least part-time, instead of full retirement.

Career goals should be seen as only one part of a person's total set of goals. For many employees, the work ethic has been replaced by a self-fulfillment ethic, which motivates them to seek leisure, lifestyle, family, and career goals without sacrificing one goal to achieve another. They see the possibility of attaining self-fulfillment in all areas of their lives and are ready to consider all the options. The possibility of "having it all" is intriguing, but if conflicts exist, many are willing to sacrifice career goals.

Identifying Career Goals

The first step in career planning and development is to help the employee identify his or her career goals. Career goals are affected by a number of factors, including the following:

1. Lifestyle and family goals
2. Stage in the person's career development
3. Continuing education opportunities
4. Work-climate preference

Lifestyle and Family Goals

Career planning should reflect the employee's family goals and desired lifestyle. Supervisors can make inaccurate assumptions about these personal aspirations. For example: At first, Dan Howard believed that Kim was not interested in a career. His experience had been that many young people worked for the agency only a few years and then left for other jobs or relocated. But one day, Kim mentioned to him, "I like working for your agency. I can walk to work and we don't need a second car. We really don't want to move from this town. All our friends and family are here."

Dan filed this information away, and during a coaching session he assigned Kim the project of reorganizing policyholder files. If Dan had continued to assume Kim would leave the agency and had neglected career planning for her, he could not have given her this opportunity for growth.

Stages in Career Development

Employees go through stages in their careers, and career goals can change at each stage. Few people set long-range career goals when young and carry these goals throughout their lives. It follows that career planning should be aided by regular, periodic discussions in which career goals are reassessed and discussed.

Trainee Stage

The trainee may be a young person just out of high school or college or someone who is changing industries. Both young employees and people changing direction are generally uncertain about their career goals for quite a few years. For this reason, they tend to rely more than other employees on their immediate supervisor for guidance. Both are usually concerned about "Where can I go?" and are uncertain of their strengths and development needs. Although concrete choices may not be possible at this point in their career, employees at the trainee stage are very interested in talking about career goals and in thinking about various possibilities.

The young employee usually enters the work world with high expectations and some uncertainty. For example, many young college graduates have high expectations, are achievement-oriented, and are eager to get ahead. These young employees often experience reality shock caused by the difference between what they expect the business world to be and what it really is. The supervisor who takes time to explain the world of work and replace unrealistic expectations with career goals and development plans can help the young employee overcome early career discontent.

Young people moving from high school to the work world experience similar uncertainty and reality shock. They may have little idea of what career paths are available or what is expected of them as employees.

People changing direction, especially those who have been laid off, also require coaching. They may have low expectations for themselves, but many have more potential in the new field than they realize. Because they are older, they have developed skills, knowledge, and habits that are transferable to the new work setting. Because they may fear failing in the new field, they need encouragement to help raise their expectations.

Early Career Employees

Early career employees are around thirty years old and have been in the work world about five to ten years. Employees in this group have become seasoned and realistic. Many experience a questioning of their priorities and values. "Is my career more important than my friends, family, or leisure time?" "Am I progressing as quickly as I should be in my career?" "Should I change organizations or career paths?" For many, this may be a time of painful reevaluation and possible change.

To coach early career employees, concentrate on realistic career paths and identify immediate development needs. You should offer career help to all, not just those who request it or seem especially promising. Do not "write off" a person who seems content and without aspirations. You may be seeing timidity rather than lack of interest. Arm yourself with knowledge about educational programs (IIA, CPCU, college, and company courses) since education is often the critical element in career development.

Mid-Career Employees

Mid-career employees are usually between forty and fifty-five years old. Sometime during this period, most people begin a second career or go through a life reevaluation. Some may wonder if the return on their investment of time and effort in their careers has been worthwhile. Some may be experiencing mid-career or mid-life crises and want to reorganize their work and private lives. Some need to give up their hopes for reaching the top and accept a more realistic vision. Others, who are satisfied with their progress and lives, need only the opportunity to review progress. Others have settled into being "good workers," and some expect advancement. A few may have "retired" from the job. Watch for "pre-retirement retirees." If allowed to drift, they will become problem employees with serious performance problems. Confront them with evidence of performance problems and questions about their career goals.

Senior Employees

Senior employees are settled in their work and anticipate retirement. For many, retirement planning is as important as career planning. For others, another crisis may develop: "Do I want a second career?"

Sometimes, employees at this stage may be looking for promotions or for new challenges. Because of retirement age laws and changing values, senior employees have more options today than ever before, and many need to discuss these with you.

Continuing Education Opportunities

An employee's acquired knowledge, skills, and education influence career goals. Today, education is not something that ends at age twenty-one or twenty-two. Many employees go back to school part-time or enroll in insurance courses. You may find yourself in the position of educational counselor. To do a good job in this area, you will need to research educational opportunities and enlist the aid of the person on your staff who is responsible for education and training in your firm.

Work-Climate Preference

Because of their personal temperament, people prefer and are better suited to certain types of work. Here are some factors to discuss.

Job Structure

Some people prefer a job that is clearly defined, with few surprises and few crises. They would be uncomfortable in a position in which there is limited supervision and in which they are required to take the initiative. Other people relish the freedom to structure their own jobs and exercise problem-solving abilities, and these employees do not need close supervision.

Job Pressure

People's ability to tolerate stress differs. Some people enjoy the pressure of working under tight deadlines and see periodic crises as challenges. Other people find that a high-production, crisis-prone environment creates too much stress, potential burnout, and perhaps health problems.

People Contacts

Some employees need to relate to other people on a continuous basis, while other people need less interaction and often see people as unnecessarily interfering with their work. People who have had repeated conflicts with others, are considered abrasive, or complain of people-stress problems should be counseled to select career paths that do not require frequent contact with others.

DEVELOPING YOUR COACHING ABILITIES

To be an effective coach, you should practice the skills described in this chapter. You will also need feedback on your coaching performance. You have two sources of feedback:

1. Your manager
2. The employees you are coaching

Your employees can probably give you the most accurate feedback, and you can elicit this feedback by asking the following questions:

1. "What would you like me to do that I'm not doing?"
2. "What can I do to help you develop your skills and knowledge?"
3. "What developmental experiences would you like?"

A good test for your developmental skills is for you to evaluate all the employees who have reported to you and ask yourself the following:

1. How many of them have advanced to higher positions?
2. Do other supervisors look to my unit to provide employees for higher-level positions?

Supervisors who are good coaches can frequently point to a number of subordinates who have advanced in the organization. Although you may lose good employees as a result of your coaching, you will also gain self-satisfaction and recognition for your ability to coach and develop employees successfully.

SUMMARY

Coaching is a means of improving performance through day-to-day communication between a supervisor and employees. To be an effective coach, you must recognize each employee's growth potential, determine where he or she is at present, and then assist and guide the employee toward desired development outcomes.

Coaching is generally described as a three-step process: objectively observing performance and behavior, guiding and eliciting feedback, and guiding development. The process works best when the supervisor is helpful and supportive, challenges employees to grow and develop, and builds a climate of mutual trust.

As a supervisor, you can expect to deal with both unsatisfactory and competent employees. Coaching employees to improve performance requires the difficult step of leveling—that is, honestly describing the specific performance or behavior you have observed. Competent performers need coaching and guidance if they are to maintain performance, grow and develop in their present jobs, and avoid complacency.

All employees, except those with severe performance problems, need career planning to help them identify their goals and acquire the knowledge and skills they need to reach those goals. Career goals are affected by lifestyle and family goals, the stage in a person's career development, continuing education opportunities, and work-climate preference.

To be an effective coach, you should practice the skills described in this chapter and seek feedback from your manager and the employees you are coaching.

Chapter 7

Improving Communication and Meetings

Your effectiveness as a supervisor depends greatly on your ability to communicate effectively with your employees and with managers. Effective communication involves speaking and listening skills, which, like other skills, should be studied and practiced in order to become proficient at them. This chapter discusses various types of communication and examines some on-the-job case situations that exemplify them. We will look at some of the barriers to effective communication and explore ways in which these barriers can be overcome. As previously stated, a supervisor's job involves getting things done through other people; communicating with those other people is a necessary part of gaining their cooperation.

COMMUNICATION PROCESS

Oral communications contains five key elements:

1. A situation
2. A sender or speaker
3. A receiver or listener
4. A verbal message
5. A nonverbal message

The first four elements are straightforward. Understanding the last is the key to improving your communication, and we will explore it at some length.

The Nonverbal Message

There is a saying in the communications field that tells us, "We cannot not communicate." When we talk and when we listen, we are sending nonverbal messages to the other person. Through these messages, we tell the other person how we feel about the information we are sending or receiving. More important, we tell the other person how we feel about him or her and ourselves. If any discrepancies exist between the verbal and nonverbal messages, most people give greater weight to nonverbal messages.

Three kinds of nonverbal signals can either support or detract from the messages we wish to convey or the responsiveness we wish to show another speaker.

Tone of Voice

How you say something often affects the other person's perception of you more than *what* you say. If you sound assertive and confident, the other person will assign greater credibility to what you are saying than if you are hesitant or use an apologetic tone. On the other hand, if your tone is hostile or critical, the other person will think you are attacking or blaming him or her. It could lead the other person, especially an employee, to withdraw in irritation and frustration.

Listen to the tone of your voice. Do you sound harsh when you don't intend to? Is a note of hesitance in your voice when you would prefer to sound confident? Watch how others react to you and adjust the tone of your voice accordingly.

Eye Contact

Eye contact can support or detract from the credibility of your message or the sincerity you project as a listener. If someone avoids eye contact or looks down when making a request, he or she is sending a contradictory nonverbal message. On the other hand, if someone maintains constant eye contact, we start to feel uncomfortable and want to get away. Staring directly at someone for a prolonged period of time conveys intimidation or even hostility. In a tense situation, when you feel uncertain about appropriate eye contact, shift your vision from the other person's eyes to between the eyes, or to the nose, or to the lower face, and then back again to the eyes.

Body Language

The way we sit or stand suggests how we feel about ourselves and others. When we sit up and lean slightly toward the other person, we convey confidence in what we are saying or interest in what the other person is saying. If we lean back or away from the other person, we suggest distance and a lack of interest.

If we get too close to the other person, we may be invading his or her "territorial boundaries," making the other person uncomfortable. Some people do not like to be touched, especially by strangers. Other people try to convey friendliness and warmth by putting an arm around another person. The person receiving this gesture may take it as an invasion of privacy. Most people in our culture prefer about eighteen inches of space between themselves and others. Some people need more. If the other person steps back, be sensitive to the nonverbal message being given to you.

Trying to attribute a certain significance to a specific body movement is difficult. Nonverbal signals tend to be very individualized. However, we can identify like or dislike and dominance or lack of dominance. When we like a person or an idea, we tend to open up, remove barriers, and move toward him or her. When we don't like a person or an idea, we close up, move away, and build defenses.

If we feel dominant toward people or in command of a situation, we are usually relaxed and project outward. If we feel we are not in command, we usually are tense, turn inward, and remain guarded.

If we have mixed feelings or haven't made up our minds, we tend to be reserved and controlled and usually project mixed signals.

Combining Verbal and Nonverbal Behavior

Any oral message we send has two parts: word content and nonverbal instructions about how to interpret the content. When the nonverbal message repeats, complements, or accents the verbal message, the listener feels confident that he or she understands. When the nonverbal message appears to contradict the verbal message, the listener will give greater credibility to the nonverbal message or be confused. Contradiction is a source of mistrust and misunderstanding.

Since most of us are not fully aware of the nonverbal messages we are sending or receiving, we often find analyzing and interpreting contradictions to be difficult. We tend to think the other person is the one who is confused.

Learn to analyze how you say something as well as what you say. The listener will provide feedback on how he or she is receiving your message. Look for nonverbal clues of irritation or anger. Also realize that negative nonverbal messages from others may have nothing to do with you. The person may simply be in a bad mood or under stress. Sometimes bringing the nonverbal message to the surface for discussion can clarify the situation. For example, you might say, "You seem upset. Is something wrong?"

Once the other person is aware that a negative message has been conveyed, he or she may be willing to explain. For example:

Supervisor: Could you give me your monthly report early?

Subordinate: Yeah, I'll do it right now. (sighing and shaking her head)

Supervisor: You seem irritated.

Subordinate: I'm sorry. I'm not irritated with you. I just got off the phone with someone who's not very cooperative.

Identifying and being willing to discuss contradictory nonverbal messages can lead to greater understanding and more effective working relationships.

LISTENING

Listening is often described as the difficult art of keeping your mouth closed and allowing the other person to talk. This suggests that listening is a passive activity. Quite the contrary is true: being a good listener usually requires a conscious effort and the deliberate exercise of skills developed through practice. Being a good listener means fighting the temptation to respond and give your own opinion or experience. It also means overcoming some common problems and bad habits.

Problems in Listening

Listening Seen as Weakness

Our society views assertiveness as a positive trait. We expect leaders to take charge of conversations and situations. We expect them to evaluate problem situations quickly and to take fast and decisive action. We value their ability to speak forcefully and with conviction that overcomes the arguments of others. The ability to influence others is virtually a definition of leadership. Rarely do we include patient listening in the picture of powerful leadership behavior.

Discomfort With Silence

Silence during a conversation is usually uncomfortable. It suggests a lack of ideas or a lack of interest in what the other person is saying. Many of us find silence so uncomfortable that we rush in with words after five or ten seconds. These words typically interject new ideas or opinions. They often steer the conversation in a new direction instead of helping the speaker pursue his or her line of thought. Ironically, this redirection may occur just when a speaker pauses to summon the words or the courage to reveal deeper thoughts.

Interrupting

When we know that interrupting someone is irritating, why do we continue to do it? Sometimes we become overstimulated by what the other person says and feel compelled to express agreement or disagreement. Sometimes we think that we will not have a chance to comment on a point if the speaker goes on to other points.

To break the bad habit of interrupting, you first have to recognize that you are doing it. Watch for body language and facial expressions that signal irritation on the part of the person talking and for comments such as "Let me finish."

Intermittent Listening

Why do we often "tune out" the speaker for a few seconds? In some cases, we make a quick judgment that the speaker's ideas have little value or that we have heard them before. More likely, we are formulating or rehearsing what we plan to say. Discipline is required to break the habit of intermittent listening; you literally force yourself to pay attention.

Resisting the Message

At times we listen poorly because we disagree with the message. Careful listening carries an element of personal risk; being open means being vulnerable. We may hear ideas or feelings that threaten us. We may hear things that call for us to change our perceptions, plans, or priorities. We may hear negative statements about things we value or people we like. We may hear criticisms of our supervisory style or its results or be attacked on more personal grounds.

You can expect that your defense mechanisms (discussed in Chapter 5) may be triggered by comments you hear or by apprehension about what may come next in a conversation. Being a good listener requires recognizing your own feelings and reactions and, in turn, controlling the expression of them. For example, you may feel the urge to explain a decision you made that is being criticized, but you can consciously refrain from doing so.

Failing To Verify Understanding

We often hesitate to verify our understanding of what has been said. Verifying may seem like criticizing the speaker for being unclear or admitting one's own difficulty in understanding. There is also the feeling that restating what has just been said is a waste of time.

Becoming an effective listener requires mastering the techniques that encourage the expression of ideas and feelings. Some of these techniques are referred to as active listening.

Active Listening

Active listening is a conscious process of eliciting information, perceptions, and feelings. Active listening does more than obtain information; it contributes to the development of trust and a good working relationship.

Elements in Active Listening

Active listening consists of three elements: attention, suspension of judgment, and response.

Attention

Most of us admit that our attention span is short. We become distracted by the sights and sounds around us and by our own thoughts. Active listening demands a concentrated effort to pay complete attention to what the other person is saying.

One helpful technique is to pay frequent attention to the nonverbal signals given by the listener. In effect, you pause periodically to scan for messages conveyed through body language and facial expressions. Another suggested technique is to mirror the posture and gestures of the speaker, when appropriate.

For example, when he or she leans forward, you should lean forward. After listening for a length of time, we have a natural tendency to evaluate what is being said and to draw conclusions, partly in an effort to summarize and simplify what the person is saying.

Suspension of Judgment

Evaluations should be deferred or, at least, be considered tentative until confirmed by additional evidence. You must withhold judgment, especially good/bad and right/wrong judgments about the message or the speaker. If you give any hint of disapproval, you give the person reason to become cautious about sharing with you. The recommendation to withhold judgment is valid for active listening in any situation. It is particularly important when the speaker is a member of your unit. Any indication that you disapprove is likely to inhibit the statements, if not the thinking, of an employee.

Response

Active listening requires giving appropriate responses. The overall guideline for responding is to avoid introducing a new idea. In active listening, you want the speaker to maintain control of the conversation. You can achieve this by paraphrasing the speaker's comments and checking your understanding of them. You should not interject a thought that steers the discussion in another direction. Pushing the conversation in a new direction is not likely to help the speaker to reveal ideas and feelings that lie beneath the surface, which is a goal of active listening. Exhibit 7-1 describes the paraphrase response.

Exhibit 7-1

The Paraphrase Response

How can you practice active listening in your day-to-day communication with others? Active listening often employs three steps: (1) listening to a message, (2) paraphrasing, or restating in your own words, the message you received, and (3) "feeding" the paraphrased message back to the speaker for confirmation. For example, you might say, "What I hear you saying is... Is this correct?"

Communication experts agree that active listening is one of the best ways to listen to someone because it requires you (1) to process in your own mind what the speaker is saying (in order for you to paraphrase it) and (2) to check your understanding of what was said by repeating to the speaker what you have heard.

Although active listening speeds up understanding, it actually slows down the communication process because it takes time. The advantages, however, should far outweigh this drawback.

Answering Questions

You may be asked for information or for your perception, opinion, or feelings about something. The general guideline is to give a direct answer when asked a direct question; however, sometimes you should not follow that guideline. Here are some of the questions that, as you judge them in context, you may decide not to answer directly.

- A question that seems premature. In such cases, your judgment is that the speaker should explore the topic more before you give the information or opinion requested.
- A question that requires you to criticize others.
- A question that asks you to take one side in a dispute.
- A question that you cannot answer without exceeding your authority.
- A question that seems to evade the issue. Perhaps the person feels pressure and seeks relief by trying to change the subject. A response that sticks to the topic is recommended.

In suggesting that you make judgments about which questions to answer directly, we are not contradicting the second element in active listening, suspension of judgment. Suspension of judgment refers to the evaluative judgment about the speaker or his or her statements and involves your approval or disapproval. Deciding how to answer questions should involve your evaluation of the questions and the progress of the discussion, not of the speaker or the ideas being expressed.

A number of specific response techniques allow you to encourage the speaker without communicating judgment or taking control. These are known as *nondirective responses* because of their ability to support but not steer the speaker's thoughts.

Nondirective Responses

Nondirective responses are techniques that encourage the other person to open up, to speak freely, and to express ideas and feelings that may be suppressed. Nondirective responses rarely come naturally; they are usually learned and used knowingly. As the word *nondirective* indicates, such responses do not direct (or redirect) the flow of the conversation. Instead, they convey support for the speaker in his or her effort to discuss a matter of importance.

The following are nondirective responses:

- Asking open-ended questions
- Asking for clarification
- Perception checking
- Reflecting
- Empathizing
- Silence or nonverbal response

We have stressed that taking command and dominating a conversation are rarely the most effective ways to persuade, motivate, or influence other people. You can use the nondirective techniques as a means to guide two-way communications. In most conversations, you will also use the following directive communication techniques:

- Telling or explaining
- Identifying problems or disagreeing
- Recommending, suggesting, or requesting

When used appropriately, the nondirective techniques are powerful. Let's now discuss them in detail.

Asking Open-Ended Questions

Open-ended questions start with who, what, when, where, why, or how. They allow the other person a great deal of freedom to express ideas, opinions, and feelings.

For example: Jessie Hamilton supervises four underwriters in a personal lines department. For several weeks, the unit has had a backlog of work. Jessie realizes that this puts a burden on her staff, especially the two senior underwriters. One of these senior underwriters, Chuck Wilson, tells her in an off-handed manner, "There must be a way to solve this problem. I'm getting awfully tired of working overtime while other people aren't busy."

Jessie wonders whether Chuck is just expressing discontentment or whether he has an idea for solving the problem. She decides to find out, so she asks Chuck to come into her office.

Jessie: I know this backlog has been a burden to you. What suggestions do you have for solving the problem?

Chuck: Well, like I said, underwriters are sitting around who don't have that much to do.

Jessie: Who are these underwriters? (open-ended question)

Chuck: Our less experienced people, especially the new trainee.

Jessie: How could they become more productive? (open-ended question)

Chuck: Well, I haven't really thought it through clearly, but if I could assign specific tasks to the new trainee, then I could get through more applications in a day.

Asking for Clarification

Asking for clarification requires using both open-ended and direct questions to encourage the other person to specify exactly what he or she means.

For example: Jessie Hamilton is meeting with her manager, Tom Dunn; the rating supervisor; and the policywriting supervisor. She has written a proposal for changing the workflow and procedures for all three units. Her manager has distributed the proposal, and they are going to discuss it.

Rating Supervisor: I don't think Jessie's plan is workable.

Jessie: You don't like anything about the plan? (asking for clarification)

Rating Supervisor: No, that isn't true. I think the procedures are very good.

Jessie: Can you identify what you primarily dislike? (asking for clarification)

Rating Supervisor: Yes. I don't like the workflow from my unit to yours.

Jessie: What don't you like about it? (asking for clarification)

Rating Supervisor: The work first comes into your unit, then goes to ours, then back to you. Once the work comes into my unit, I want to finish it. None of this back and forth business.

Jessie: If I change the workflow, would you accept the plan? (asking for clarification)

Rating Supervisor: Yes, basically. But I have a few more suggestions.

People often speak in generalizations. For example, the rating supervisor said he did not think the plan was workable. When Jessie asked him to clarify what he meant, she found out it was only the workflow, not the entire plan, that he disliked.

Asking for clarification is helpful when someone talks in abstractions or uses terms you don't understand. For example, an information technology specialist is explaining how changes in a computer program will affect Jessie's underwriting unit.

IT Specialist: This specific change is transparent to the user.

Jessie: What do you mean by transparent? (asking for clarification)

IT Specialist: Oh, as a user of the program, you won't even notice the change.

Jessie: Does it affect my unit or me at all? (asking for clarification)

IT Specialist: No. That's what I mean by transparent. You won't notice it.

Perception Checking

Perception checking means describing, in a tentative fashion, what you think the other person means. This allows the other person to confirm or correct your perception or inference.

Misinterpreting what a person says is easy, as is making assumptions about how he or she feels or what's bothering him or her. If the other person is upset or hostile, do not respond with irritation, even if you think the hostility is directed toward you.

For example, Jessie is passing by Chuck's desk when she remembers a report she wants on an agent.

Jessie: Could you give me a written report on the loss ratio for the Smith agency for the last six months?

Chuck: How soon?

Jessie: As soon as possible.

Chuck: And as soon as possible, I'll get to the rest of this stack of files on my desk.

Jessie: You sound annoyed. (perception checking)

Chuck: Yes, I am. Do you mean that you want me to drop everything and do it now? (perception checking)

Jessie: No, I don't. I mean when you have the time. I know you are busy. No rush. Two weeks from now would be fine.

There is a risk in perception checking. The other person may take the opportunity to tell you what really annoys him and it may be you. On the positive side, this is the way good relationships are built and maintained. If you start using this technique, chances are your subordinates may copy it.

Reflecting

To reflect is to repeat part of a sentence or a word that the other person has said. In reflecting, the listener breaks in and merely mirrors or echoes what has been said. The purposes of reflecting are as follows:

- To encourage the other person to continue talking
- To assist him or her in analyzing a situation
- To defuse defensive remarks, when necessary

For example, Jessie is talking to her manager, Tom Dunn, about the new trainee, John.

Jessie: I'm so angry. I just can't believe he made this mistake.

Tom: Mistake? (reflecting)

Jessie: I assume that John made the mistake.

Tom: You assume. (reflecting)

Jessie: All right. I am assuming. Before I accuse John, I had better ask some questions and find out what really happened.

In this conversation, Tom has led Jessie to analyze her assumptions further and to arrive at a tentative course of action.

To reflect, select the key phrases to repeat so that the other person will elaborate on these ideas or feelings. Reflecting should move the conversation forward by singling out the point to be developed next.

For example, Jessie asks John what he did with the Roberts' file for two weeks.

John: I put it in my desk drawer.

Jessie: In your desk drawer. (reflecting)

John: Yes. I was going to work on it Wednesday because I knew Chuck wanted the information Thursday. But I was absent Wednesday. So I called the office and told Helen to get the file and give it to Chuck. I guess she forgot.

Jessie: She forgot. (reflecting)

John: I should have checked when I came back, but I assumed that she had given it to Chuck. I really am sorry. I should have remembered to check.

Reflecting should be used with discretion, because its overuse can become annoying. But when used in conjunction with open-ended questions, clarification, and perception checking, reflecting guides discussion forward by asking the speaker to go deeper into issues of significance.

Empathizing

Empathy is the ability to identify with how someone feels. For example:

Chuck: When agents call me and ask for quotes time after time and don't give us the business, I get angry and frustrated.

Jessie: That is frustrating.

Empathizing means responding to or echoing the feeling rather than the content of the person's statement. Disclosing how you feel encourages the other person to reveal more of his or her feelings. Such disclosures often require a certain amount of trust–trust that the information will be held in confidence and will not be used against him or her.

Silence or Nonverbal Response

Silence is both a requirement and an effective technique for listening. When you ask a question or use any nondirective technique, you are asking for the other person to respond. Give the person time to think. The silence may seem long to you, but it is not for the other person, who is trying to formulate a response. As long as the other person is not giving you nonverbal clues that the silence is uncomfortable for him or her, wait for the person to speak. Silence can put the burden of explaining on the other person, but it can also communicate more strongly than words.

Gestures and non-word spoken responses encourage the speaker to continue and do not redirect the flow of ideas. "Uh-huh" and "umm" are two positive nonverbal responses.

DIRECTIVE COMMUNICATION TECHNIQUES

The primary purpose of directive communication is to provide the other person with information you think he or she needs or wants. Giving information and instructions is essential in supervising others–so essential that we should review the following techniques:

1. Telling and explaining
2. Identifying problems or disagreeing
3. Influencing

Telling and Explaining

As a supervisor, you must give directions and assignments, and explain and interpret company or agency policies or plans. Here are some guidelines for telling and explaining.

Set a Clear Communication Objective

What do you want the other person to do as result of this message? Take some action? Agree or disagree? File it away for future reference? Having an objective in mind will help you select the best way to present your message.

Analyze Your Audience (Your Listener)

What's the person's knowledge of the subject or background with the situation? What level of abstraction is best? For example, you could ask yourself: "How much detail or background do I need to give?" "What's this person's likely reaction?" "Will I need to sell my ideas?"

Determine Where and When to Talk

The length and importance of the discussion are the determining factors. Don't hold key conversations on the spur of the moment. For important conversations, set a time and place aside where you will not be interrupted.

Obtain Feedback

To determine whether the other person understands you, request feedback. Asking the person to repeat the message may suggest that you doubt his or her ability to understand. You should ask questions about the message, such as "Do you see any problems in this?" or "How do you think this will work out?"

Identifying Problems or Disagreeing

As a supervisor, you will often have messages to deliver that subordinates would prefer not to hear. We have put these challenging communications under the heading "Identifying Problems or Disagreeing" to suggest their touchy nature.

Discuss Performance or Behavior, Not Personality

When you are identifying problems or disagreeing, there is high potential for conflict. You therefore want to reduce defensive reaction from the other person. You should not sound as though you are blaming the other person, but rather you should make clear that you object to a specific kind of behavior or performance level, or that you disagree with a specific position or decision. The techniques previously recommended for discussing performance should be recalled in this context.

Speak in Specifics

When identifying problems or disagreeing, avoid broad generalizations. State specifically what you disagree with. Avoid words such as "always," "never," and "all." For example, don't say, "You never get to work on time." Instead, say, "You have been late two days out of five this week."

Send "I" Messages

Send "I" messages instead of "you" messages when disagreeing or identifying difficulties.

When we are upset, we tend to state our dissatisfaction in "you" messages, which imply that the other person is in some way to blame for how we feel. For example, Tom Dunn, Jessie's manager, is talking with Jessie, the underwriting supervisor.

Tom: You have not been doing your job as a supervisor. Your subordinates are all goofing off. They are bothering other people, and you're going to have to put a stop to it immediately.

Although this may be an accurate evaluation, there is a more constructive way to deliver criticism. Let's rephrase the above "you" message into an "I" message.

Tom: I believe there is a serious problem in your unit. I see you working very hard, but I observe your subordinates goofing off. They are disrupting the entire department, and I can't tolerate this situation.

In the preceding example, Jessie is less likely to become defensive. She cannot reject how Tom perceives the situation because Tom has assumed responsibility for his own feelings and perceptions.

Be Assertive, Not Hostile

You should be assertive when identifying problems or disagreeing. You can show a great deal of conviction about how you feel and confidence in your perceptions. Hostility, however, is quite different from assertiveness. Hostility implies that the other person is to blame. "You" messages, judgmental phrases, generalizations, a loud and angry tone of voice, and unwavering eye contact all express hostility and blame. Hostility can act as an automatic red flag to the other person and trigger a defensive reaction.

Influencing

As a supervisor, you often seek to influence others in deliberately gentle ways—ways that do not fit into the preceding categories of *telling and explaining* and *identifying problems or disagreeing.* You recommend, suggest, urge, and request action rather than give commands or direct orders.

We have all been taught that it is polite, and usually more successful, to express our needs as requests. You should therefore label your messages carefully, saying, "I recommend," "I ask," "I urge," and so on.

CONDUCTING MEETINGS

How many times have you attended a meeting and left thinking, "What a waste of time"? This section will provide you with ideas and techniques that should help you lead meetings that will prevent such thoughts. Although this section is designed primarily to aid you in becoming a better meeting leader, it also contains suggestions for being a better meeting participant. The discussion then includes ways of analyzing group behavior, whether the group is your meeting audience or your work unit.

Types of Meetings

Let us look at types of meetings and their objectives. This should enable you to determine whether a meeting is needed to attain a given objective. It should also help you plan meetings by highlighting the need for having a clear objective.

Following are the most common types of meetings called by supervisors:

- Downward communication
- Information-gathering
- Problem-solving
- Attitude-adjustment

Downward communication meetings are frequently called by supervisors when they need to give information to their employees, perhaps to explain a new change. Alternatives to the downward communication meeting are memos, notices on a bulletin board, and electronic mail messages. You must decide which method will best help your unit members understand the message. If a written message would be ignored or could be misunderstood, or if you want to promote discussion, a meeting is warranted.

Information-gathering meetings should be called when you need information or opinions from employees. Imagine you have been asked to recommend a more efficient procedure for handling the mail. Your staff members are likely to have some good ideas on the subject. Maybe they deal directly with the mail, are aware of problems, and have ideas on how to solve them. A meeting is a good way to get people to share ideas and give feedback. In some cases, you should ask each employee to give you his or her ideas in writing. Writing can clarify ideas and make thought more deliberate. It can also be more efficient to have the ideas expressed in writing.

Problem-solving meetings can be useful when your unit faces a serious problem, such as increasing error ratios or a work backlog. Instead of using an authoritarian leadership style, which would involve telling people what must be done, you may wish to use the participative approach, which gets employees involved in solving the problem, increasing the likelihood that the solution will be accepted. Problem-solving meetings can be "brainstorming" sessions—that is, attempts to generate many potential solutions. Brainstorming invites one person to feed on the ideas of another. Participants are encouraged to voice all of their ideas, since no idea is discarded. The ideas are evaluated later. Because of the importance of interaction between employees and the desire for acceptance of the solution, writing does not offer a good alternative to problem-solving meetings.

Attitude-adjustment meetings are often used when you or higher management has made a decision and it must, in turn, be shared with your subordinates. The decision to lengthen the time between salary adjustments could be grounds for an attitude-adjustment meeting. These meetings differ from downward communication meetings in that you must convince your staff to accept the decision.

There are alternatives to the attitude-adjustment meeting. You can simply put the decision in writing and distribute it, or you might discuss the decision with each person to get reactions and to answer questions. Both of these approaches may be less costly than a formal meeting, but they lack employee interaction. If your unit is likely to view the management decision negatively, hold a meeting to allow employees to express their feelings. This will give you some direction as to what further action may be needed in implementing the decision.

Meeting Effectiveness

As meeting leader, you will be responsible for achieving objectives, choosing participants and evaluating their satisfaction with the results, beginning and concluding the meeting on time, and conducting the meeting cost effectively. How well you attend to these responsibilities will determine the effectiveness of your meetings.

Effective Meetings

An effective meeting achieves its objective in the minimum amount of time, satisfies its participants, and is cost effective.

Participant satisfaction is the most difficult factor to evaluate. Satisfaction does not necessarily mean "happy," as a meeting's goal may be to develop solutions to problems or to give bad news, such as a reduction in staff. Satisfaction generally comes from understanding; reasons for a decision were given and the meeting provided a chance to discuss them openly. You may find it difficult to determine how satisfied participants are, but you should always make an effort to do so.

Ineffective Meetings

Here are eleven of the most frequent meeting problems and a few suggestions on how they can be avoided or at least minimized.

No Stated Purpose

Every meeting should have an objective that is stated in writing before the meeting.

No Agenda

Every meeting should have an agenda, which should be prepared and circulated in advance among participants. For some meetings, the objective may serve as the agenda. The agenda should help people prepare for the meeting and let them know in advance how long the meeting will last.

Wrong People Attend

Who attends a meeting should be determined by its objective. Only those who can offer valuable information and insight should attend.

Wrong Time

Schedule meetings at convenient times. Interest will decrease if the meeting runs into lunchtime. Participants should be notified of the meeting time in advance.

Inconvenient Location

Hold your meetings in a convenient place. The room should be of adequate size, with all the equipment you plan to use at hand. Try to select a location that is as free from interruptions as possible.

Late Start

Start meetings on time. Those who arrive late will learn, through embarrassment, to avoid tardiness. Good planning can guarantee that meetings end on time. Interest drops when a meeting runs late, especially when people have made other plans.

Interruptions

Interruptions are costly. They disrupt the continuity of your meeting. (Side conversations between participants can have the same effect.) You must let everyone know that interruptions are not welcome. Set aside a specific break time when messages can be delivered. You should also indicate what interruptions will be welcome, such as questions to clarify a point.

Wandering

Stick to the agenda. If participants go off on tangents, stay in control and bring them back to your subject. Suggest that the group can take up other issues if time permits once all agenda items have been handled.

Lack of Interest

Participants will not necessarily be interested in your subject. Conduct meetings with participants in mind. Try to connect your subject with the concerns of participants. Ask questions, especially of those who do not appear to be attentive.

Inadequate Time

Allow enough time so that participants can digest what is being said. Do not simply state a position. Clarify points, give examples, and obtain feedback to see that points are understood. Encourage participants to ask questions.

Lack of Conclusion

Be sure participants know what has been accomplished when you conclude a meeting. Close by summarizing the meeting. Let everyone know what will happen next. If assignments are to be made, make them. If additional meetings are needed, schedule them. If actions are agreed on, make a plan for accomplishing them. Do not forget to follow up on results.

Role of the Meeting Leader

The role you play in leading a meeting will depend largely on the type of meeting and its objectives. Your role should become clear during the process of planning the meeting.

Different Roles for Different Meetings

Meeting leaders have different roles for different types of meetings. Your role as meeting leader in a downward communication meeting is that of communicator of information. You are likely to do most of the talking. Remember, sending information from the front of the room does not mean communication has taken place. You should ask questions to see that the information is understood. In the downward-communication meeting, your goal is to get people involved in the information you are giving.

Your role as leader of an information-gathering meeting is to encourage participation and develop ideas. The kind of information desired should be clarified at the outset. Participants must be encouraged to offer their ideas and interact. You must keep the meeting on track and under control while encouraging free thinking and openness. Provocative statements stimulate thought.

Your role during a problem-solving meeting may change during the meeting. You will be an information communicator when you state the problem. You will have to stimulate participation in the problem-solving process. You may also contribute your own ideas. Finally, you must make conclusions and summarize the solutions. Playing these roles while not allowing your own ideas to dominate the session is difficult.

Your role during an attitude-adjustment meeting is to encourage the expression of feelings. Using the techniques of active listening is appropriate. Although you want to encourage the free expression of feelings, you must not lose control of the meeting. You might ask, "Do others feel this way?" as a way to maintain control while encouraging the expression of feelings.

Planning the Meeting

Effective meetings are carefully planned. You must plan what you want to happen and how it will happen. State specific objectives as conditions that should exist at the end of the meeting. Once objectives have been determined, decide who should be invited to the meeting. Prepare an outline of the material to be covered before the meeting. As you outline the material, keep the participants in mind—what is their interest in and knowledge of the subject and so on. As you outline, check your own knowledge of the material and anticipate questions. If necessary, do some research so that you can answer all foreseeable questions.

*[Handwritten margin note: * Leaders goal is to get people involved in the information you are giving *]*

As you outline what you are going to say, decide how much detail is needed. Some people can talk from brief notes, say on 3" x 5" cards. Others need a detailed speech outline before they are comfortable. Few people can speak before a group with no notes at all. Even the most confident speaker usually relies on a topic-heading outline.

The outline should have a minimum of three parts: (1) the opening or introduction, (2) the body, and (3) the close. Your opening might start with a simple welcome.

After the introduction, state the subject of the meeting and the objectives you wish to accomplish. Four or five objectives for a one-hour meeting are probably enough. Make clear what is to be accomplished. You could say, "Since the objective of this meeting is to solve the missing file problem, I will need your suggestions." State the "ground rules" for the session. For instance, if your meeting is to run one hour, say so. Let people know whether they should ask questions as they wish or wait until after you have finished speaking. These steps make it clear to everyone how the meeting will be run.

The body of the outline is determined by the type of meeting—that is, downward communication, information-gathering, problem-solving, or attitude-adjustment. Try to outline logical, sequential steps from the simple to the complex, from the known to the unknown. The sample outline in Exhibit 7-2 illustrates these steps.

Most meetings close with a simple summary of the key points of the meeting. Relating these key points to the objectives should tie the meeting together. Try to close on a "high note," or a positive statement calling for action. Finally, thank your audience for attending.

The final preparation step is to study and rehearse your outline. If you feel unsure about yourself, ask a friend or family member to listen to your rehearsal and comment on it. Is it understandable? The great public speaker Dale Carnegie gave the same talk on personal growth and development for more than fifteen years and is said to have rehearsed before each presentation. Why not help yourself? Find a quiet place to talk your outline through out loud. Otherwise, read your outline over several times to yourself, evaluating whether you feel comfortable about what you are going to say.

Making a Presentation

Not every supervisor is a great public speaker; however, the ability to express yourself clearly and effectively in front of a group of people is almost essential to being a successful supervisor. Fortunately, this skill can be developed through practice. Perhaps the two most important qualities a meeting leader must project are self-confidence and enthusiasm. Both come from a thorough knowledge of the subject and a positive attitude. In addition to self-confidence and enthusiasm, you should also have skill in the techniques of speaking, using audio-visual aids, and getting participation.

Exhibit 7-2

Sample Meeting Outline

Subject:	First Quality Circle Meeting
Objective:	To understand the purpose, rationale, and processes involved in quality circles.
Materials:	Two overhead slides, projector, screen, two handouts

Method	Outline
	I. Introduction
Lecture	a. Welcome
Show slide	b. Objectives
	c. Meeting details
	d. Background—firm's desire to involve employees in decision making
	II. Body
Lecture	a. Define quality circle and its voluntary nature
Show slide	b. State ground rules and areas of involvement
Handout	c. Describe role of steering committee, supervisor, facilitator, members
Discussion	d. Tell how circle can provide members a chance to be recognized as experts, give two-way communication, and an opportunity to improve the quality of work
Exercise	e. Introduce facilitator, who explains problem-solving process
	f. Facilitator explains brainstorming technique
	g. Use brainstorming to choose a name for the group
	III. Close
Handout	a. Summarize key points based on objectives
	b. Evaluate meeting
	c. Announce next meeting
	d. Thank audience for attending

Techniques

A good speaker uses variety. Vary your style from serious to the lighter side. Humor can be used to make a point effectively. Some people have a natural sense of humor and can tell jokes and stories well, while others cannot. Determine your effectiveness at telling a joke before trying it in front of a group. Another way to vary your presentation is to go from straight talk to discussion and then to questions and answers.

Vary the tone of your voice. Adjust the speed of your delivery and the loudness of your voice. Good eye contact with the audience is vital, and you may need to practice it consciously over a series of meetings. Avoid distracting mannerisms, but use a variety of gestures to add emphasis to your message. Use clear, simple language. As you speak, pause occasionally for emphasis and allow your message to sink in. Use the language of your audience and remember that short sentences are more easily remembered than long ones. Use frequent examples to make your points more clear. Examples involving real situations will help the message get through. Taping a meeting is an excellent way to improve your skill. As you listen to the playback, you can study tone, speed, loudness, word choice, illustrations, and other aspects of your speaking.

Audio-Visual Aids

Your message can be made more effective, as well as more interesting, through the use of audio-visual aids. We tend to learn more and more easily when we see as well as hear. Audio-visual aids are powerful tools for emphasizing key points or simplifying complex ones. If you use aids, they must be carefully selected and prepared.

Getting Participation

The most effective meetings actively involve the participants. To get active participation, you must stimulate a desire to come to the meeting. This begins with your meeting announcement. Once in the meeting, you can channel thinking toward your objectives by skillfully asking questions. The best questions will not be answerable with "yes" or "no." Questions like "How do you think this idea will work?" will usually elicit responses and sometimes even debate. Open-ended questions require more thought and often help participants express their feelings. Use questions to involve everyone ("Ann, we haven't heard from you yet.") as well as to quiet the "know-it-all" ("Bill, you have given us a number of good ideas, but now we need to hear from someone else.").

Team activity fosters involvement. Small discussion groups make it possible and easy for everyone to contribute. Persons who hesitate to speak in large groups usually lose their shyness in team activities. Simply dividing a large meeting into small groups to "discuss" something is unwise. As leader, you must give a specific topic or question and a time limit for the team activity. By having team "reporters" present each team's ideas, all participants get to share the information. Exhibit 7-3 summarizes some Do's and Don'ts for successful meetings.

Evaluating Meetings

How can you tell whether a meeting has been a success? Leader and participants should consider whether the meeting achieved its objectives. The leader should consider his or her own reactions to the meeting and seek feedback from participants.

You have several ways of getting your audience's reaction to a meeting. You may ask people to tell you how they feel before they leave. (Was this meeting worth your time? What are you going to do now?) You can often obtain valuable feedback by contacting one or two people right after a meeting. You might seek the views of those closest to you or those you know to be objective and candid. Be very direct in this process and ask for feedback on specific items.

Exhibit 7-3

Do's and Don'ts for Successful Meetings

Do…

- Give adequate notice.
- Be sure facilities are adequate and ready.
- Start and end your meeting on time.
- Plan your agenda to meet your objectives and follow it.
- Be enthusiastic to keep the meeting interesting.
- Use some showmanship to gain attention.
- Get audience participation.
- Use audio-visual aids as part of your presentation, if they are applicable.
- Supplement your message with printed materials.
- End your meeting with a brief summary of key points.
- Find out what participants think of the meeting.

Don't…

- Go to your meeting poorly prepared.
- Use the same format for each meeting.
- Be too formal. Be well organized, but informal.
- Try to cover too many subjects in one meeting.
- Make your meetings one-sided by talking too much.
- Let the meeting deteriorate into a gripe session.
- Overlook feedback. Have a question-and-answer period.
- Run more than sixty minutes without a break.

Reactions are sometimes gathered by way of a printed form that each participant completes before leaving. The sample form in Exhibit 7-4 is easy to use and elicits valuable information.

Summarize the evaluation findings by category and look for trends and the majority reaction. If most attendees rated your meeting as poor or fair, look carefully at the comments and suggestions. If you *really* want to improve your next meeting, make plans to correct your weaknesses and to build on your strengths.

Problems in Conducting Meetings

Facilitating productive discussion in meetings is rarely easy. You have undoubtedly felt frustrated in meetings when people talk too much or too little, when arguments become heated or prolonged, or when the discussion seems fruitless and endless. Poorly conducted meetings produce inferior results, damage relationships, and create stress for participants. In contrast, a well-run meeting provides far-reaching organizational benefits and personal satisfaction.

Exhibit 7-4

Meeting Evaluation Form

Circle Your Response

1. Rate the meeting.	Poor	Fair	Good	Excellent	
2. Were the time and place satisfactory?				Yes	No
If no, why not?					
3a. Were the objectives clear?				Yes	No
b. Were the objectives reached?				Yes	No
4. Was the length sufficient?				Yes	No
5a. Rate the leader. Was he or she prepared?				Yes	No
b. Rate the presentation.	Poor	Fair	Good	Excellent	
6a. Rate the subject. Was it relevant?				Yes	No
b. Interesting?				Yes	No
c. Understood?				Yes	No
7. How satisfied are you?					

Very satisfied   Satisfied   Unsatisfied   Very unsatisfied

8. Any other comments or suggestions?

You face a dilemma when conducting meetings: how can you maintain control and yet allow full participation?

The objective of a meeting should govern the amount of control you exercise when conducting it. For instance, downward communication meetings call for tight control, at least for a major portion of the meeting. You may limit questions and discussion to a predetermined place on the agenda.

Most meeting objectives make discussion valuable, if not essential, to success. Can you imagine a problem-solving meeting that succeeds without a relatively free discussion? However, we know that a good discussion is not totally free and uncontrolled. The leader guides it, stimulates and echoes contributions, and acts swiftly to overcome obstacles as they arise.

Most of the problems that confront you in leading meetings call for early identification and fast action. Let us now consider some of the most common problems.

Hidden Agendas

A hidden agenda is a concern that affects a person's behavior in a meeting but that is not openly identified by the person. We usually think of a hidden agenda as a question or demand that a person brings to the meeting. At times hidden concerns may arise spontaneously during a meeting; however, as commonly used, the hidden agenda is a strong concern brought to the meeting. Sometimes hidden agendas are revealed when a person's comments seem to be off the track. A person with a hidden agenda usually seems to be dumping a preexisting idea or feeling at the first opportunity. Such a person may be aware of his or her concern but not admit it openly, and at other times, the person is not in touch with the idea or feeling that manifests in his or her behavior.

To illustrate a hidden agenda, consider a meeting at which you will ask the members of your unit to establish the criteria to be used in reallocating their assigned territories. Your objective is to have the unit members decide on the criteria. You attempt to keep the discussion centered on *criteria* and do not allow members to talk about who will get which territory. John argues that travel should be equalized among unit members as much as possible. Arlene contends that seniority should be a major criterion. John has a hidden agenda that he is not aware of: he does not want a territory requiring many overnight trips. Arlene's hidden agenda is that she does not want to be assigned to Chicago. Arlene may be well aware of her concern over the Chicago assignment, yet she does not admit it openly. You may have a hidden agenda of your own in running the meeting. For instance, your unrecognized concern may be that you want a clear consensus among unit members. You may not care what the group decides as long as everyone agrees.

The hidden agendas in this instance are not especially devious or damaging. Nonetheless, they impair communication as long as they remain hidden. How good can communication be when a person is talking about one issue while thinking about another one?

You should attempt to bring hidden agendas into the open. If you suspect that a person's comments reveal a hidden agenda, ask questions or state your observations and ask for the person's reaction.

If you think that a given meeting will be impeded by hidden agendas, consider starting the meeting by asking participants to state their concerns about the subject and meeting objective. You might ask participants to say how they feel about the subject before proceeding with the agenda.

Dominating Persons

What should you do when the discussion is dominated by one person or by a small number of participants? Asking specific questions of other participants usually helps, since asking the overactive participants to "give the others a chance" may not overcome the hesitance of those who have not spoken. Dividing the meeting into smaller discussion groups is also an effective way to disrupt the pattern of domination.

Arguments

Meetings can suddenly become tense when discussion turns into argument. Arguments are marked by repeated back-and-forth exchanges between participants. Those engaged in arguing usually challenge the statements of one another and seem more intent on "winning" than on finding the best answer.

Most arguments have a win/lose character, and you must try to transform them into win/win collaboration. One useful guideline is to insist that others speak before the arguing parties are allowed to speak again. Another useful tactic is to summarize the positions and redirect the discussion to an underlying or related issue.

✳ Status Differences

Differences in the informal status and formal rank of participants may hamper discussion. We are often hesitant to contradict people with greater knowledge, standing, or experience. When conducting meetings, ask for the ideas of lower-status persons before turning to those of higher standing. You might also ask high-status individuals to concentrate on particular aspects of the topic.

Obtaining Consensus

Complete agreement in organizational meetings is a rarity. Consensus is normally the desired outcome, if only because it takes too long to reach a unanimous decision. Consensus means that all views have been fairly heard and that a majority opinion has emerged. Under consensus, those who do not agree with the majority decision believe that their thoughts have been understood and have received careful consideration. Achieving consensus is usually preferable to voting on important issues.

To move a group toward consensus, you should summarize views, integrate them when possible, and focus discussion on points of disagreement. You will often sense when consensus has been reached. When this happens, summarize the conclusion and verify that participants are ready to move on to the next item.

The problems you may encounter in running meetings have only been highlighted in this section. We urge you to study the techniques used by leaders whose meetings you consider effective. You will find that good meetings do not happen by chance; they result from careful planning and assertive leading.

Let us now turn to communications in a broader sense, organization-wide communications.

ORGANIZATIONAL COMMUNICATIONS

Communications flow downward, upward, and across organizational lines in a marvelously intricate network. Objectives, policies, and strategies must be communicated downward so that everyone will be moving in the same direction. Management needs feedback (upward communication) on progress toward key objectives in order to make decisions and take corrective actions. Communications flow horizontally between and among peer supervisors and managers so that objectives, workflow, and procedural changes mesh.

Every organization, no matter how small or large, is in a constant state of change. Without adequate communications, departments, units, and individuals will not achieve teamwork and change will not be smooth.

Barriers to Organizational Communications

Communications never flow perfectly because of a number of barriers. When a directive or policy is communicated downward, there is likely to be distortion and loss of information at each level. For example, the principals of an agency develop a marketing program. They understand the need for the plan, but when they communicate it to the next level of managers, they fail to explain the need. When these managers communicate it to the supervisors, they inadvertently convey their lack of enthusiasm. When the supervisors communicate it to the staff, the program is seen as a new reporting system rather than a major new marketing effort as the principals originally intended.

A research study that was conducted in 100 representative industries throughout the United States showed that one-way communication from top management to the technical or clerical level diminishes in its effectiveness as it progresses downward. When the directive goes from corporate to the next lower level of management, only sixty-seven percent of the communication is understood. When the message reaches the third management level, only fifty-six percent is understood; on the second level, only forty percent; and on the first-line supervisory level, only thirty percent. When supervisors communicate to technical or clerical workers, only twenty percent of the original corporate message is received.

Superiors and subordinates often cannot agree on the most elementary facts about the subordinate's responsibilities and authority. Many research studies have reported that there is only about a thirty percent agreement between a superior's and a subordinate's definition of the subordinate's job. Managers, supervisors, and other workers frequently complain that they don't know what their superiors expect from them or where they stand.

The positive point in this research information is that peer employees, whether managerial, technical, or clerical, usually communicate with ninety percent effectiveness. The problem is the distortion and loss of information as it goes from one level to the next. There are a number of reasons for this, especially screening of information and organizational distance.

Screening of Information

Management's communication downward is often one way with little opportunity for asking questions, clarifying ideas, or checking perceptions. The communication channels that management primarily uses are discussions, meetings, memos, and reports. The information that management selects to tell employees is often screened because management believes that employees do not need or want to know what is behind a decision.

The distortion and loss of communication as the information travels upward is as great as or perhaps greater than when it travels downward. Employees tend to screen what they tell their superiors in order to look good. This tendency can be reinforced by the supervisor's dissatisfaction when given negative information. Employees quickly learn how much negative feedback their supervisors are willing to hear and refrain from exceeding this limit.

Organizational Distance

Employees at different levels in an organization have different objectives, problems, information needs, and values toward work. The lack of knowledge about the role and problems of other units creates barriers to communication. Simply not knowing the people in another unit results in organizational distance.

Overcoming Barriers

The effects of these barriers can be reduced so that communication can flow more easily. We recommend the following techniques.

Use Two-Way Communication

As a supervisor, you need to listen and gain feedback from employees. The nondirective techniques are ideal for *eliciting* information. The following is an ideal format for *giving* information either to an individual or a group:

1. Tell and explain.
2. Ask open-ended questions to signal that questions and responses are welcome.
3. Encourage questions and responses.
4. Summarize key points and agreements.

Encourage Employees To Provide Information

The following is recommended in order to encourage upward communication from employees:

- Maintain an open-door (and open-mind) climate.
- Encourage the expression of feelings as well as facts.
- Ask employees for their opinions.
- Reward employees for reporting problems.
- Provide feedback, and follow through on problems employees identify.
- Obtain answers to employees' questions even if they seem unimportant to you.

Communicate Upward

How can you overcome the normal tendency to minimize bad news and exaggerate good news when communicating to your superiors? Here are some guidelines:

- Give both sides of the story.
- Initiate requests for help; do not wait until problems become major.
- Use "I" messages.
- Observe the chain of command; do not bypass your superior and go to his or her manager without approval.

Communicating Within Informal Groups

When people are brought together to perform a task, they quickly assemble themselves into informal groups. These groups develop as a result of people's social needs to interact, gain acceptance, and belong.

Informal groups are developed on every level: clerical, technical, supervisory, managerial, and executive. Individuals in every group compare ideas and values and almost subconsciously agree on group norms. *Norms* define how individuals are expected to behave in specific circumstances to be members of the group in good standing. For example, one group may have a norm of high productivity and cooperation. Another group may develop a norm that cooperation with management is discouraged. Norms are *enforced*; members are spoken to, teased, rebuked, and ostracized for violating norms.

Communicating With Peer Supervisors

Many decisions and changes in workflow and procedures require coordination among supervisors. The formal communication channel, which is primarily designed to carry information downward and upward, may not adequately meet this need for peer coordination. You should take the initiative for informing other supervisors and asking for their opinions and cooperation. You should also see yourself as a member of an informal group of peer supervisors and identify the norms and expectations of that group.

Communicating With Employee Groups

A supervisor should not be a member of an employee group because that group's norms will often conflict with what is expected of the supervisor. A supervisor who tries to "be one of the gang" can only maintain membership in the employee group if he or she conforms to the group's norms. Nonetheless, supervisors can and should communicate frequently with employee groups in an informal way. Here are some guidelines:

1. Identify the informal leader or leaders of the group.
2. Gain cooperation of the informal leaders by keeping them informed and asking for their ideas and recommendations.
3. Allow an appropriate level of group interaction during work.
4. Encourage members of the group to help one another in work-related tasks.
5. Resolve conflicts that affect unit performance. This may mean getting the two conflicting parties together to talk through their problem and agree on a solution.
6. Represent the group to higher management if problems or complaints are justified and only higher management can take action.

WRITTEN COMMUNICATION

A written message, whether it is an e-mail letter, a memo, or a report, is one-way communication with no feedback or, at best, delayed feedback from the reader. Consequently, the message needs to be logical, clear, and concise. The reader does not have the opportunity to raise questions or seek clarification.

The first step in writing is to define your objective. What do you want the reader to do or know as a result of reading your communication? Do you want your reader to: approve a recommendation? take some action as a result of the letter or memo? change his or her mind? learn some piece of information?

Write your objective down. Rewrite it. Make it as clear, concise, and specific as you can. Next, jot down key points that support your objective. As you think of key points, keep your reader in mind. What previous knowledge does the reader have of the situation you are describing? This will determine how much detail you will need to give. What is the reader's attitude toward the subject?

An objective and key points provide a guide for you to follow as you write. You may spend as much time thinking and preparing as you will writing, but the quality of the written piece will be much better than if you tried to organize and write at the same time.

Develop a Business Style

All writers have a writing style. All good writers have a writing style that is clear and concise. For business writing, the best style is a standard, journalistic style. You are not aware of any change in style from one newspaper article to another, but the writing is clear and concise. Following are some of the basic guidelines for good, journalistic writing.

Use the Active Voice

You put action into your writing by using the active voice. The active voice asserts that the subject of the sentence performs the action that the verb denotes. In contrast, the passive voice shows that the subject of the sentence does not act but is the object or the receiver of the action. The following example shows the difference that the active voice makes:

I threw the ball. (Active voice)

The ball was thrown by me. (Passive voice)

The active voice sounds more forceful and certain than passive voice. For example:

The marketing department developed a new, exciting product. (Active voice)

A new, exciting product was developed. (Passive voice)

The passive voice frequently fails to identify who did what, so the reader may be confused. For example:

The decision was made not to expand the homeowners market this year. (Passive voice)

But who made the decision? This bit of information may be very important for the reader to know to interpret the message properly. Let's change the preceding sentence from passive to active voice:

The marketing manager has decided not to expand the homeowners market this year. (Active voice)

Occasional use of the passive voice is acceptable, especially when the person or thing doing the acting is not important or relevant. Nonetheless, a good rule of thumb is to use the active voice.

Use Simple, Concrete Words

Some business people believe they would improve their written communications if they could improve their vocabulary. People who have extensive vocabularies find that when they write, they cannot use some of their favorite words because many readers will not know the meaning of these words. Using "big" words that may be misinterpreted does not make for good writing. Some business people not only try to use big words, but worse, they also convert simple words into complex words or constructions. For example, they write "utilize" for "use." Following is an example of a memo written to impress rather than to communicate:

TO: Staff

FROM: Supervisor

It is now time to pay attention to a more extensive effort. You are all aware that we have seen some detrimental increases in expenditures. To whatever extent it is humanly possible, we should all try to minimize expenditures and simultaneously work more efficiently. Let us utilize every means available to minimize expenditures and increase office efficiency.

I hope we can all achieve some measure of success to report at our next staff meeting.

What does the preceding memo say? Following is an example of a memo written to communicate the same message:

TO: Staff

FROM: Supervisor

In the last six months, our agency expenses rose ten percent over budget. In the next six months, we need to cut expenses and increase production.

Please review all budgeted expenses under your control for the remainder of the year and identify items that could be eliminated or reduced. Also identify ways we could change workflow or procedures to reduce the time it takes us to rate the policies in the unit.

Be prepared to report your recommendations at our next staff meeting on December 3 at 8:30 A.M.

The second memo is more concrete, uses simpler words, and lets the reader know what's expected.

Omit Needless Words and Phrases

First drafts are usually littered with extra words and phrases that can confuse the reader. Almost any written material can be reduced by omitting needless words and phrases. For example, replace "at the present time" with "now" or "in spite of the fact that" with "although."

Use Short Sentences

Long, compound, complex sentences can get writers into grammatical difficulties. Any compound sentence can be separated into at least two simple sentences. Complex sentences usually contain clauses beginning with such words as since, although, or because.

If you add a few phrases beginning with who, which, or that to the compound, complex sentence, the probability of confusing your reader increases. For example:

> The producers not meeting their expected sales quotas means that the agency will have reduced revenues, and this, in turn, affects our operating expenses, which continue to rise, resulting in a loss of $5,000 for the year.

Let's restructure this sentence into one simple and one compound sentence:

> We will have a $5,000 loss this year for two reasons. The producers did not meet their expected sales quotas, and our operating expenses continued to rise.

When you reread your first draft, look for long sentences. Restructure them up and see if the message is not clearer. Complex ideas do not require complex-compound sentence structures.

Use Short Paragraphs

Journalistic style requires short paragraphs. You should evaluate the sequence of sentences and paragraphs in your writing. Reread your copy. Analyze the flow of ideas.

Write Short Letters, E-Mails, and Memos

Written documents that are only one page long are more likely to be read than longer ones. Try to set two pages as a maximum length for most business writing. Many people read only the beginning and the end of documents, which can lead to serious miscommunication. Avoid using one written piece to explain two or more subjects.

Select the Right Tone and Format

When we talk, we are aware that *how* we say something is as important as what we say. When we write, we should be equally concerned about how we phrase our ideas, what words we select, and how the written message may sound to the reader. How we write our ideas is referred to as *tone*. How we sequence our ideas is referred to as *format*.

Dashing off a memo, an e-mail, or a letter without considering tone or format can get the best writers into difficulty.

Writers need to think carefully about the tone of their messages and to reread, edit, and proofread all written communications before sending them.

Because writing is one-way communication, we frequently use the directive communication techniques of telling or explaining, identifying problems and difficulties, and making recommendations or requests.

Telling and Explaining

We usually write memos to unit members, managers, or supervisors to keep them informed, to document critical decisions or meetings, or to give status reports. The amount of internal mail may equal the amount of external mail in some organizations. Supervisors also may send letters to outsiders to keep them informed.

The key to telling or explaining is to strike a balance between overloading the reader with excessive information and being certain you give the reader enough information. This is another reason the concise, easy-to-read journalistic style is adaptable to most business communications. If you can present all of the important information in a concise way, your reader will be grateful and you will have communicated effectively.

Format, or the sequence of ideas, is important for telling and explaining. If you are telling good news, then put the good news in the first paragraph. Give supporting details in the body, and then close by referring to the good news again or to its benefit to the reader or to you. If the news you are telling is bad, do not start the letter or memo with the bad news unless you want to shock the reader. Give an introduction to the bad news in the first paragraph.

Identifying Problems or Disagreeing

Memos and letters that identify problems are probably the most difficult ones to write. You want the reader to get your message, but you do not want to create problems by offending him or her. Delete harsh phrases and words. Reread the memo or letter or ask a friend to read it. Aim for a neutral rather than a negative tone. For example, instead of writing, "You claim that you sent the letter to me on February 15," rephrase your letter to read, "I received your letter on March 8."

Remember that the techniques you use for identifying problems and disagreeing in face-to-face communications are equally applicable when writing.

Recommending and Requesting

An internal memo to management making a recommendation and an external letter requesting that the reader take some action are two common business communications. Following is a good format for making a recommendation:

1. Identify the problem in the first few paragraphs.
2. Recommend your solution.
3. List benefits of your solution.

You might title each of these sections for easy identification.

SUMMARY

Your effectiveness as a supervisor depends greatly on your ability to communicate effectively with your employees and with managers. This chapter examines oral and written communications, the two ways in which you will communicate.

Any oral message you send consists of two parts: word content and nonverbal instructions about how to interpret the content. These instructions may come from your tone of voice, your eye contact, or your body language. When your nonverbal message repeats, complements, or accents your verbal message, the listener feels confident that he or she understands. When your nonverbal message appears to contradict your verbal message, the listener will generally give greater credibility to the nonverbal message. Because contradiction is a source of mistrust and misunderstanding, you should be aware of the nonverbal messages you are sending and receiving.

Communicating is a two-way process, which means it requires a speaker (to send the message) and a listener (to receive the message). Although you listen to others every day, you may not always "hear" them. Being a good listener usually requires a conscious effort and the deliberate exercise of listening skills. This chapter discussed several problems that interfere with listening and described the process of active listening to help eliminate such problems.

Nondirective responses and directive communication techniques were also discussed. Nondirective responses encourage others to express and to understand ideas and feelings that may be suppressed and include asking open-ended questions, asking for clarification, perception checking, reflecting, empathizing, and silence or nonverbal responses. Directive communication techniques provide the other person with information you think he or she needs or wants to know and includes telling and explaining, identifying problems or disagreeing, and influencing.

Your supervisory role is likely to require you to conduct meetings. This chapter discussed the four most common meetings supervisors call: downward communication, information-gathering, problem-solving, and attitude-adjustment. Also discussed were meeting effectiveness, your role as the meeting leader, making presentations, evaluating meetings, and common problems in conducting meetings.

Without adequate organizational communications, departments, units, and individuals will not achieve a sense of teamwork and implementing change will be difficult. Screening of information and organizational distance often present barriers to organizational communications. Using two-way communication, encouraging employees to provide information, and communicating effectively to upper-level management can help to overcome such barriers.

Besides communicating orally with employees and managers, you are likely to communicate with them in writing. Because written messages are one-way communications and offer little or no opportunity for feedback, they need to be logical, clear, and concise. Suggestions for developing a business style, writing short letters and memos, and selecting the right tone and format were given.

Chapter 8

Fair Employment Laws and Regulations, I

Fair employment has become one of the most important areas of human resource management. The reason is the widespread recognition that all individuals should have the right to employment based on their own abilities. Numerous laws and regulations regarding fair employment practices have been enacted by federal, state, and local governments. The overall purpose of fair employment laws and regulations is to give every individual equality of opportunity in employment and to prevent discriminatory employment practices based on race, religion, national origin, sex, age, or handicap.

Because they spend the greatest amount of time with employees, supervisors have greater exposure to potential fair employment problems than do other managers. Supervisors have major personnel responsibilities, including interviewing and selection, training, performance evaluation, promotions, salary administration, discipline, and termination. These and other personnel responsibilities of the supervisor are subject to a variety of employment laws and regulations. Failure to give adequate attention to fair employment practices and other employment laws and rules can be very costly to the company and to the supervisor. Supervisors can be personally charged with fair employment violations, and your company may be subjected to fines and other damages.

As a supervisor, you are involved in nearly every aspect of personnel policy, and your actions help to prevent fair employment violations. You have a responsibility to abide by fair employment laws and regulations in all of your relationships with employees. The objectives of this chapter and Chapter 9 are to help you fulfill your fair employment responsibilities. This chapter provides introductory material and reviews the principal fair employment law, Title VII of the Civil Rights Act of 1964, and an important amendment, the Pregnancy Discrimination Act. Also included is a description of the Equal Employment Opportunity Commission established by Title VII and the Americans With Disabilities Act of 1990. Chapter 9 reviews other important fair employment laws and regulations, including those applicable to federal contractors, and summarizes the prohibitions of all of the fair employment laws and regulations.

Employment law is a highly specialized field within the legal profession. Should a question or problem arise, the organization will normally seek the advice of law firms that specialize in employment law.

As supervisor, you should immediately report all fair employment questions and incidents to your manager, since alleged fair employment violations trigger legal or quasi-legal proceedings. Your attempts to handle a fair employment complaint on your own might make a problem worse.

FAIR EMPLOYMENT

Historically, employment opportunities in the United States have not been distributed equally among all groups. Even today, unemployment among blacks and many other minorities is higher than among whites, and the average wages of minority group members and women are less than those of white men. More women occupy low-paying clerical and service jobs than men, who predominate in the professions and management.

The causes of such unequal treatment are complex. Some of it is undoubtedly the result of past conscious discrimination. Much of it is the result of employment patterns based on stereotyped assumptions, which, in turn, also have their roots in past conscious discrimination.

Most employment discrimination today is probably unintentional. It occurs not because employment opportunities are consciously closed to certain groups, but because not enough action is taken to make the opportunities available to those groups.

Government involvement in fair employment has developed over a long period of time. Early limitations on employer freedom of action came with the Railway Labor Act of 1926 and the National Labor Relations Act of 1935, both of which prohibited employers from discriminating against applicants and employees because of union or organizing activities. The Fair Labor Standards Act of 1938 regulated minimum wages, overtime pay, and child labor. In the 1940s, states and municipalities began to pass fair employment laws.

Presidential Executive Orders in the 1950s and 1960s restricted racial discrimination by government employers and employers under contract with the government. In 1963 Congress passed the first United States employment discrimination law, the Equal Pay Act, to prohibit pay discrimination between male and female employees.

Not until 1964, however, with the passage of the Civil Rights Act, did Congress provide for federal legal enforcement for equal employment opportunity. Title VII of this act is the keystone of fair employment legislation. It prohibits employers from discriminating because of race, color, sex, religion, or national origin in all practices, privileges, and conditions of employment. After this, other laws were enacted to prohibit discrimination on the basis of age, handicap, and pregnancy.

Federal and State Fair Employment Laws and Regulations

Every property-liability insurance company is subject to fair employment laws and regulations. Federal laws apply to all firms engaged in interstate commerce, which would include all insurance companies, brokers, or agencies except those that operate solely within a single state. State and local laws and regulations apply to all firms operating within the boundaries of these governmental bodies.

Laws are enacted by legislative bodies such as the United States Congress or a state legislature. Laws also establish regulatory agencies. A regulation is a rule of a regulatory agency such as the Equal Employment Opportunity Commission or a state fair employment commission. Regulations issued by these agencies generally have the same force and effect as laws.

The principal federal fair employment law and other major employment laws follow:

- The Equal Pay Act of 1963, prohibiting sex discrimination in the payment of wages
- The Civil Rights Act of 1964, prohibiting discrimination on the basis of race, color, sex, national origin, and religion
- The Age Discrimination in Employment Act of 1967, prohibiting age discrimination
- The Rehabilitation Act of 1973, prohibiting discrimination against individuals with a handicap
- The Pregnancy Discrimination Act of 1978, prohibiting pregnancy discrimination
- The Immigration Reform and Control Act of 1986, prohibiting the hiring of aliens not authorized to work in the United States and prohibiting discrimination on the basis of citizenship or national origin
- The Americans with Disabilities Act of 1990, prohibiting discrimination against those with a mental or physical disability who are capable of performing the essential functions of a job

In addition, several presidential executive orders applying to federal government contractors and subcontractors also prohibit discrimination on the basis of race, color, religion, national origin, sex, age, and handicap. These laws and orders are described more fully in this chapter and in the next.

Definitions

Many specialized terms are used to discuss or describe the subject of fair employment. You must understand the more commonly used terms if you are to comply with fair employment laws and regulations.

Fair Employment Practice

For our purposes, fair employment practice is a legal term referring to an employment-related action or a decision of an employer that does not violate a law or a regulation prohibiting certain kinds of discrimination. The most common prohibitions are employment-related decisions based on race, religion, sex, national origin, age, and handicap. This definition excludes actions that may be viewed as unfair in an everyday sense but that do not violate a fair employment practice law or regulation. For example, giving a relative a promotion over other, more qualified employees may be viewed as unfair, but it is not illegal; therefore, for our purposes, it is not an unfair employment practice.

Equal Employment Opportunity

This term is frequently used as a synonym for fair employment practice. Equal Employment Opportunity (EEO) means all individuals are given the same opportunities regardless of their race, sex, age, religion, national origin, or other such classification.

Equal Employment Opportunity Commission

The Equal Employment Opportunity Commission (EEOC) is a federal agency responsible for enforcing the federal fair employment laws. The EEOC has the power to institute lawsuits, to issue guidelines and regulations that have the force of law, to render decisions, and to assist employees who believe they have been discriminated against and employers who desire help in complying with the law.

Civil Rights

This term has an application beyond matters of employment. In this text, we are concerned only with its meaning in respect to employment as it refers to the rights of applicants and employees to be treated by the employer without regard to race, sex, color, religion, age, or other prohibited classifications. Civil rights laws establish and define these rights.

Protected Groups

Protected groups are legally identified groups that are specifically protected— by laws—against employment discrimination. Examples are women, people older than forty, and blacks. These groups are also sometimes referred to as a "protected class" or a "minority group."

Discrimination

You should be able to distinguish between legal and illegal discrimination. Illegal discrimination refers to employment practices that violate the prohibitions contained in fair employment laws or regulations. An example of illegal discrimination is the treatment of individuals or groups based on race, sex, religion, or similar classifications. A legal discrimination is an employment decision that is based on a factor that is not prohibited by law or regulation, such as an ability or a skill necessary to perform the job.

Intent Versus Effect

Discriminatory intent refers to an action or a practice in which there is a conscious motivation or attempt to discriminate. Discriminatory effect refers to actions that result in discrimination but that were not motivated by an attempt to discriminate; for example, a vision requirement for pilots that screens out many older people. In most cases, unless the employer can establish a clear business necessity, an employment practice is illegal if its effect discriminates against a protected group, regardless of the employer's intent.

Prima Facie

Prima facie discrimination is a legal term referring to evidence that does not have to be proven because it is accepted at face value. For example, a *prima facie* case of racial discrimination can be established by a minority person who was rejected for a position for which he or she was qualified. The complainant does not have to prove discrimination. To defend itself, the employer must show that it did not discriminate illegally, which it could do by showing that it hired a more qualified applicant for the job.

Bona Fide Occupational Qualification (BFOQ)

A BFOQ is a genuine and legitimate requirement necessary for the performance of a job. An employer may discriminate legally against protected groups if a BFOQ can be established, but this exception is limited to a very narrow area by the courts. A male sex requirement for modeling men's clothing is an example of a BFOQ. Few, if any, BFOQs apply to the insurance business.

Class Action

A class action is a lawsuit filed by one or a few persons on behalf of all persons affected by the discriminatory practices of an employer. The complainant represents all members of a class of people.

Conciliation

Conciliation refers to informal procedures the EEOC and other fair employment enforcement agencies use to eliminate employer discrimination and to obtain remedies for affected persons. Conciliation efforts rely on persuasion and take place outside the courtroom. An employer is not required to comply with requests made during the conciliation process.

Injunction

An injunction in a fair employment case is a court order directing an employer to stop certain discriminatory practices or to perform a specific act, such as employing or promoting an individual.

Liquidated Damages

Liquidated damages are a penalty that employers who willfully discriminate may be required to pay to an individual who was discriminated against. Liquidated damages are generally equal to and in addition to the amount of any back pay due to the individual.

Affirmative Action

Affirmative action is positive action by an employer to eliminate and prevent illegal employment discrimination. An affirmative action program involves the development of specific action plans to provide protected groups with equal employment opportunities. This contrasts with a passive approach in which the employer does not discriminate but takes no active steps to guarantee equal employment opportunities.

Supervisory Responsibility

As a supervisor, your job involves many different personnel functions, such as recruiting, selection, salary administration, performance evaluation, promotions, transfers, training, coaching, discipline, and termination. Because every one of these personnel responsibilities is affected by fair employment laws, you must know how to avoid unlawful discriminatory practices when you supervise.

When a supervisor violates a fair employment law, the company bears the responsibility. The supervisor plays an essential role—perhaps the most important in the organization—in ensuring that the company's policies and practices are applied without illegal discrimination. The supervisor's responsibility is to carry out, on a daily basis, the company's commitment to equal employment opportunity.

Knowledge

To meet these responsibilities, you must possess a thorough understanding of federal, state, and local fair employment laws and regulations. To prevent violations, you need to know the specific kinds of discrimination that must be avoided in your day-to-day dealings with job applicants and subordinates. You must also be completely familiar with your company's fair employment policy.

Self-Awareness

As a supervisor, you must be aware of your prejudices and dislikes. Although no one can completely eliminate prejudices, recognition is the first step in preventing them from interfering with your supervisory responsibilities. Be willing to confront yourself and to make an objective assessment of the validity of your beliefs.

Active Support

Supervise your unit in compliance with fair employment laws and the company's fair employment policy. Establish and maintain a fair employment environment within your unit and communicate to all employees your support for equal employment opportunity.

TITLE VII - CIVIL RIGHTS ACT OF 1964

Title VII of the Civil Rights Act of 1964 is the most comprehensive of the fair employment laws. It covers almost all forms of discrimination in the employment and pre-employment process, including classifying employees or applicants on a basis that could adversely affect their status. It also created the Equal Employment Opportunity Commission (EEOC), the federal government's principal enforcement agency for fair employment practices.

Coverage and Application

Title VII covers employers, employment agencies, and labor organizations. Under the act, an employer is any company engaged in interstate commerce with fifteen or more employees. Most insurance organizations are therefore covered by the act. All individuals are protected, but only from certain types of discrimination.

Illegal Discrimination

Discrimination on the basis of race, color, sex, national origin, or religion is prohibited in practically every area of employment. This includes but is not limited to the following situations:

* Recruiting
* Selection
* Employment advertising
* Training programs
* Performance evaluations
* Promotions
* Compensation and benefits
* Terminations and layoffs
* Counseling and discipline
* Hours and breaks
* Special privileges

Age discrimination is not covered in Title VII. Some have argued that Congress intended to cover it but human error occurred in the final drafting of the act.

Bases of Discrimination

Title VII does not require that you hire someone who is incapable of doing the job. You can discriminate on the basis of ability, but you cannot discriminate on the basis of race, color, sex, national origin, or religion. The wording of these provisions is shown in the accompanying box.

Title VII—Civil Rights Act of 1964

It shall be an unlawful employment practice for an employer:

(1) to fail or refuse to hire or to discharge any individual, or otherwise to discriminate against any individual with respect to his compensation, terms, conditions, or privileges of employment, because of such individual's race, color, religion, sex, or national origin: or

(2) to limit, segregate, or classify his employees or applicants for employment in any way which would deprive or tend to deprive any individual of employment opportunities or otherwise adversely affect the status of an employee, because of such individual's race, color, religion, sex, or national origin.

Race and Color

Although the express legislative purpose of Title VII was to increase employment opportunities for blacks, the act protects all racial groups, including whites. Discrimination because of the race of an individual's spouse or friends is also considered racial discrimination because race is playing a role in the employment decision. Examples of racial discrimination are paying minorities less than non-minorities for the same work and preventing them from advancing.

Using tests that screen out a higher percentage of minorities will be considered discriminatory unless the employer can clearly demonstrate that the tests measure factors that are essential to performance on the job. Recruitment and selection methods that eliminate most minority candidates are generally considered discriminatory.

Employment practices that limit, segregate, or classify employees on the basis of race are specifically prohibited by Title VII. Physical segregation of employees by race with respect to company facilities or activities is a clear violation of Title VII.

Sometimes racial discrimination arises from employment practices that in themselves are not motivated by discrimination but that substantially restrict the employment opportunities of a particular race. Unless justified by business necessity, these practices can have a discriminatory effect and are therefore in violation of Title VII. In other words, you can be charged with illegal discrimination if your employment action has a discriminatory effect regardless of whether it was your *intention* to discriminate.

Sex

Many believe that stereotypes about women and traditional concepts regarding job roles may be the biggest obstacle to compliance with the ban on sex discrimination in Title VII. Title VII requires that both men and women be treated the same. Beliefs about "male jobs" and "female jobs" are not valid unless you can prove that sex is a bona fide occupational qualification (genuine job-related requirement) for the job. The courts have interpreted sex to refer to gender only and not to sexual preference, so discrimination against homosexuals is not prohibited by the act.

Sexual Harassment

Much, but not all, sexual harassment is prohibited sex discrimination. It is generally considered sexual discrimination under Title VII for a supervisor to request sexual favors from an employee as a term or condition of employment. It is sex discrimination because the sexual requests are employment conditions that are being imposed on persons of the opposite sex. The factors that determine the existence of sex discrimination are (1) whether the request is or is perceived as a condition or term of employment and (2) whether the person making the request is acting with the actual or implied authority of the employer. Supervisors, as representatives of the company, are generally considered to be acting within the scope of their authority in employment matters. They deal with the daily terms and conditions of employment and are capable of giving an unfavorable performance evaluation, withholding promotions or salary increases, giving preferential hours, and other special treatment or favors. There are two types of sexual harassment: *quid pro quo* and hostile environment harassment.

Quid Pro Quo Harassment

Quid pro quo harassment is defined as a member of management using his or her authority to solicit sexual favors in exchange for promised continued employment, pay, or future career opportunities. The phrase *quid pro quo* is Latin and means "something in return."

Here is an example of *quid pro quo* harassment:

> Tom is Jean's supervisor. Tom is very attracted to Jean, but Jean makes it clear to Tom that she is not interested in him. Tom knows that getting promoted is important to Jean. He tells Jean, "I will make sure you are taken care of at ABC if you will spend some of your time taking care of me." Jean listens to this offer and decides that the career opportunity outweighs her personal feelings for Tom. She and Tom begin a relationship that includes sexual relations. Their relationship continues for a few months, but Jean realizes that she does not want to continue it further. Jean has met and fallen in love with someone else. She tells Tom that their relationship is over.

> A month later, Tom completes a periodic appraisal of employee performance. Tom appraises Jean overall as a "4" performer, the second lowest level on the company's five-point scale, and comments very negatively on Jean's interpersonal skills. Her previous overall appraisal was "2," the second highest level on the company's scale.

Jean believes that she is a victim of sexual harassment. Is Jean's complaint valid? If so, what constituted the sexual harassment?

Jean's complaint is valid. Tom should be fired. In getting Jean to enter a sexual relationship, Tom clearly engaged in *quid pro quo* harassment; that is, he used his management position, and the authority it gave him, to make decisions about Jean's employment and to bargain for sexual favors from her. The sexual relationship was not welcomed by Jean. The fact that she entered into it voluntarily does not make a difference. The link to job success was what caused her to agree to the relationship with Tom. Tom has engaged in a very serious kind of sexual harassment, one for which ABC, despite its policy against sexual harassment and its lack of knowledge of Tom's improprieties, could be held liable.

Hostile Environment Harassment

The second type of sexual harassment is hostile environment. This occurs when employee conduct produces an offensive work environment. The key to this type of sexual harassment is that the employee who is bothered by the offensive environment *tells* the other employee(s) of the discomfort it is causing. If the conduct is continued, it constitutes sexual harassment.

Decide whether or not this example describes hostile environment harassment:

> Louis and Helen both work at a product lab in the Midwest as pricers, responsible for different product families. They work for the same manager, whose secretary arranged travel together for both of them to a product-pricing training program in White Plains. Their tickets placed them next to each other on the plane to New York. The plane was filled to capacity. Louis thought he would entertain Helen with his complete repertoire of X-rated jokes. Helen encouraged him to stop, but he continued to barrage her with vulgarity. She was so upset that she refused to share a rental car and took a limo without him. She also rearranged her return reservations so that she would not be traveling back to the lab with Louis. When they got back to the lab, she complained to their manager that she had been subjected to sexual harassment by Louis and that ABC should do something to make sure Louis never did such a thing again to her or anyone else. The manager told Helen that he empathized with her but that he could do nothing about it because the incident occurred on Sunday evening, which is nonwork time, and on a plane, which is off company premises. Helen then issued a complaint stating that she suffered sexual harassment and that the manager should have disciplined Louis for harassing her.

Is Helen's complaint valid? What if the secretary had arranged for different flights for these two employees, but Helen decided to switch her flights to those Louis had because she wanted company on the trip? What if Louis had behaved like a gentleman on the trip to White Plains and on the weekend after the training program, Helen and Louis decided to rent a car and drive up to Cape Cod for a couple of days to sightsee before returning home, and Louis told offensive jokes in the car on the way to Cape Cod?

Unwelcome vulgar jokes can constitute sexual harassment when told in the work environment. Helen made it very clear that the jokes were unwelcome, yet Louis continued to subject her to them. Although it is not clear that a court would hold ABC liable for such conduct occurring on a commercial flight, Louis should be counseled for harassment of Helen since the company had placed them together on the flight. If the jokes had been told in the car en route to a weekend of voluntarily arranged sightseeing, the company is not likely to be held responsible. Even if the vulgar jokes had been told on the flight, but with the joint travel arrangements having been made voluntarily by the two employees, it is still not clear whether discipline would be called for. This case illustrates the range of situational factors that may be considered in determining whether harassment occurred.

EEOC Guidelines

The EEOC has issued sex discrimination guidelines that advise employers of attitudes or activities that may lead to or even constitute sex discrimination. These include the following:

- Assumptions about the employment characteristics of women that differ from men. For example, refusing to hire a young woman into a training program on the grounds that she might get married and quit or refusing to hire a woman with children on the grounds that she will have a higher absentee record because of sick children.

- Beliefs about the relative mental or physical abilities of the sexes, such as women are less aggressive, men are more analytical, or men are more mechanically inclined or able to perform certain physical activities.

- Using the gender preferences of customers, other employees, or yourself as a basis for employment decisions. Examples are hiring only male underwriters because agents prefer them or male supervisors because employees say they will not work for a female boss.

Specific Standards

Certain standards, if applied by the company, must be uniformly applied to all employees. Areas in which sex and other kinds of discrimination frequently take place relate to marriage, children, grooming, rules, and discipline.

Marital Status   Refusal to hire individuals based on their marital status—if the rule is applied to one sex only—is illegal. Refusal to hire either married or single people if the rule applies both to men and women in the job category is permissible. Instructing employees of one sex that they can't marry but not telling the other sex the same thing is discriminatory.

Children   Rules regarding employees with children are illegal if applied to only one sex. Any such rule must be uniformly applied to both sexes.

Grooming   Grooming standards that are not imposed on one sex may not be imposed on the other. The standards do not have to be identical for both sexes, but they need to be comparable. The standards for one sex must not be more stringent than for the other sex. For example, a dress code would be questionable if it defined standards related to clothing and jewelry for women but did not cover these items for men.

Rules and Discipline

Different rules or discipline cannot be based on the employee's sex or race. For example, you cannot refuse to hire or discharge a man because of a heterosexual affair or a child born outside a marriage unless the same rule applies to women.

National Origin

"National origin" refers to the country in which a person was born or from which his or her ancestors came. To discriminate on the basis of national origin is illegal, but Title VII does not prohibit discrimination based on citizenship. You do not have to hire an alien, but you cannot discriminate on the basis of different origins or citizenships. For example, you cannot refuse to accept Hispanic aliens while accepting white European aliens. An employer that refuses to hire aliens should make sure it is not a pretext for discrimination on the basis of national origin. (A later act, the Immigration Reform Control Act of 1986, also prohibits discrimination on the basis of citizenship or national origin.)

Religion

Religion is defined as a deeply and sincerely held conviction. It includes all aspects of religious observance and practice and includes the beliefs of atheists. It is not limited to the traditional denominations such as Protestant, Catholic, or Jewish.

The law says that "religion includes all aspects of religious observance and practice." It may therefore be a discriminatory practice not to hire a person because of the clothing or appearance required by the religion or to refuse to hire or to fire an individual who refuses to work on his or her particular Sabbath or religious holiday.

The employer is expected to make a *reasonable accommodation* of the religious observances of employees. Title VII permits religious discrimination if the employer "is unable to reasonably accommodate an employee's religious observance or practice without undue hardship on the conduct of the employer's business." The company can apply a rule that infringes upon a particular religious observance or practice only if it can show that it cannot reasonably accommodate the religious practice without "undue hardship."

Problems typically arise when an employee has a religious objection to working on his or her Sabbath or religious holiday. If the work to be performed on these days is not essential to the company's business, the employee must be granted leave. The accommodation problem arises when someone else must be assigned to perform the work. The Supreme Court ruled that seniority rights of other employees take precedence over the protection of religious beliefs, and the employer does not have to incur more than minimal expenses for such things as overtime and loss of efficiency. The employer is not required to assign objecting senior employees to work for an absent junior employee or to pay any significant premium overtime pay.

Discriminatory Practices

In addition to prohibiting discrimination in hiring and promotion, Title VII prohibits more subtle forms of discriminatory action.

Segregation

Clear discrimination exists when employees are segregated into particular jobs, work classifications, or work areas based on sex, race, national origin, or any of the other illegal bases of discrimination. This is true even if there is no difference in working conditions, opportunities, compensation, or any other terms or conditions of employment. *Separate* is not considered *equal* because segregation tends to deprive individuals of employment opportunities by placing them in positions of psychological inferiority. This, in turn, can undermine their morale.

Compensation

Compensation in the form of salary or benefits is an important term of employment. As such, compensation discrimination, or awarding salary or benefits on the basis of sex, race, color, religion, or national origin, is prohibited by Title VII. This overlaps with the prohibitions on pay discrimination between the sexes in the Equal Pay Act.

Harassment

Harassment refers to situations in which the employer or its officials deliberately make an employee's working conditions so intolerable that the employee is forced into an involuntary termination, or what is referred to as a *constructive discharge*. Harassment also includes situations in which the company knows that the employee is being harassed by fellow employees and fails to take prompt and forceful corrective action. This is known as a hostile environment. Some examples of illegal harassment are the following: racial, ethnic, or sexist remarks or jokes; excessive supervision of members of a protected class; or requiring employees to participate in religious exercises.

Employment Advertisements

Title VII prohibits companies from using advertisements relating to employment that indicate "any preference, limitation, specification, or discrimination based on race, color, religion, sex, or national origin." This prohibition also applies to notices of job openings that may be posted on a company bulletin board or placed in an internal newsletter. Implicit or explicit references to age, sex, race, national origin, or marital status should be avoided in all employment-related notices or advertisements.

Retaliation

It is an unlawful employment practice for an employer to discriminate against an individual who files charges with the EEOC, who participates in an EEOC investigation or court proceeding, or who opposes practices that are made unlawful by Title VII. The purpose of this provision is to protect employees who exercise their rights under the act. Examples of such discrimination include taking any of the following actions because an applicant was previously involved in a discrimination complaint: refusing to hire an applicant, withholding a salary increase or privileges, discharging an employee, placing an employee on probation, or making things more difficult for that employee.

Bona Fide Occupational Qualifications (BFOQ)

Title VII provides that discrimination is permitted when sex, religion, or national origin is a "bona fide occupational qualification reasonably necessary to the normal operation of that particular business." However, there are severe limits on the use of a BFOQ as a reason for discrimination against a protected group. A BFOQ does not apply to race or color, nor to discrimination between categories of current employees; it applies only to hiring and referrals. Establishing a BFOQ is difficult and is generally limited to situations in which sex or national origin is inherently part of the qualification for the job, such as acting in a theatrical performance.

Statistical evidence about the ability of many members of a class of people cannot be used to establish a BFOQ. For example, if a job requires lifting heavy mail sacks, you cannot exclude women because statistics show that many women cannot lift heavy weights. The requirement in this example would be that all or nearly all women must be unable to perform the job. In reality, many women can lift heavy loads.

To establish a BFOQ, an employer must establish the following:

- All or nearly all of the class of people cannot perform the duties of the job safely and efficiently.
- The occupational qualification must be reasonably necessary to the essence of the company's business. Customer preference does not satisfy this requirement. For this reason, airlines cannot limit cabin-attendant jobs to women, and insurance companies cannot limit marketing-representative jobs to men.

Conceiving of any job in an insurance company or agency for which a valid BFOQ could be established is difficult.

Title VII Complaints

Individuals who believe they have been discriminated against cannot simply file a Title VII lawsuit. They must follow a complicated set of federal and state administrative procedures before they can file a suit.

Title VII Enforcement and Remedies

The agency created to enforce Title VII is the Equal Employment Opportunity Commission (EEOC). Before victims of discrimination can sue on their own behalf, they must use the EEOC and the appropriate state or local fair employment agency complaint-resolution process. A more complete description of the structure and functions of the EEOC is provided later in this chapter.

Filing a Complaint

Discrimination victims must file a written charge under oath with the EEOC. Ordinarily, the charges must be filed within 180 days of the discriminatory act. Somewhat different procedures apply if the state or local jurisdiction also has its own fair employment laws.

The EEOC has exclusive jurisdiction over the complaint for 180 days. This means that the individual cannot act on his or her own, such as by filing an individual lawsuit. The EEOC will attempt to eliminate the discrimination by persuasion. If this does not produce acceptable results, the EEOC can file a lawsuit in a federal district court. If the EEOC elects not to sue, the charging party will be notified of his or her right to file a private lawsuit in federal court. This notice is referred to as a "right to sue" letter. Receipt of a "right to sue" letter is necessary before an individual can sue the employer. If the EEOC finds that there is no reasonable cause to believe that a discrimination violation has occurred and decides not to take action, an individual can still file a private suit after receiving the "right to sue" letter.

Remedies

A number of remedies are available to the courts when a company has been found to have engaged in an unlawful employment practice. The courts may order the company to refrain from engaging in the unlawful practices and can order affirmative action, which may include reinstatement or hiring of employees, back pay, or other remedies. A general rule is that the injured party is to be placed, as nearly as possible, in the situation he or she would have occupied if the discrimination had not occurred. To accomplish this, courts have ordered back pay, front pay (wages people would have received in a position that was illegally denied to them), retroactive seniority, hiring and job-referral quotas and goals, and the reimbursement of attorneys' fees and court costs. Punitive and similar damages are not available under Title VII. The employer can also recover attorneys' fees from the complaining party if a discrimination claim is frivolous, unreasonable, or groundless.

Class Action Suits

Class action suits have been used widely in connection with Title VII. A class action suit is a suit in which the charging party sues as a representative of all members of a class of people. For example, if a black employee believes that he or she and all other black employees are being discriminated against, that employee can file charges on behalf of all black employees. If discrimination is proved, damages or remedies will be awarded to the entire class of affected persons. Successful class action suits are generally very costly to the employer. Most of the multi-million dollar discrimination awards have resulted from class action suits.

Proving Violations

The charging party in a Title VII suit initially has only to establish a prima facie case of racial discrimination. *Prima facie* means that facts are assumed to be true unless proven false by other evidence. A *prima facie* case is established by showing the following:

- The complainant was a member of a protected class.
- The complainant applied for a job opening for which he or she was qualified and was denied the job.
- The company continued to seek applicants.

You can see that it is easy to file a charge. It is also easy for the company to answer the charge.

Defending Complaints

To defend a Title VII charge, the company has only to show a legitimate nondiscriminatory reason for its action. Examples of this are job qualifications, seniority, performance on an objective test, past work record, or experience. The company is, however, required to present factual evidence in support of its actions. If an employee is fired for absenteeism or substandard performance, for example, the employer must present some evidence that retained employees do not have similar work records. Similarly, if an applicant is not hired because he or she lacked a particular qualification, the employer must demonstrate that the individual who was hired *did* possess that qualification.

Title VII provides an employer with three defenses it can use to disprove charges of discrimination. First, it is not an unlawful employment practice to apply different terms or conditions of employment according to a bona fide seniority or merit system if these differences are not the result of an intention to discriminate on an illegal basis. For example, it is legal to lay off employees with the least seniority first or to pay more productive employees higher salaries if these actions are part of established policy. Second, a company can rely on a professionally developed, validated ability test if the test is not designed, intended, or used to discriminate on an illegal basis. Third, discrimination is permitted when sex, religion, or national origin is a "bona fide occupational qualification reasonably necessary to the normal operation of that particular business"—the BFOQ defense previously mentioned.

THE PREGNANCY DISCRIMINATION ACT OF 1978

The Pregnancy Discrimination Act is of special importance to insurance supervisors because a large percentage of insurance employees are young women. Before 1978, the Supreme Court had ruled that an employer's failure to include pregnancy in a package of employee disability benefits was not sex discrimination under Title VII. In response to this decision, Congress passed the Pregnancy Discrimination Act, amending the Civil Rights Act of 1964 (Title VII). The amendment requires that pregnant women or women with related medical conditions must be treated on the same basis as other job applicants and employees—that is, on the basis of their ability or inability to perform the job.

Coverage and Application

The Pregnancy Discrimination Act applies to all employers covered by Title VII. As stated in the discussion of Title VII, this includes most insurance organizations. The pertinent provision of the act follows:

> The terms "because of sex" or "on the basis of sex" include, but are not limited to, because of or on the basis of pregnancy, childbirth, or related medical conditions; and women affected by pregnancy, childbirth, or related medical conditions shall be treated the same for all employment-related purposes, including receipt of benefits under fringe benefit programs, as other persons not so affected but similar in their ability or inability to work.

Pregnancy Discrimination

Pregnancy discrimination is differential treatment of employees because they are pregnant. A pregnant employee must be treated on the same basis as all other employees—that is, on the basis of ability or inability to perform the job.

An employer cannot discharge, deny seniority to, refuse to hire or promote, exclude from training, or require a mandatory leave of an employee just because she is pregnant. In addition, pregnancy cannot be excluded from medical or disability benefit plans. There is no requirement for a company to provide medical or disability benefit plans, but if it does provide such plans, pregnancy and related conditions must be treated on the same basis as all other disabilities.

The act does not require that pregnant employees receive any special treatment but requires that they be treated on the same basis as an employee with any other disability. A practical guide is to ask yourself if you would make the same decision if the employee had any other disability. For example, to require a pregnant employee to take a leave of absence because she could not perform all aspects of the job is illegal if you allowed employees recovering from heart attacks or other illnesses to remain on the job without having to perform the entire job.

Supervisors should not automatically equate pregnancy with disability, although the condition will inevitably result in a disability or the inability to perform the job for a period of time. Pregnant employees should be treated as capable of performing the job until they demonstrate they can no longer do so. They should then be given the same rights, privileges, and treatment as any other temporarily disabled employee. If your employer has a salary continuance plan based on seniority for employees on sick leave, it must also grant salary continuance based on seniority to an employee disabled by pregnancy. Similarly, although there is no legal requirement to make reasonable accommodation for a pregnant employee who cannot perform her work in the normal manner, if a company ordinarily makes a reasonable accommodation for employees with other disabilities, then it must do the same for pregnant employees. As is generally true throughout the field of fair employment, consistency of treatment is a paramount consideration.

Employers can require pregnant employees to furnish medical certification of disability or recovery, providing they have the same requirement for employees with other kinds of disabilities. Under this act, employers do not have to provide female employees with a leave of absence for child-rearing purposes after recovery from pregnancy.

Exceptions and Enforcement

Since the Pregnancy Discrimination Act is an amendment to Title VII, the provisions of Title VII with respect to exceptions and enforcement apply equally to the Pregnancy Discrimination Act. Any BFOQ reasonably necessary to the normal operation of the business or other legitimate, nondiscriminatory reasons can be used by the company to support its actions. Employees claiming pregnancy discrimination must file a charge with the EEOC, which has exclusive jurisdiction over it for 180 days. The EEOC will first attempt conciliation and then has the option to file a complaint in federal district court or to issue a "right to sue" letter. After receiving a "right to sue" letter, the employee is free to file a private suit in the federal district court. Remedies for pregnancy discrimination violations are the same as for Title VII violations.

THE EQUAL EMPLOYMENT OPPORTUNITY COMMISSION

The Equal Employment Opportunity Commission (EEOC) was created by Title VII of the Civil Rights Act of 1964 to enforce the provisions of this act. Initially, the EEOC had weak enforcement powers and was not effective. Over the years, however, it has been strengthened considerably with significant enforcement powers, and the scope of its activities has been expanded to the enforcement of other fair employment laws. An understanding of the EEOC is important because it is the most active and visible federal fair employment agency. The likelihood is high that if you are ever confronted with a fair employment practice complaint, the EEOC will become involved.

Structure and Purpose

The EEOC is headed by five commissioners who are appointed by the President. The agency operates through district offices and sub-offices located in major cities throughout the United States. The broad purpose of the agency is the prevention of unlawful employment practices. It has administrative and enforcement powers with respect to Title VII, the Equal Pay Act, and the Age Discrimination in Employment Act.

Powers and Authority

The principal roles of the EEOC are interpretation, investigation, conciliation, enforcement, and education.

Interpretation

The EEOC has the power to issue regulations and interpretive guidelines. Formal regulations issued by the EEOC have the full force of law. Guidelines do not have the strength of formal regulations but do indicate the policy of the commission and are entitled to "great deference" by the courts. Interpretations include important definitions, procedures, and standards and methods of compliance.

Investigation

The commission is empowered and obligated to receive charges of discrimination and to conduct investigations to determine whether there is reasonable cause to believe the charges are true. It has the authority to subpoena and examine any evidence relevant to the charges and to require the attendance and questioning of witnesses.

Conciliation

The commission has the authority to attempt to eliminate discrimination through conciliation, persuasion, negotiation, and other informal methods.

Enforcement

The agency can file suit in the federal district courts to obtain compliance. The suits may be filed in its own name or on behalf of individuals alleging discrimination. The agency does not have to wait for a complaint to be filed but can initiate court action whenever it encounters a "pattern or practice" of discrimination.

Education

The agency has the responsibility of providing employers charged with discrimination the necessary technical assistance to comply with the law, to study and report on relevant matters, and to conduct other educational and promotional activities in the interest of fair employment.

Complaint Handling Procedures

Complaints may be initiated by individuals who believe themselves to be the victims of discrimination or by the EEOC itself. A complaint is made by filing a charge in writing through the mail or in person at any office of the EEOC. The complaint must be made in writing and under oath and filed within 180 days of the alleged discriminatory act. The EEOC must give notice of the charge to the accused employer within ten days of filing.

Deferral Agencies

If the location where the violation occurs has a state or local fair employment commission or agency with adequate powers to deal with the problem, the EEOC must refrain from processing the complaint for sixty days to allow the local agency an opportunity to resolve the complaint. During this period, the state or local agency has exclusive jurisdiction over the complaint. The EEOC defers jurisdiction to these state or local agencies, known as *deferral agencies*. When such an agency exists, the notice requirement for filing a complaint with the EEOC is within 300 days of the discriminatory act or within thirty days of the notice of termination of the state or local proceedings. The shorter of the two periods applies. A state or local agency's failing to take action does not prevent the EEOC from taking its own action.

Conciliation

Neither an individual nor the EEOC has the power to sue an employer under Title VII unless there has first been an attempt at conciliation. The law requires that if there is a probable cause that the discrimination exists, the EEOC must first attempt to eliminate the discrimination by informal methods of conference, conciliation, and persuasion. The employer does not have to agree to any conciliation agreement, and it is not binding unless the employer's consent is obtained.

The EEOC generally issues a conciliation agreement and includes any remedies it believes are necessary to correct the discrimination. For its part, the EEOC agrees not to process the charge further. The conciliation agreement also notes that no judgment on the merits of the charge has been made.

Lawsuits

After the failure of conciliation, the EEOC can institute a lawsuit in a federal district court. If the EEOC decides not to sue and terminates its action because it believes it has no jurisdiction or there is no reasonable cause to believe the discrimination occurred, it will issue a "right to sue" letter to the individual who filed the complaint. Only after individuals have received a "right to sue" letter can they file a private discrimination suit. At this point, individuals can sue even if the EEOC decides that no reasonable cause exists to believe discrimination occurred. In any event, if the EEOC has not disposed of a charge within 180 days after receiving it, individuals have the right to request and receive a "right to sue" letter.

THE AMERICANS WITH DISABILITIES ACT

Act Requirements

The Americans with Disabilities Act of 1990 (ADA), which applies to all employers with fifteen or more employees, prohibits employers from making decisions based solely on the basis of a disability. Generally, the act specifies that an employer may not reach any employment decision solely on the basis of an individual's disability. An employer may not classify an applicant or an employee because of his or her disability in a way that adversely affects his or her opportunities or job status. Employers may not discriminate against qualified disabled applicants or employees in recruitment, hiring, promotion, training, layoffs, pay, leave policies, position assignments, or benefits.

The key to complying with the act is to define job positions clearly. The act does not require an employer to hire a disabled person who is unable to perform the work required by a position. The key word is *required*, as the act forces an employer to look at a job position and determine:

- What the components of the job position are
- What elements are essential to the employee's performance
- What components of the job position are convenient but not essential to be performed

Once these three factors have been determined, the act requires that as long as an individual with a disability is otherwise qualified for a position, with or without reasonable accommodation, the employer cannot make an adverse employment decision based solely on the disability.

Disability

What is a disability? The act defines a disability as "a physical or mental impairment that substantially limits one or more of the major life activities, a record of having such an impairment, or being regarded as having such an impairment." The act does not list what should be considered an impairment; rather, the guidelines are established by the EEOC and the courts. These guidelines cover not only what most people would consider to be disabilities, but also the perception of an impairment. For example, a person with a facial disfigurement cannot be denied a job position as a receptionist if he or she is capable of performing the essential functions of the position. Likewise, courts have held that an obese person cannot be denied a position he or she is capable of performing on the grounds that the long-term prognosis is not good for the person's health.

Accommodation vs. Burden

The act requires employers to make reasonable accommodations for employees. Reasonable accommodation involves the removal of unnecessary restrictions or barriers.

For example, your company has an opening for an underwriting position in one of its regional offices. Among the requirements are five years of underwriting experience and the ability to travel to the home office every other month. An applicant applies who is wheelchair bound. If that applicant is in every way qualified, the company cannot discriminate against the person because he or she would require modification of the work space to accommodate the wheelchair. Additionally, if the person needed additional time to travel to the home office because of the disability, that extra time would also be considered a reasonable accommodation.

What is considered an undue burden is less clear. The EEOC (and the courts) would make a final determination based on the individual situation. An example given by the EEOC is that a small day-care center might be required to spend a nominal amount to equip a telephone for use by a secretary with impaired hearing, while a large school district might be required to supply a teacher's aide to a blind teacher.

Employer Restrictions

Employers must also work to eliminate discrimination in the way in which they ask questions of potential employees. Saying "Do you have any physical disabilities that would prevent you from doing the job?" is inappropriate. You may say, however, that "This position requires you to be on the job five days a week for eight hours a day. In addition, you will occasionally be required to lift 100-pound boxes. Can you meet this requirement?"

Overall, the act is designed to promote the employment of people who are capable of performing a job but who might otherwise be overlooked because of a disability.

SUMMARY

In recent years, fair employment has become one of the most important areas of human resource management. Numerous laws and regulations regarding fair employment practices have been enacted by federal, state, and local governments to give every individual equality of opportunity in employment and to prevent discriminatory practices because of race, color, religion, national origin, sex, age, or handicap.

Because you as a supervisor will spend the greatest amount of time with employees, you will have greater exposure to potential fair employment problems than do other managers. As a supervisor, your job involves many different personnel functions, such as recruiting, selection, salary administration, performance evaluation, promotions, transfers, training, coaching, discipline, and termination. Because all of your personnel responsibilities are subject to a variety of employment laws and regulations, you must know how to avoid unlawful discriminatory practices.

This chapter is intended to help you fulfill your fair employment responsibilities by providing introductory material and by reviewing the principal fair employment law, Title VII of the Civil Rights Act of 1964; an important amendment, the Pregnancy Discrimination Act of 1978; and the Americans with Disabilities Act of 1990. Also discussed was the Equal Employment Opportunity Commission (EEOC) established by Title VII. Chapter 9 will review other important fair employment laws and regulations, including those pertaining to equal pay, age discrimination, and federal contractors.

As a supervisor, you have a responsibility to know what these laws prohibit and whom they protect and to supervise your unit accordingly. In the event that a fair employment question or incident should arise, you should report it to your manager, since alleged fair employment violations usually trigger legal or quasi-legal proceedings. Remember, you do not have to hire people because they are in a protected group, but you do have to give all applicants and employees the full opportunity to be judged and treated on the basis of their abilities.

Chapter 9

Fair Employment Laws and Regulations, II

The preceding chapter introduced some of the fair employment laws and regulations for which you, as supervisor, are responsible for knowing about and complying with.

This chapter covers four other important federal laws—the Equal Pay Act, the Age Discrimination in Employment Act, the Immigration Reform and Control Act, and the Family and Medical Leave Act of 1993—as well as laws and regulations that apply to firms doing business with the federal government. Brief comments are made regarding state and local fair employment requirements. At the end of the chapter, the requirements of all of the fair employment laws and regulations are summarized in terms of what you can and cannot do as a supervisor and remain in compliance with the law.

THE EQUAL PAY ACT OF 1963

The Equal Pay Act of 1963 is an amendment to the Fair Labor Standards Act of 1938. The act prohibits discrimination on the basis of sex in determining the rates of pay to employees.

Coverage of the Act

The Equal Pay Act applies to all employers not specifically exempted who are engaged in interstate commerce. In addition to private business firms, the Equal Pay Act applies to labor unions and to employees of federal, state, and local governments.

The key provisions of the Equal Pay Act read as follows:

> No employer having employees subject to any provisions of this section shall discriminate, within any establishment in which such employees are employed, between employees on the basis of sex, by paying wages to employees in such establishment at a rate less than the rate at which he pays wages to employees of the opposite sex in such establishment for equal work on jobs the performance of which requires equal skill, effort, and responsibility and which are performed under similar working conditions.

The Equal Pay Act applies to virtually every insurance organization, including many insurance agencies because they are engaged in interstate commerce. A small company, brokerage firm, or agency with one covered property or exposure insured in another state is engaged in interstate commerce and is therefore subject to the provisions of the Equal Pay Act.

Sex Discrimination Prohibited

The act prohibits an employer from paying wages to employees of one sex at a rate less than that paid to employees of the opposite sex if they are working on jobs that require equal skill, effort, and responsibility and are performed under similar working conditions. The term "wages" includes overtime pay and contributions for benefits. Although not designed to protect men, the act protects men as well as women.

Exceptions are allowed if the payment is made under a seniority system, a merit system, a system that measures earnings by quantity or quality production, or a differential based on any factor other than sex.

The Equal Pay for Equal Work Standard

The concept of equal work is defined by the Equal Pay Act as jobs requiring "equal skill, effort, responsibilities" that are "performed under similar working conditions." These are the four separate elements that must be independently satisfied for work to be considered *equal*.

Jobs do not need to be identical to be equal, only *substantially equal*. In determining whether jobs are substantially equal, courts look at the duties actually being performed on the job, not at job classifications, job descriptions, or job titles.

Equal Skill

Skill includes the experience, training, education, and ability required to perform job duties. The key question is not whether an individual possesses additional training or skills, but whether his or her job requires or uses those additional skills. If tasks requiring additional skills consume an insignificant portion of an employee's time, they do not justify a pay differential. In addition, "equal skill" does not mean identical skill. If the jobs are basically of the same character, the degree of skill can be compared.

Equal Effort

Effort is the physical or mental exertion needed to perform a job. Greater physical or mental exertion justifies more pay. To justify greater pay, it must be shown that there are additional duties that meet the following criteria:

- The additional duties are performed by those receiving the extra pay.
- The additional duties are a significant, regular, and recurring part of the job.
- The additional duties are substantial.
- The additional duties are commensurate with the pay differential.

- The additional duties are available on a nondiscriminatory basis.

If women are not given an opportunity to perform the additional duties that command greater pay, the employer cannot justify unequal pay.

Equal Responsibility

Responsibility is the degree of accountability required in the performance of the job. Responsibility relates to the importance of the job and to the economic or social consequences that result from the employee's actions and decisions. The potential consequences of errors or mistakes and the extent to which the job is supervised should also be considered in comparing responsibility.

Similar Working Conditions

Working conditions refers to the physical surroundings and the hazards of a job. An unpleasant working environment or outdoor work could justify greater pay than a more pleasing work environment or indoor work.

The Protected Class

The protected class under the Equal Pay Act is all employees, male and female. Most pay discrimination cases involve women receiving less pay than men, and the Act was designed to correct and prevent this kind of inequality. Nevertheless, it also protects male employees who are paid less than female employees in the same job. Unlike the Fair Labor Standards Act, which exempts certain administrative and professional positions from overtime pay and other requirements, the protection of the Equal Pay Act extends to executive, administrative, professional, and outside sales employees. No category of employee is excluded from the coverage of the Equal Pay Act, but the Act does have a provision for excluding small retail and certain other businesses.

Violations

Employees with equal-pay complaints may file suit in a state or federal court or may file a complaint with the Equal Employment Opportunity Commission (EEOC), which can then go to court on behalf of the employee. An employee who is successful in proving pay discrimination can receive the amount of underpaid wages as unpaid back wages and sometimes an additional equivalent amount as "liquidated damages." Reasonable attorney fees and court costs may also be recovered by the employee. The act states that an employer who is in violation of the act cannot reduce the wage rate of any employee in order to comply with the act. For example, an employer who is paying men at a higher rate in violation of the act cannot reduce their pay to obtain equality. The pay of the women must be increased in such instances.

Retaliation

The Equal Pay Act prohibits retaliation against an employee who makes an equal-pay complaint even if the charge proves to be groundless. This provision is contained in most fair employment laws in order to protect employees' rights to pursue legal action if they think they have been discriminated against.

Defenses

The law provides the employer with certain reasons or defenses that can be used to justify pay differences. An employer can legally maintain a pay difference for equal work if the difference is based on a seniority system, a merit system, or a production evaluation system (quality or quantity) that is uniformly applied to men and women. In addition, a pay difference can be justified if it is based on any factor other than sex. A shift differential under which night work is paid at a higher rate than day work or a *bona fide* training program that warrants higher pay on completion are examples of such factors. These defenses are not valid, however, if one sex is excluded from participating.

THE AGE DISCRIMINATION IN EMPLOYMENT ACT OF 1967 (ADEA)

Age discrimination has been receiving increasing attention in recent years. The number of age discrimination complaints has risen dramatically for a number of reasons. The elimination of the mandatory retirement age, in most instances, has changed the work situation. A company might have previously elected to "carry" older, poorly performing employees because they had only a few years left before retirement. Now, however, with the work life potentially lengthened, many companies are no longer willing to continue this practice. The proportion of older persons in the work force is increasing, and many employees want to work longer for a variety of reasons, including fulfillment of economic and social needs.

The stated purpose of the ADEA is "to promote the employment of older persons based on their ability rather than age; to prohibit arbitrary age discrimination in employment; to help employers and workers find ways of meeting problems arising from the impact of age unemployment."

Coverage of the Act

The ADEA prohibits discrimination by employers against older workers. It is similar, but not identical, to Title VII in coverage and exemptions. It applies to all firms engaged in interstate commerce if they have twenty or more employees. This would include most insurance companies, brokerage firms, and large agencies. The act contains the following provision:

It shall be unlawful for an employer—

(1) to fail or refuse to hire or to discharge any individual or otherwise discriminate against any individual with respect to his compensation, terms, conditions or privileges of employment because of such individual's age;

(2) to limit, segregate, or classify his employees in any way which would deprive or tend to deprive any individual of employment opportunities or otherwise adversely affect the status of an employee, because of such individual's age; or

(3) to reduce the wage rate of any employee in order to comply with this chapter.

Except as permitted by the act, you cannot discriminate against an individual because of his or her age in hiring; firing; determining wages, benefits, hours, training, career development, vacation, or sick leave; or in any other terms or conditions of employment.

Employment Advertisements

The act prohibits any notices or advertisements relating to employment that indicate any preference, limitation, or discrimination based on age. Advertisements implying age with terms like "boys," "girls," "students," "recent graduates," and so on generally are illegal.

Retaliation

The ADEA prohibits retaliation on the same basis as Title VII. Employees cannot discriminate against individuals because they have opposed illegal age discrimination or because they have filed charges, testified, or participated in an age discrimination matter.

The Protected Class

The ADEA prohibits discrimination on the basis of age against individuals who have reached the age of forty or above. Although the act initially limited the upper age to sixty-five and then seventy, all upper limits have now been removed. An employer may not discriminate against anyone in the protected age group by giving more favorable treatment because of age to someone younger or older.

The act is not limited to protecting older employees from discrimination in favor of younger employees. If the victim of discrimination is older than forty, the age of the person favored is not relevant. Therefore, a violation occurs if you select, on the basis of age alone, a person aged sixty-five over one aged forty-five. The act also protects the forty-five-year-old against age discrimination. Your decision must be based on a factor other than age, such as ability or experience.

If a person favored is within the protected age group and the other person is outside the protected group, there is no illegal discrimination or protection under the act. You could select, on the basis of age alone, a person aged forty-seven over one aged thirty-five. Also permissible is having a minimum age requirement that is below forty because this would favor everyone in the protected group.

Exceptions and Exemptions

There are a number of exceptions and exemptions to the ADEA's prohibition against age discrimination.

Bona Fide Occupational Qualifications

Discrimination is not illegal if age is a bona fide occupational qualification (BFOQ); that is, a qualification that is reasonably necessary to the normal operation of the business. Examples are actors required for youthful roles or models for products aimed at the youth market. To establish a BFOQ, a company would also have to show that all or nearly all individuals within the protected class would be unable to perform the duties of the job. The cost of hiring, training, or retraining older workers is not an acceptable BFOQ defense. Even if many older persons might not qualify for a particular job, each person must be given an opportunity to qualify as an individual. There are few, if any, positions in the insurance business for which a BFOQ based on age could be established.

Factors Other Than Age

Reasonable factors other than age may be used to discriminate. The ADEA specifically states that it is not unlawful "to discharge or otherwise discipline an individual for good cause." You can discriminate on the basis of performance, experience, work record, and other reasonable non-age factors that are required for performance of the job. However, customer or co-worker preference for a person of a particular age is not an acceptable reason.

Seniority

The ADEA allows you to observe the terms of a bona fide seniority system, providing that doing so is not a deception to avoid the other provisions of the act.

Benefit Plans

Benefit plans cannot be used as an excuse to fail to hire any individual.

One intent of the ADEA was to allow employers to observe the terms of bona fide employee benefit plans, such as retirement, pension, or insurance plans, that are not deceptions to avoid the provisions of the act. This intent was thwarted by a 1989 Supreme Court decision that generally exempted employee benefit plans from the ADEA. Congress responded in 1990 by passing a law that amended the ADEA and thereby restored benefit protection to older employees. The 1990 law, the Older Workers Benefit Protection Act, requires employers to provide older employees with benefits that are at least equal to those provided to younger employees unless the employer can prove that the cost of providing a benefit is greater for an older employee than for a younger one.

Enforcement and Remedies

The ADEA can be enforced by aggrieved individuals or the EEOC, and a broad range of remedies is available to correct violations. Class actions are also permitted, but under ADEA, all members of the affected class must file their written consent with the court in order to be included in the suit. Although this limits the use of class action suits under the ADEA, they still can be quite substantial in cost.

Private Suits

Victims of age discrimination can bring suit in state or federal court; however, they must first file a complaint with the EEOC within 180 days of the date the discrimination took place. The filing of the complaint with the EEOC must be in writing and need only name the defendant and give a general description of the discrimination.

EEOC

Procedures for handling age discrimination complaints under the ADEA differ somewhat from Title VII procedures. The EEOC can sue on behalf of individuals who suffer age discrimination, but it must first attempt voluntary conciliation or persuasion. If the EEOC institutes a suit before the individual files suit, then the individual cannot bring his or her own private suit. The EEOC can also obtain court orders (injunctions) directing the employer not to commit future violations of the act.

Remedies

A victim of age discrimination can recover unpaid compensation and reasonable attorney fees. If the discrimination was willful and intentional, the employer may also have to pay liquidated damages (an additional penalty payment) equal to the unpaid compensation. The ADEA also gives the courts authority to grant judgments requiring employment, reinstatement, and promotion. In order to comply with the requirements of the ADEA, an employer cannot reduce the wages or benefits of favored employees. It must increase the benefits of the injured employee.

ADEA Complaints

An ADEA complainant must only establish a *prima facie* case of discrimination. This can be accomplished by showing that he or she was a member of the protected class and was rejected for a position for which he or she was qualified. It is not necessary to prove that the employer had a motive to discriminate because of age. The employer must then provide evidence that its behavior was nondiscriminatory.

The legal rules for age discrimination cases are not as well established as for Title VII, and some differences in application have occurred. For example, some courts have held that it is necessary for the complainant to show that a person outside the protected group was selected for a position for which he or she was denied, while other courts have not made this requirement. Some courts also have required that in order to establish a case, the employee must show that the employer was aware of his or her age.

Defending Complaints

To defend itself successfully in an age discrimination case, the employer must show good cause for its action. This can be done by showing that its action was based on reasonable factors other than age or on one of the exceptions permitted by the law. Some examples of these permitted exceptions are termination or discipline for insubordination, absenteeism, or inability to perform and failure to hire because no position was open or the applicant was unqualified. Objective evidence is not always required. The courts have accepted subjective performance evaluations of employees as the basis for termination decisions. In hiring decisions, however, subjective evaluations will generally not be accepted.

LAWS AND REGULATIONS APPLICABLE TO FEDERAL CONTRACTORS

The fair employment laws we have discussed so far have been laws passed by Congress. A more limited group of employers must be concerned about additional fair employment requirements. These employers are federal contractors and, as such, are subject to Presidential Executive Orders and the Rehabilitation Act of 1973.

Federal Contractors

A federal contractor is a business that has entered into a contract to provide goods or services to the federal government. Direct subcontractors of these businesses are also considered to be federal contractors. Fair employment requirements are a part of the contract between the government and the contractor, and therefore the basis for the firm's legal obligation is contractual. The firm has voluntarily entered into a government contract in which it agrees to observe certain employment practices. The contractor is free to decide not to enter the contract, but once it does, it is bound to comply with its terms. Since the duty of nondiscrimination is contractual, the remedies for noncomplying contractors are also contractual and consist mainly of cancellation of the contract and court orders requiring the contractor to perform whatever work was contracted for.

Insurance Companies as Federal Contractors

You might wonder why it is important for insurance companies to know about requirements for federal contractors. Many insurance companies are federal contractors or subcontractors. Many life insurance companies, either directly or as reinsurers, participate in writing group life insurance plans for federal government employees and servicepeople and thus are federal contractors. Many of these companies are affiliated with, or are the parent companies of, other property and liability companies. Other insurance companies are federal contractors because they lease office space to the federal government or because they provide property and liability insurance to federal agencies or to other agencies and organizations receiving federal funds.

Many states and localities have established local requirements patterned after the federal ones. Having a thorough understanding of federal-contractor requirements will help you to understand and comply with the particular fair employment requirements in your locality.

Affirmative Action

Federal contractors cannot satisfy their fair employment obligations with a passive approach to equal employment. They are generally required to prepare an *affirmative-action program*, which is a written plan containing the following elements:

1. Identification of any areas in which protected classes are underused
2. A corrective action plan to remedy the situation; that is, to achieve full use of protected class members
3. Specific goals and timetables for achieving the plan

Affirmative-action plans also generally include auditing and reporting procedures and requirements that the contractor take whatever steps are necessary to ensure that protected class members receive equal opportunity. These requirements might call for the contractor to advertise that it has a policy of equal employment opportunity, participate in various training programs, or contact and work with community service organizations and programs.

Office of Federal Contract Compliance Programs (OFCCP)

The Office of Federal Contract Compliance Programs (OFCCP) is a federal agency within the Department of Labor. The OFCCP is responsible for the enforcement of Presidential Executive Orders and the Rehabilitation Act of 1973.

Handling Complaints

Discrimination complaints against a federal contractor can be initiated by the individual discriminated against or by the OFCCP. An employee of a government contractor does not have a private right of action against his or her employer and therefore cannot individually sue for violation of obligations imposed contractually by the government. Only the OFCCP can bring a suit against an employer. Complaint-handling by the OFCCP is similar to the EEOC's handling of Title VII complaints, as discussed in Chapter 8. Informal means of obtaining compliance are attempted first. In addition, the OFCCP will generally refer complaints that are also violations of Title VII to the EEOC for handling under the act rather than process the complaint under its authority.

Contractors with more than fifteen employees must file an annual compliance report with the OFCCP and are subject to compliance reviews. The OFCCP periodically conducts compliance reviews (audits) to determine whether the contractor is meeting its nondiscrimination and affirmative-action obligations. An OFCCP audit includes the following activities:

1. A desk audit, or the submission and review of the affirmative-action plan and supporting data to the OFCCP
2. An on-site visit of the contractor's premises and a review of additional information, including interviews with employees
3. A deficiency notice and, if necessary, a conciliation agreement

Presidential Executive Order 11246

An Executive Order is an order issued by the President of the United States. The principal executive order requiring fair employment practices is Executive Order 11246, signed in 1965. This order affects all companies holding government contracts in excess of $10,000. It requires that a nondiscrimination clause be included in all contracts with the government. Other fair employment executive orders have been issued; however, these amended Executive Order 11246. When we refer to Executive Order 11246, these amendments are included.

Nondiscrimination Requirements

The prohibitions on discrimination in Executive Order 11246 are similar to the discrimination prohibitions in Title VII and other fair employment laws. For some employers, this means overlapping or duplicate fair employment requirements. Some companies not engaged in interstate commerce may not be subject to Title VII but may be subject to Executive Order 11246 because they have a government contract. An example of this might be a small, local insurance firm that leases office space to the government for a post office facility.

A company that is subject to Title VII and is a government contractor cannot assume it is fulfilling its government-contractor obligations merely by complying with Title VII. Executive Order 11246 involves additional requirements, such as compliance reviews and formal affirmative-action plans.

In electing to do business with the government, a contractor agrees to comply with the nondiscriminatory provisions of the contract *during* the performance of the contract. The requirements of Executive Order 11246 are not limited to the work performed under the specific contract with the government. During the term of the contract, they apply to *all* work performed at any facility, including those that have nothing to do with the specific government contract. All operations of the contractor are covered.

Executive Order 11246 requires that certain provisions be included in every government contract in excess of $10,000. A key provision of Executive Order 11246 is the following:

During the performance of this contract, the contractor agrees as follows:

(1) The contractor will not discriminate against any employee or applicant for employment because of race, color, creed, or national origin. The contractor will take affirmative action to insure that applicants are employed, and that employees are treated during employment, without regard to their race, creed, color, or national origin. Such action shall include, but shall not be limited to, the following: employment, upgrading, demotion, or transfer; recruitment or recruitment advertising; layoffs or termination; rates of pay or other forms of compensation; and selection for training, including apprenticeship.

Later amendments added prohibitions against sex, age, and handicap discrimination.

In addition to nondiscrimination on the basis of race, color, religion, sex, national origin, age, and physical handicap, a federal contractor agrees to do the following:

- Include a policy statement of nondiscrimination in all employment advertisements
- Comply with all of the requirements of Executive Order 11246 and with the rules and regulations of the Secretary of Labor
- Furnish all information required under the regulations
- Include in every subcontract or purchase order a provision similar to Executive Order 11246

A government contractor agrees to comply with the rules and regulations promulgated by the Secretary of Labor. In some cases, these go beyond the requirements of Title VII. An important example is an OFCCP regulation that requires federal-contractor employers to grant leaves of absence to women after childbirth even if the employer has no general leave policy. Title VII does not clearly require this.

Affirmative-Action Requirements

Executive Order 11246 requires the contractor to take affirmative action. This means that the contractor will not passively administer a nondiscriminatory employment program. Active steps must be taken to ensure "full and equal employment." As discussed in the previous section, an affirmative-action program includes identifying any areas where protected classes are underused, developing a corrective plan including goals and timetables, auditing, and reporting to determine whether the company is meeting its goals. The OFCCP has issued regulations that define the specific contents and method to be used in developing an acceptable affirmative-action program. A contractor's compliance with the program is judged not only by whether the goals have been achieved but also by whether the contractor has made a "good faith effort" to reach its goals. Contractors subject to Executive Order 11246 are required to have a written affirmative-action plan if they meet the criteria for number of employees and contract amount.

Compliance Reviews

Contractors that are required to have a written affirmative-action plan must file an annual compliance report with the OFCCP. In addition, the OFCCP has an active compliance review program to determine whether contractors are meeting their obligations under the executive order. The OFCCP follows a standardized procedure to conduct compliance reviews. The first step is a desk audit of the contractor's affirmative-action program, followed by an on-site review at the contractor's facility to look into matters not fully addressed in the affirmative-action plan. If problems are discovered, the compliance officer will request that the contractor sign a written conciliation agreement, which specifies the corrective action to be taken by a specified date.

Enforcement and Penalties

Interpretation, administration, and enforcement of Executive Order 11246 are the responsibilities of the OFCCP. The OFCCP has the authority to issue rules and regulations relevant to Executive Order 11246 with which federal contractors must comply. To avoid duplication in fair employment compliance activities, the OFCCP coordinates its efforts with those of the EEOC. The OFCCP may, and usually does, refer Title VII individual complaints of discrimination to the EEOC for handling instead of handling them under the executive order.

Complaints

Complaints may be initiated by an individual who feels discriminated against, by the OFCCP as a result of a compliance review, or by an outside community or advocate-type agency. Complaints filed by individuals must be made in writing to the OFCCP within 180 days of the alleged violation. Class action complaints do not have to identify the individual(s) making the complaint. The OFCCP must first make every effort to eliminate the discrimination. If this fails, the OFCCP can issue an administrative order requiring the appropriate relief. Individuals do not have the right to sue on their own behalf.

Remedies and Penalties

If violations of Executive Order 11246 are found, the remedies are appropriate relief to overcome the discrimination, including back pay and retroactive seniority. Penalties for failure to correct the problem are suspension or termination of the contract and elimination or disqualification from future government contracts.

The Rehabilitation Act of 1973

The Rehabilitation Act of 1973 is designed to broaden employment opportunities for people who are handicapped. It imposes obligations on federal contractors as well as agencies of the federal government and programs receiving federal funding. Our discussion is limited to Section 503 of the

Rehabilitation Act, which applies to government contractors in a manner similar to Presidential Executive Orders. Section 503 places an affirmative-action obligation on federal contractors to hire and promote people with handicaps. This area is of special interest and application to insurance organizations because of the nature of insurance work. Insurance is a "knowledge" industry in which it is much easier to make a "reasonable accommodation" for a handicapped person than in manufacturing or service industries, which require greater use of manual or other physical skills.

The Rehabilitation Act applies to federal contractors and subcontractors with a contract of $2,500 or more and requires these employers to take affirmative action in the employment of individuals with handicaps. The act contains the following provision:

> Any contract in excess of $2,500 entered into by any Federal department or agency for the procurement of personal property and non-personal services (including construction) for the United States shall contain a provision requiring that, in employing persons to carry out such contracts, the party contracting with the United States shall take affirmative action to employ and advance in employment qualified handicapped individuals.

The Rehabilitation Act does not prohibit discrimination on the basis of handicap by federal contractors. Department of Labor regulations that implement the act require federal contractors not to discriminate against people with handicaps.

Affirmative-Action Plans

Contractors with fifty or more employees and a contract of $50,000 or more must have a written affirmative-action plan that includes steps to accommodate workers with disabilities. The affirmative-action plan does not have to go into as much detail as affirmative-action plans for Executive Order 11246. It concentrates more on what the contractor is doing to provide reasonable accommodations for handicapped persons.

Handicapped Individuals

A handicapped person is one who has a physical or mental impairment that substantially limits one or more major life activities, has a record of such impairment, or is regarded by others as having such impairment. Life activities include such things as walking, seeing, hearing, speaking, working, taking care of oneself, and performing manual tasks. A person is substantially limited if he or she has difficulty obtaining, retaining, or advancing in employment because of a physical or mental condition.

In addition to covering handicaps such as blindness, deafness, and missing limbs, the act covers diseases such as cancer, heart disease, epilepsy, and AIDS. It also covers learning disabilities, emotional disorders, mental retardation, and sometimes disfigurement or obesity. Alcohol abuse that prevents an individual from performing the duties of the job or that constitutes a threat to the property or safety of other people is excluded from the definition of handicap, although people who have successfully completed a substance-abuse program are protected under the ADA.

Reasonable Accommodation

Section 503 of the Rehabilitation Act does not use the term "reasonable accommodation." Regulations implementing the act define a handicapped individual as "one who is capable of performing a particular job with *reasonable accommodation* to his or her handicap." Some realignment of job duties to accommodate the handicapped individual can be required. For example, the responsibility for occasionally answering a telephone could be removed from a hearing-impaired individual and assigned to another person. Some accommodation could involve financial costs. For example, an employer might have to purchase telephone amplifiers for hearing-impaired employees or construct special ramps to accommodate wheelchairs. This contrasts with Title VII's requirement of reasonable accommodation for religious practices. The difference is that the employer voluntarily enters into the federal contract and thus agrees to these requirements. Nevertheless, large financial outlays or expensive realignments of work assignments would generally be considered unreasonable and would not be required under this act.

Enforcement and Penalties

Enforcement of the Rehabilitation Act is similar to that of Executive Orders. The OFCCP is the enforcement agency, and complaints are handled in a similar fashion to Executive Orders. An employee alleging discrimination may file a written complaint within 180 days of the alleged violation. Complaints are referred to the employer if the employer has an internal review procedure. If not resolved within sixty days of referral or if there is no internal review procedure, the OFCCP will investigate the complaint and attempt to secure compliance through conciliation. Individuals cannot bring private suit under Section 503.

Penalties available to the OFCCP are the withholding of payments on the contract, cancellation of the contract, or disqualification from future contracts. In addition, judicial enforcement of the affirmative action clause in the contract may be obtained by the OFCCP.

IMMIGRATION REFORM AND CONTROL ACT OF 1986

The Immigration Reform and Control Act of 1986 combines fair employment provisions with those that address other employment problems.

Employment of Aliens

The act prohibits employers from knowingly hiring, recruiting, or referring for work aliens who are not authorized to work in the United States and provides penalties for employers who violate this prohibition. Aliens may not be permitted to work in the United States because their immigration status does not allow them to work or because they entered the country illegally.

The act is addressed to the employer; it establishes a schedule of fines for the employer, not the illegal alien employee. It also makes special provisions for foreign agricultural workers and gives amnesty to certain undocumented aliens already in the country.

The act requires the employer to verify the citizenship of prospective employees. A new employee must attest in writing that he or she is a citizen or a permanent resident alien, or that he or she is otherwise legally authorized to work in the United States. The employer must retain this statement.

Discrimination Provisions

The Immigration Reform and Control Act of 1986 prohibits employment discrimination based on national origin or citizenship. It established a new enforcement position, the Special Counsel for Immigration-Related Unfair Employment Practices, in the Department of Justice. Employers with fifteen or more employees are already prohibited from discrimination on the basis of national origin by Title VII of the Civil Rights Act of 1964. Thus, the effects of the law are to add citizenship status discrimination to the list of illegal employment actions and to extend coverage to employers with four to fourteen employees.

STATE AND LOCAL FAIR EMPLOYMENT LAWS

Most states and many local governments have enacted broad fair employment laws with anti-discrimination provisions that parallel the federal laws. You should become completely familiar with the state and local laws that apply to your area.

Coverage and Application

State and local laws apply to employers within their political boundaries. Individual state and local laws would have to be consulted for exceptions and exemptions from the coverage of a particular law. Many of these laws go far beyond federal law and are much more complete. Some states have taken an extremely aggressive approach to expanding the coverage of fair employment requirements by law and interpretation. Most of the larger states, including New York, California, Illinois, and Michigan, fall into this category. State agencies and courts frequently rely on the federal rules and interpretations for guidance; however, they are not compelled to do this. Depending on the provisions of the particular law, the requirements may be more or less stringent than requirements under federal laws and regulations.

Prohibited Discrimination

State and local laws generally prohibit the same kinds of discrimination as do the federal laws, including race, religion, national origin, age, sex, and handicap. Some states go beyond these requirements and prohibit discrimination based on sexual preference and marital status. The definition of "handicap" is frequently expanded to include AIDS, alcoholism, and obesity. You must examine your state laws to familiarize yourself with such important differences.

Relationship to EEOC

Federal laws require that state and local procedures be followed before taking a discrimination case to the federal courts if the state and local agencies have the power to obtain relief for the complainant. State and local agencies are evaluated by the EEOC to determine whether they meet the requirements specified in the federal law. Agencies that meet the requirements are designated as Deferral Agencies, a list of which is published by the EEOC. These agencies have sixty days within which to take exclusive action on discrimination charges. Other state and local agencies that do not meet the requirements for Deferral Agencies in the federal law are referred to as Notice Agencies and, although not entitled to deferral by the EEOC, are generally notified of any discrimination charges filed with the EEOC.

SUMMARY OF FAIR EMPLOYMENT REQUIREMENTS

Let us now summarize the requirements of all of the fair employment laws and regulations we have covered.

Illegal Discrimination—What You Cannot Do

As a supervisor, you cannot treat employees differently or otherwise discriminate on the basis of age, race, citizenship, national origin, religion, sex, pregnancy, and in most cases, handicap or disability.

In addition to these legal requirements, your firm has its own requirements, often important to its survival. The insurance industry is extremely competitive today. News reports of mergers and acquisitions are commonplace, and experts predict that less competitive companies will go out of business or be acquired by more successful companies.

Productivity improvement is a vital concern of every insurance organization. Productivity improvement requires that supervisors base their personnel decisions on the willingness and ability of employees to perform the requirements of the job. This organizational requirement corresponds perfectly with the legal requirement not to discriminate. If you make decisions on the basis of ability, you will also comply with the legal requirement not to discriminate on the basis of personal characteristics that are unrelated to the job. See Exhibit 9-1 for a list of the forms of illegal discrimination.

Most discrimination is unintentional and indirect. For example, asking a female job applicant to explain what provisions she has made for child care is a subtle form of sex discrimination because this is not a question that would generally be asked of male applicants. It tends to eliminate female applicants from being selected if the interviewer is not satisfied that adequate child-care arrangements have been made to ensure regular work attendance. You must be aware of such subtle discrimination so that you can avoid it in your supervisory activities.

Exhibit 9-1

Forms of Illegal Discrimination

- Age
- Race
- Color
- National Origin
- Citizenship
- Religion

- Sex
- Pregnancy
- Handicap/Disability
- Retaliation
- Harassment

Age Discrimination

You may not discriminate against individuals who are forty or older. You would practice discrimination not only by giving preferential treatment to those who are younger than age forty but also by preferring one group within the protected age category over other groups in that category. Firing a sixty-five-year-old employee on the basis of age and replacing him or her with a forty-year-old employee still constitutes age discrimination.

Race and Color Discrimination

The term "race" is subject to varying interpretations that may differ from the meaning of the term in everyday language. Such distinctions are not important because regardless of the definition, employment discrimination based on race or color is not allowed. Race and color categories include people with black, brown, red, or white skin, or Asians, Indians, Hispanics, and so on. For administrative purposes, the EEOC and the OFCCP group minority individuals in the following general categories:

- Black
- Asian/Pacific Islander
- American Indian or Alaskan Native
- Hispanic

The term "minority employee," however, can be misleading because in a given situation, a white person might be a minority person. The point is that all persons are equally protected from discrimination.

National Origin and Citizenship Discrimination

You cannot discriminate against individuals because of place of origin. Whether the persons or their parents were born or raised in Italy, Mexico, Czechoslovakia, China, Nigeria, Indonesia, or anywhere else is irrelevant. National-origin protection also applies to individuals who are married to persons of a specific national origin or who are members of, or associated with, organizations or institutions identified with a particular national origin.

You cannot discriminate on the basis of citizenship, although you must comply with the law that aliens be authorized to work in the United States.

Religious Discrimination

You may not discriminate against an individual because of religion. Protected individuals may be Catholic, Mormon, Protestant, Jewish, Black Muslim, or Jehovah's Witnesses, or they may believe in any other faith if it is a sincerely held religious belief or conviction. The law requires that reasonable accommodation be made to religious requirements with respect to work days and times. This means that employers must grant unpaid time off for religious observances in many situations. Also protected are individuals with no religious beliefs, such as atheists.

Sex Discrimination

You must grant women and men equal opportunity and treatment. This is a particularly troublesome area because of the stereotypes many people hold about what women can and should do. These stereotypes can permeate the thinking of even the most conscientious supervisor. The insurance business is basically a knowledge industry, and intellectual capacity and motivation are not higher in one sex than in the other.

Pregnancy Discrimination

Pregnancy discrimination is a form of sex discrimination against women. Pregnant employees must be treated the same as any other employee. When pregnancy results in a condition of disability or the inability to perform the job, women must be treated the same as any other disabled employee. Just as the law requires employers to be "color blind," it requires them to be "pregnancy blind." This includes making reasonable accommodations for a pregnant employee on the same basis as for any other disabled employee.

Pregnancy should be viewed as consisting of two stages. The first stage is when the pregnant employee is not disabled and is fully performing the job or most of the job. Some accommodation may be necessary, such as not requiring the employee to lift heavy cartons. This is no different than if an employee recently suffered a severe backstrain and is not required to do any incidental heavy lifting.

The second phase of the pregnancy is the disabled stage. This occurs late in the pregnancy when the employee can no longer perform the job. At this point, the employee should be treated the same as any other employee who is unable to work because of a disability such as a heart attack or hospitalization for an operation. The trick here is to think beyond the term "pregnancy" and to handle the condition as a "disability" when it becomes a disability.

Handicapped and Disability Discrimination

Fair employment requirements for people with handicaps and disabilities are less clear. In addition to the nondiscrimination provisions applicable to federal contractors, many states and localities require nondiscriminatory treatment of these individuals. In addition, most companies have policies stating that they desire to hire people with handicaps or disabilities. Keeping an open mind in this area will lead to the widespread realization that many handicapped or disabled individuals are capable of fully performing various jobs with minimum accommodation.

Retaliation and Harassment

Retaliation and harassment can be viewed as special forms of discrimination. Retaliation refers to actions taken against an employee because of his or her involvement in a fair employment discrimination complaint or investigation. Harassment is a form of indirect discrimination in which an attempt is made to intimidate the employee, with the focus being sex, religion, race, or any of the other prohibited forms of discrimination.

Retaliation

An employee who believes he or she is the victim of discrimination has the right to file a complaint and take what actions are necessary to enforce the right to nondiscriminatory treatment. Similarly, employees have the right to testify in any fair employment hearing or lawsuit. Employees also have the right to *oppose* unlawful discrimination practices of an employer. To protect these rights, the law does not permit an employer to retaliate against an employee for involvement in any of these activities. Supervisors cannot use these activities as the basis for an unfavorable performance evaluation, withholding a promotion, deferral of a salary increase, or any other punitive action.

Harassment

Harassment is the creation of a work environment or working conditions that are offensive or intolerable to an employee and that are motivated by or directed at the employee's protected class status. Racial, ethnic, sexist, or religious jokes; teasing; or other kinds of unfavorable treatment of a protected-group individual are considered harassment. Harassment also occurs if other employees engage in such conduct and the supervisor is aware of it and fails to take corrective action. Harassment is an illegal activity. Supervisors have the responsibility to prevent it from occurring and to take prompt and appropriate action if it does occur.

Sexual harassment is a special form of harassment. It is illegal to create or tolerate a hostile environment. It is also illegal to engage in *quid pro quo* harassment, in which favorable treatment is promised in return for sexual favors.

Legal Discrimination—What You Can Do

So far we have concentrated on what you cannot do as a supervisor. In practice, there is much you *can* do. Your overall objective is to achieve the goals of your unit so that the objectives of your organization are accomplished. This requires employees with the necessary knowledge, skills, and motivation to perform the work that you supervise. The law places no barriers in your way here; you have every right to select and differentiate on the basis of merit and ability. In a sense, all the law requires is that you be a fair supervisor and base your decisions on reasonable job-related criteria.

Bona Fide Occupational Qualifications

A bona fide occupational qualification (BFOQ) is a normally prohibited factor that is allowed as an employment qualification in a specific case. To establish a BFOQ, you must show that all or practically all persons of a particular class cannot perform a given job. If you are successful in establishing a BFOQ, you can then legally discriminate against the class that is unable to perform that job.

Very few attempts to establish BFOQs have been successful, and most of these have been related to sex. Some examples of these are theatrical roles and certain clothing models. In some instances, religion may also be a BFOQ. A church-operated school can legally hire only members of its own faith to teach religion in its school. The desires or preferences of customers or employees are not sufficient to establish a BFOQ. A BFOQ also cannot be established on the basis of beliefs (whether valid or invalid) about the willingness, ability, or propriety of persons from one sex engaging in particular work activities.

Men and women must be given an equal opportunity for all positions based on their *individual* abilities. Women should be given the same opportunities as men for any position, including but not limited to marketing representatives, underwriters, safety engineers, mail clerks, and print-shop machine operators. Similarly, men should be given the same opportunities as women for all positions, including secretaries, telephone operators, raters, and file clerks. Remember that you can always discriminate against an individual who does not have the *ability* to perform a particular job.

Valid Performance Standards

Employers should establish valid performance standards for each job. These standards should be based on the duties and responsibilities of the job. The standards should be reasonable and objective and, when met, constitute full performance of the job. The standards should apply evenly and equally to persons of all classes.

Ideally, standards should be quantified and performance measured in such terms as quality, quantity, cost, and time. Be careful not to overstate standards by setting them so high as to be unrealistic and unattainable. When excessive standards are applied to a member of a protected group, they may become the basis for a discrimination charge.

Standards may be established for any *work-related* traits, activities, or results that are necessary for effective performance on the job. Examples of permitted standards are the number of cases rated or underwritten, error rates, transmittals handled per unit of time, calls made or answered, attendance, work-related appearance, training progress, work attitude, and work-related interpersonal relations.

Examples of prohibited standards are quantity, quality, or time standards applied differently to men and women or to minorities, appearance rules prohibiting hairstyles unique to a particular minority or gender, attitude standards restricting statements of support for a particular sex or race, and rules that attempt to restrict interpersonal relations between protected groups and other employees.

Job-Related Selection

The essence of selection is differentiation. You may differentiate on the basis of job relatedness. An individual can be required to have the knowledge, skills, experience, training or education, and motivation necessary for successful performance of the job. For example, an applicant for a rater position can be required to possess the necessary basic mathematics skills; an applicant for a file-clerk position can be required to know the alphabet; a safety-engineer applicant can be required to have the necessary technical education; and an applicant for a supervisory position can be required to have the necessary years of related experience and the necessary training, communication, evaluation, and other supervisory skills.

However, selection cannot be made on the basis of criteria that are not required to perform the job. Asking for education and experience requirements that are not related to the position or that successful incumbents in those positions do not possess would be improper.

Job Performance

You can always legally differentiate between individuals who are satisfactorily performing the job and those who are not. This requires fair and objective evaluation. The presence of valid job-performance standards helps to ensure objective assessment of job performance. Remember, however, that the same standards must apply to all individuals in the same job and that the same evaluation system and procedures must be used. If two persons are fully trained and have identical jobs, you cannot expect fifty transactions per week from one and thirty-five from the other. Equally wrong would be to keep production records only on the one who was a minority. The same standards, rules, and treatment should apply to all.

The same training, coaching, and other on-the-job assistance must be provided to all individuals to enable them to perform the full requirements of the job. You must recognize, however, that no two individuals are alike and that some require more training and coaching than others. If a protected class member has the capability to perform the job but requires a reasonable amount of additional training because of his or her status, the training must be provided. The courts have ruled that this is sometimes necessary to eliminate the effects of past discrimination.

When it is established that an individual cannot perform the job, that person must be treated the same as other employees who are not performing. Often, a discrimination complaint is successful not because of an invalid evaluation of substandard performance but because of the way the situation was handled.

An example is maintaining a file on substandard minority employees when this practice is not followed for other substandard employees. You must follow the same procedures for all employees who are unable to perform their work.

THE SUPERVISOR'S FAIR EMPLOYMENT RESPONSIBILITY

Overall responsibility for fair employment policies and practices in a large organization is generally assigned to the human resources department. The legal department is also likely to be involved. In a small organization, the fair employment responsibility may remain with the owner, manager, or managers. The human resources department or other central authority is generally responsible for monitoring and evaluating fair employment activities, filing reports, and answering complaints. As a supervisor, you are the person responsible for carrying out the company's nondiscriminatory policies in your unit. Your actions are considered the actions of the company. The company will be held responsible for your intentional and unintentional discriminatory acts. In addition, you can be personally sued as a defendant in a discrimination case.

Knowledge of Laws and Regulations

As a supervisor, you are responsible for having a general knowledge of fair employment laws and regulations. This includes the federal fair employment laws discussed here and in the preceding chapter and the regulations that apply to federal contractors if they apply to your organization. You are also responsible for understanding and complying with any state and local fair employment laws that apply in your area. You may need to show some initiative to find out what laws apply and what they require.

In practice, you are not expected to memorize the provisions of these laws and regulations or to keep abreast of the latest rulings. You should, however, be aware of the various protected groups and the specific kinds of prohibited discrimination and have an in-depth understanding of the employment-related activities that are subject to fair employment regulation. To that end, we will now summarize fair employment requirements with a focus on what you should and should not do.

Application of Fair Employment Practices

Knowledge of the provisions of laws and regulations is not enough. You must also know how to interpret and apply them in your everyday supervisory activities. Most discrimination complaints arise from the unintentional actions of supervisors and managers, not from a conscious discriminatory posture by the organization.

Violations of the law are determined by the result of the discriminatory action or practice and *not by the intent*. In the eyes of the law, unintentional discrimination is still discrimination. Many times, EEO complaints have arisen because of a seemingly innocent question or action by a supervisor or manager. You need to be fully aware of the subtleties of discrimination and not invite charges of discrimination because of carelessness or ignorance.

We do not want to encourage you to supervise in a defensive manner. We instead hope to provide you with the knowledge and skills to supervise in a positive manner so that all employees are treated fairly and objectively and your supervisory decisions regarding them are based on their performance and ability. Remember that fair employment makes good management sense. Decisions based on sex, age, or minority status do not increase productivity; decisions based on merit and ability do. There is great personal challenge in achieving this. You are asked to overcome the natural tendency to show favoritism to those who are like you. This favoritism may be slight and subtle. No matter how minor it is, you are called to rise above this ordinary human tendency when dealing with employees.

Covered Supervisory Activities

Fair employment requirements have broad application and extend into almost every personnel area and activity. You need to know the fair employment pitfalls associated with each of these areas. The more important of these areas are summarized in Exhibit 9-2. You should assume that there are no exceptions and develop the habit of practicing fair employment in every aspect of supervision.

Recruitment and Selection

The hiring of new employees may be the most critical area in achieving truly fair employment. No opportunities are available to members of protected groups if they cannot get in the door. Hiring is the area in which unintentional discrimination is most likely to occur. Conducting a truly nondiscriminatory interview requires a generous measure of self-discipline. You must refrain from asking questions that could result in illegal discrimination.

Criteria for Interview Questions

Job-related selection standards provide the basis for fair employment practices. Requirements that are not job-related may impose unnecessary barriers to the selection of minorities, women, and older employees. Courts have consistently ruled that selection standards are illegal when they are not job-related and exclude a high percentage of minority or female applicants or any other group protected by fair employment laws. This also includes men when they are excluded from jobs normally held by women.

The following questions serve as criteria for guiding questions in an employment interview:

1. Is the question job-related? How?
2. Is the information necessary to determine the applicant's qualifications for the job?
3. If the applicant is a woman, would you ask the same question of a man?
4. If the applicant is a minority, would you ask the same question of a non-minority?
5. Can the question be interpreted as discriminatory? How?

Exhibit 9-2

Activities Requiring Fair Employment Supervision

Recruitment and Selection
    Recruitment Advertisements and Notices
    Job Posting
    Referrals
    Testing
    Interviewing
    Hiring
    Job Assignments

Training and Development
    On-the-Job Training
    Formal Training Programs
    Informal Training Programs
    Educational Assistance Programs
    Career Counseling

Promotions

Transfers

Salary Administration
    Performance Evaluation
    Salary Actions
    Job Classifications and Grades
    Job Titles

Discipline
    Substandard Performance Counseling

Terminations
    Discharges
    Layoffs
    Recalls

Terms and Conditions of Employment
    Benefit Plans
    Productivity Standards
    Work Assignments
    Leaves of Absence
    Overtime Opportunities
    Hours
    Time Off
    Rest Periods
    Work Rules
    Assignment of Work Space, Equipment, and Materials

Guidelines for Interviewing

Exhibit 9-3 summarizes the areas usually covered in an employment interview. Great care is needed to probe these areas without eliciting information that can lead to illegal discrimination.

Exhibit 9-3	
Interview Subject Area	
Interview Area	Information Needed or Furnished
Job History	Past and present positions held, duties and responsibilities, likes and dislikes, specific accomplishments and disappointments, reasons for job changes
Education and Goals	Formal education record, career goals and objectives, ideal job, other self-development activities, short- and long-range job objectives
Other People	Relationships with peers, subordinates, and bosses; type of people applicant works best with; ideal boss
The Company	Department and company objectives, expectations and values, specific duties and responsibilities, opportunities for advancement, other significant factors affecting the job
Compensation	Compensation system, salary range for the position, salary review schedule, salary growth opportunities

Lawful and Unlawful Pre-Employment Questions

Exhibit 9-4 contrasts the lawful and unlawful questions that may be asked during a pre-employment interview. Avoid such natural conversational subjects as marital status or living arrangements. In addition to refraining from asking unlawful questions, you should discourage an applicant from giving you the improper information on his or her own.

Discipline and Termination

Many supervisors find it difficult to discipline and terminate employees. Problems rarely go away by themselves, and prompt action is usually best. Problems that may result in disciplinary action should always be discussed with the employee. With the possible exception of a warning after a first offense, a written record should be kept and the employee asked to sign it.

We recommend a three-step approach in matters involving disciplinary action:

- Step 1—Identify the problem. Meet with the employee and review the standards. Clearly identify, and obtain the employee's agreement on, the nature of the problem. Focus on the problem, not the person.

Exhibit 9-4

Lawful and Unlawful Pre-Employment Questions

Type of Question	Lawful Questions
Name	What is your full name?
Residence/Address	What is your address?
Age	Are you under eighteen or over seventy? Do you meet the minimum age requirements as set forth by law, and can you furnish proof of age or a work permit if hired?
Marital Status	This job will frequently require working at night—can you meet this requirement? We have a one-year training program—can you meet this requirement?
Pregnancy/Children	The hours for this job are from 7:30 A.M. to 4:00 P.M.—can you work this schedule?
Religion	None
Race or Color	None
Birthplace or National Origin	Are you a United States citizen? If not a citizen, do you have a work visa? Do you speak, read, or write a specific foreign language (if a BFOQ)?
Education	What schools did you attend? What courses did you take, and what were your grades?

Possible Unlawful Questions

Did you change your name? What was it before? What is your maiden name? What was your father's surname?

Do you own or rent? Where do your parents reside? Who else lives with you? How long have you resided at your present address?

How old are you? What is your birthdate? When did you graduate from school? Do you have a birth certificate or baptismal certificate?

Are you married, single, divorced, engaged, etc.? Do you plan to get married? How long do you plan to work?

Are you pregnant or do you plan to get pregnant? How many children do you have? How old are your children? Who will take care of your children? How would your husband feel about your traveling?

Do you consider yourself a good Christian? What church do you attend? What is the name of your minister/pastor? What societies do you belong to? Do you know this is a Protestant organization?

Any question that would indicate race or color.

Where were you born? Where were your parents (or spouse) born? Are you native-born or naturalized? What country are you a citizen of? What foreign language do you speak (when not job related)?

Isn't that a Catholic school? What kind of students (nationality, race) did they have at your school? Is English your native language?

Do you have a good credit rating? Can you give us some credit references? Where do you have charge accounts? Have you ever had your wages garnisheed or been declared bankrupt? Do you have any loans outstanding? What is the name of your bank?

Have you ever been arrested or convicted of any crime?

What is your weight or height? Will you change your hairstyle if you are hired? Would you give us a photograph (before hiring)?

What kind of discharge did you receive? Did you receive an honorable discharge?

Do you have any handicaps?

- Step 2—Develop a corrective action program. With the employee, develop a program of corrective action to solve the problem. The program should clearly identify the actions the employee should take and should be expressed in measurable terms when possible. The program should also specify your role in helping to solve the problem; for instance, by providing additional training. The program should specify the timetable for following up on and solving the problem.
- Step 3—Identify consequences. Clearly identify and communicate to the employee the consequences of not solving the problem as specified in the timetable.

Documentation

Adequate records are important to the defense of discrimination complaints regarding discipline or termination. If a complaint is filed, the first thing the investigator is likely to request is the file of written records relating to the action. Records should be accurate, complete, and specific. Serious discipline problems and all termination situations should be completely documented. The documentation should contain a description of the problem that is expressed in objective and measurable terms. The documentation should include dates, critical incidents, a description of the performance standards and the actual level of performance, and the reasons for your decisions.

Do not overdo documentation by keeping written records of every incident that occurs. Small problems that are dealt with informally, for instance, need not be documented. If they develop into recurrent or significant problems, however, documentation should begin, and you should then include a record of the prior informal, undocumented discussions. Treat all employees alike in all your documentation activities. Documenting problems for only some employees is itself a discriminatory act. Establish guidelines to be followed for all employees and then apply them to everyone.

THE FAMILY AND MEDICAL LEAVE ACT OF 1993

Most of the laws covered in this course deal directly with the hiring, promotion, transferring, and termination of employees. The Family and Medical Leave Act of 1993 (FMLA) deals directly with the treatment of current employees who need to take extended (or sporadic) leave because of family and/or medical problems.

Criteria for Leave

This act requires employers to grant their eligible employees up to twelve weeks of unpaid leave with the right to reinstatement to their current job or an equivalent one. The law affects all employers with fifty or more employees (either at the main work site or within seventy-five miles of it). The law further states that an employee is eligible if he or she has been employed for a minimum of one year and has worked at least 1,250 hours during the current year.

The four reasons that require the leave to be made available are:

- the birth of a child and/or in order to care for a newly born child,
- the adoption of or the foster-care placement of a child,
- the need for the employee to care for a spouse, child, or parent with a serious medical condition, and
- a serious medical condition that prevents the employee from being able to perform his or her duties on the job.

An employee is permitted to use the full twelve-week period at one time, can take it intermittently, or can work a reduced-day work schedule. Additionally, the twelve-week period is available during any twelve-month period.

Usually, the full twelve weeks must be taken consecutively for the birth, adoption, or foster-care placement of a child, but one can obviously see how serious illness could cause the leave to be taken sporadically.

Employees are required to give thirty days' advance notice to their employer if the notice is practical. If the leave is because of an emergency, notification is required as soon as is practical. Employers can require an employee to provide medical notes to certify that an employee's medical condition (or one of his or her relative) is valid.

Serious Medical Condition

The FMLA defines "serious medical condition." It is a physical or mental illness, injury, or impairment that involves one of the following:

- any period of incapacity or treatment in connection with inpatient care at a recognized healthcare institution,
- a period of incapacity that requires absence from work, school, or normal daily activities in excess of three days that also requires continuing treatment by a healthcare provider, or
- continuing treatment by a healthcare provider for a chronic or long-term health condition that is either incurable or so serious that if left untreated, would result in a period of incapacity in excess of three days.

Other Requirements

The FMLA does not require that an employee be paid for leave that is taken under its regulations. Employers may continue to pay employees at their discretion or permit the use of unused sick or vacation leave, but there is no requirement for them to do so. The act does require employers to continue to pay for any health insurance coverage that is normally provided to the employee without charging the employee any additional money. Finally, employers are required by the act to reinstate the employee to his or her previous position (or an equivalent one) at the end of the leave period. Any seniority that would have been earned during the leave period is also earned.

Although an individual supervisor would not be required to make the decision of whether a particular leave situation qualifies under FMLA, supervisors need to be aware that this type of leave can be taken and that they might have to cover for the work that the employee would have done while he or she is on an FMLA leave.

SUMMARY

Supplementing the discussion of fair employment laws and regulations in the preceding chapter, this chapter covered three additional important federal laws: the Equal Pay Act of 1963, the Age Discrimination Act of 1967 (ADEA), and the Immigration Reform and Control Act of 1986. The Equal Pay Act prohibits discrimination on the basis of sex in determining the rates of pay to employees; the ADEA prohibits discrimination against people forty and older; the Immigration Reform and Control Act prohibits employers from knowingly hiring, recruiting, or referring for work aliens who are not authorized to work in the United States and from discriminating against prospective employees on the basis of national origin or citizenship.

Also discussed were laws and regulations that apply to federal contractors or subcontractors; that is, firms doing business with the federal government. Federal contractors and subcontractors, which include many insurance companies, are subject to Presidential Executive Order 11246 and the Rehabilitation Act of 1973.

Also covered was the Family and Medical Leave Act of 1993 and its implications for providing fair leave treatment to all employees.

As a supervisor, you have a direct, personal responsibility for the maintenance of fair employment in your unit. Our national goal is clear: to achieve full access to jobs and fair treatment at work for all. To you as supervisor, the rules and the pitfalls may seem numerous. We have given you some specific guidelines in the sensitive areas of hiring and discipline. We urge you to review fair employment requirements periodically (especially the state and local laws that apply to your area), to act with caution in employment matters, and to integrate into your responsibilities the underlying objective of fair employment. To assist you, a summary of the requirements of all of the fair employment laws and regulations discussed in Chapter 8 and this chapter was provided.

Index

Page numbers in boldface refer to definitions of Key Words and Phrases. Page numbers in italics refer to exhibits.

Sexual harassment, 8.9

Situational theory of leadership, Fiedler's, 4.11–4.13

Social system, supervisor's, 2.4–2.9, 2.24

Staff authority, **1.20**

Staff tasks, **1.19**

Structural cues, 5.4

Supervision, **1.1**

    improving proficiency at, 1.14–1.16

    causes of failure at, 2.21–2.24

Supervisor

    employee expectations of, 1.26–1.27

    management expectations of, 1.16–1.18

    promotion to role of, 2.20–2.21

    relationships with employees, 2.16–2.18

    relationships with managers and executives, 2.9–2.14

    relationships with other supervisors, 2.14–2.16

Supervisory duties, 1.3–1.5, 2.23, 2.24

Supervisory functions, 1.6–1.7

Supervisory skills, 1.9, 1.12–1.14

Support system, **2.18**–2.20

T

Tannenbaum's and Schmidt's continuum of leadership behavior, 4.18–4.19

Termination, 9.25–9.27

Theories of leadership, 4.10–4.19

Theory X and Theory Y, McGregor's, 4.17–4.18

Title VII—Civil Rights Act of 1964, 8.7–8.16

    bases of discrimination under, 8.8

    complaints and, 8.14, 8.16

    coverage and application of, 8.7

    enforcement and remedies of, 8.14

    illegal discrimination under, 8.7

Training, 1.14

V

Valence, 3.13, *3.14*

Values, **5.3**

Vroom's expectancy theory, 3.12–3.15

W

Withdrawal, 5.12

Written communication, 7.27–7.32